Entertaining
with Friends

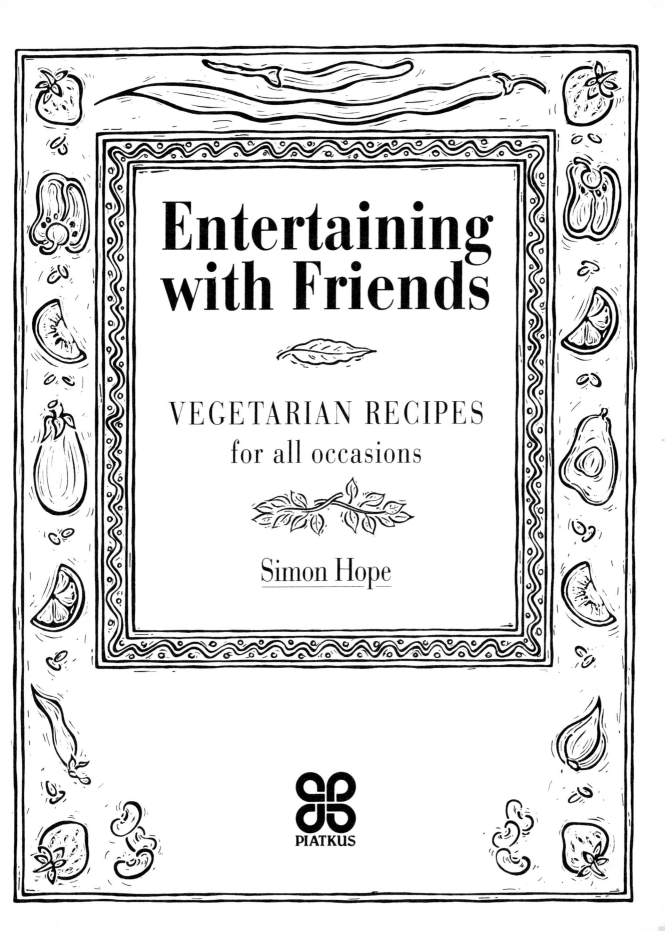

Entertaining with Friends

VEGETARIAN RECIPES

for all occasions

Simon Hope

PIATKUS

For Kate

Copyright © Simon Hope 1993

First published in 1993 by
Judy Piatkus (Publishers) Ltd,
5 Windmill Street,
London W1P 1HF

**The moral right of the author
has been established**

*A catalogue record for this book is available
from the British Library*

ISBN 0–7499–1285–5

Designed by Paul Saunders
Illustrations and cover artwork by Lorraine Harrison
Photographs by James Murphy
Styling of photographs by Roisin Nield
Food prepared by Karen Samuel and Simon Hope

Typeset by Selwood Systems, Midsomer Norton
Printed by Butler & Tanner Ltd, Frome and London

CONTENTS

Acknowledgements vi

Introduction vii

1 Breakfasts and Brunches 1

2 Informal Meals 22

3 Lunch and Dinner Parties 46

4 Entertaining Children 116

5 The Vegetarian Buffet 127

6 Picnics and Barbecues 165

7 A Vegetarian Christmas 194

8 Basic Recipes 217

Index 229

Acknowledgements

I would like specially to thank my partner Jerry Gray and head chef Karen Samuel for all their hard work, both in allowing me time to write this book and for their contribution to it. I would also like to thank the staff, present and past, of *Food for friends*, notably Vicky Martin, Phil Taylor and Philippe Persigny, for their inspiration, taste buds and dedication to furthering the future of vegetarian food in this country.

Finally I must say thank you to all my family for their loyalty, love and constructive criticism.

INTRODUCTION

Ten years ago I was busy writing *The Reluctant Vegetarian*. Vegetarian cheese and free-range eggs were almost impossible to buy in bulk, peppers were green or red and fresh herbs meant parsley. Oil was vegetable and vinegar was malt. Balsamic vinegar was something you could only buy in exclusive West End delicatessens. Now the variety and quality of foods are seemingly endless; even the average supermarket stocks products from all parts of the globe. Oil is not just oil – it comes from specific plants, seeds and nuts and is prized for being unrefined or cold pressed. The food business has exploded and the best thing is it's good for cooking, eating and entertaining in general, and you in particular.

When I wrote my first book my wife, Kate, was pregnant with Daisy, our first daughter, Aubergine the cat was having kittens, and when I wasn't writing I was working all hours of the day and night at my restaurant *Food for friends*. One of the first things to change when you have a young family and other commitments is your concept of entertaining. It's not that you change much, but your circumstances are changed immeasurably and of course permanently enriched.

Entertaining becomes something that is mostly done at home or at the homes of others with similarly clipped wings. You are no longer the doyenne of the discos but more the diva of the dinner party, and when you are, like me, in the food business too, your work is bound to influence your leisure. So cooking at the restaurant becomes an extension or reflection of cooking and entertaining at home and vice versa.

Entertaining with Friends is very much a book of *Food for friends* recipes as they have developed over the past ten years. Every chapter has its root in some part of the restaurant's not too distant past. During this time we just haven't stopped entertaining. The biggest influences have been Jeremy, my partner, and our main savoury chefs, Phil and Karen, and all the other staff, but most importantly our customers and friends, especially the ones who weren't afraid to tell us when we got it wrong.

Of course, there have been occasions when we have got it right. Breakfast at *Food for friends* happened after a trip to California in the early eighties. I was impressed by the huge and largely meatless morning feasts washed down with fresh fruit juice and good coffee. For the average vegetarian it is great to discover life beyond muesli and Marmite on toast.

Parties both at work and at home, formal and informal, have thankfully been a great feature of the past ten years. Having been trained in extremely formal catering, I of course rebelled when I left college and followed the most informal of career paths. However, I was extremely lucky to have certain disciplines under my belt and at no time do they give me more pleasure than when having a dinner or lunch party at home, or a gourmet evening at the restaurant. Out of this desire to please on all levels came the buffets and the picnics and the festive celebrations, plus countless other events over the last ten years.

Food for friends customers have always come from a broad spectrum of people, common only in their desire for good food at a sensible price. One of the movements we've noticed over the past ten years is a general tendency towards lighter foods (early vegetarian dishes could be notoriously heavy) with a greater awareness of allergies and dietetic information generally. More and more people are becoming vegetarian or vegan, especially women. There are far fewer social hang-ups, except with the 'Real Men Don't Eat Quiche' brigade, and it is quite common not to be vegetarian but to eat mostly vegetarian food for health and economic reasons (or simply because you prefer it).

So the new book was born and while my previous book, *The Reluctant Vegetarian*, illuminated the path for many from the darkness of vegetable ignorance to the light of life with little or no meat, *Entertaining with Friends* takes a step into the future – emphasising that while food is necessary, it can be fun and no matter what the occasion is, wholly or partially we have an edible vegetarian solution.

I sincerely hope you enjoy reading this book as much as I have enjoyed writing it and if you have any queries please write to me at *Food for friends*, 17A–18 Prince Albert Street, The Lanes, Brighton, BN1 1HF.

Notes

Recipes marked with a V are suitable for vegans, depending on your use of vegan margarine or oil instead of butter, sugar instead of honey etc. If there is an acceptable vegan substitute for any non-vegan ingredients I have given these as alternatives.

Recipes marked G are gluten free.

Yeast

Several recipes in this book use fresh yeast. It is quite easy to obtain and can be kept for about 6 days in the fridge, if well wrapped. Alternatively it can be frozen for up to 3 months.

I find dried yeast can be a little unpredictable, but if you want to use it, or can't find fresh yeast, then by all means do so. You will need half the quantity of dried yeast as fresh yeast. To use, dissolve 1 teaspoon of sugar in the warm liquid before adding the dried yeast, wait for about 10 minutes or according to the packet instructions, then continue as for fresh yeast.

If you want to use the 'Easy-Blend' or 'Fast Acting' types of dried yeast, follow the instructions on the packet.

Tomatoes

When fresh, outdoor home-grown tomatoes are not available (which is most of the time) always use good quality tinned Italian plum tomatoes or add sun-dried tomatoes. While a lot of flavour is lost in the tinning process, at least you are using tomatoes that have ripened and grown to maturity naturally under the sun. Fresh tomatoes that have been picked green under glass and often transported thousands of miles can never compete, even if they're beautifully red when you use them – the flavour simply isn't there.

Cheese

At the restaurants we always use vegetarian cheeses, which are cheeses made with non-animal rennet. A huge variety of these cheeses are now available but you do have to search for them. If you have a good cheesemonger or delicatessen near you, it's worth asking if they will order what you want.

Chapter one

BREAKFAST AND

BRUNCHES

Breakfast has to be one of the most important meals of the day and also one of the
easiest to miss. For vegetarians it's the one
meal of the day when their choice is not greatly
restricted. Breakfast has been going through a
sticky period, with people avoiding breakfast
saying that they didn't have time, but current
thinking is that it is the one meal that should not
be missed, for both dietary and psychological
reasons.

In essence what the experts are saying is what
we've always known in our hearts. Bodies, like
machines, need fuel and it's best to put the fuel in
before you start using your body. Psychologically
breakfast 'sets you up' for the day. You feel positive, energetic and raring to go after a good
breakfast.

Increasingly those people who were 'too busy'
for breakfast are now entertaining at breakfast. It
makes a lot of sense for business people to meet
then. A good positive meeting, when everyone is
on the ball, need not intrude into the working
part of the day.

At home, Monday to Friday, breakfast has to be
a fairly efficient affair, with simple but sustaining
foods that are quick to prepare and easy to eat.
What could be more sustaining on a cold winter's
morning than a steaming hot bowl of porridge
topped with milk or cream and honey or treacle?

At the weekend breakfast can become a wholly
different occasion. On Sunday especially it can
easily become brunch – usually from 10 to 11 in
the morning. Why not invite your friends to it?

I once went to a brunch party in Ireland. It
was a wonderfully relaxed affair with cereals and
fruit followed by scrambled eggs, mushrooms,
tomatoes and sautéed potatoes, all washed
down with hot fresh coffee and jugs of champagne and fresh orange juice. Contrary to what
you might expect, the brunch set us up for the
whole day.

The most important thing when planning any
entertaining at breakfast is to minimise the
amount of preparation on the day. If possible, set
the table the night before and prepare the bases
of any mixes you may have to make. Prudent use
of fridge and freezer are a must, because if your
meal is to be a success then you must be seen to
enjoy it too. Some corners cannot be cut; don't
be lured into thinking you can freshly squeeze
your fruit juice the night before – it won't taste
the same the next day.

For this chapter I've chosen four occasions
on which you may find yourself entertaining at
breakfast. If you haven't tried it before, now's
your chance.

BEAUJOLAIS BREAKFAST

Celebrating Beaujolais Day seems to be becoming rarer and rarer – a sad state of affairs indeed. November can be one of the dreariest months of the year and Beaujolais Day shines as a solitary gleam of light in an otherwise empty month. The race to get the wine from Beaujolais to England is a harmless bit of fun. Invariably the wine is mediocre and best served chilled, but then, what can you expect of something that has only just been opened? No – Beaujolais Day is just a jolly, a chance to let your hair down when you're normally just putting it up. Best take the day off work and invite a few of your more raucous friends around for a sumptuous breakfast combining a hint of 'La Belle France' with an unusually continental English breakfast.

MENU

BEAUJOLAIS BREAKFAST OR BRUNCH

SERVES 8

Red Grape Juice or Freshly Squeezed Orange Juice

—·—

A Selection of Yeasted Pastries
(Pain au Chocolat, Pain aux Raisins and Croissants)
served with
unsalted French butter and apricot conserve

—·—

Poached Eggs on Hot Walnut Toast with
Deep-fried Brie,
Roast Cherry Tomatoes and Madeira Mushrooms

—·—

To Drink: Coffee or hot chocolate
and of course, Beaujolais Nouveau
To Finish: Ice-cold Muscat Grapes

COUNTDOWN

Day before

1. Buy or make the Walnut Bread and freeze if desired.

2. Prepare the breadcrumbs for the Brie. Season with salt, pepper and paprika.

3. Wash the cherry tomatoes. Allow 4 for each guest.

4. Put a saucepanful of acidulated water (see page 8) on the stove ready for the morning (it's the sort of thing you might forget).

5. Set the table – try to use large French coffee cups or bowls.

6. Clean the button mushrooms and chop some parsley.

On the day

1. Take the bread and yeasted pastries out of the freezer.

2. Curl the butter, squeeze the juice and turn on the oven.

3. Open the wine – still cold from transit. Make the coffee.

4. Heat the Yeasted Pastries. While they're in the oven prepare the brie for frying (dip in flour, egg and breadcrumbs).

5. Brush the cherry tomatoes with a little olive oil and season with salt, pepper and some oregano. Put in a roasting dish ready to go into the oven.

6. Slice the bread to fit your toaster or put it ready to toast under the grill.

7. Bring the acidulated water to a gently rolling boil.

After eating your pastries and quaffing a few glasses of Beaujolais you'll feel much more like cooking. As soon as you remove the yeasted pastries from the oven put the cherry tomatoes in – with 8 plates to warm.

After such a hearty start to the meal people won't mind waiting 10–15 minutes for their next course. There is, after all, the Beaujolais to sup.

8. Next, cook the mushrooms and while they're simmering, deep fry the Brie. Drain on kitchen paper and keep in a warm dish in the oven with the tomatoes. Finally, poach the eggs in the acidulated water and toast the Walnut Bread.

To serve: Perch the poached eggs on the Walnut Toast surrounded with the Brie, tomatoes and a spoon of Madeira Mushrooms. Sprinkle with parsley if desired.

⟦V⟧ ⟦G⟧ *Freshly Squeezed Orange Juice*

As long as it is just that, there's nothing nicer to start the day. Choose your oranges carefully. Fresh Spanish are best at this time of the year – don't even contemplate anything from the other side of the equator. Size is not important but they must be sweet and juicy. As with lemons, often the juiciest types have thin skins. If you haven't already got a juicer you're happy with, choose mechanical rather than electric and make sure it uses a proper leverage system to save your biceps and to extract the maximum juice possible. Keep the juice in a covered jug in the fridge until you are ready to pour it. Vital vitamins will be destroyed by exposure to air and light.

Yeasted Pastries

These delightful puffs of mouthwatering pastry are best served hot. If using a microwave, minimise the amount of time they are exposed or else they will become tough. Of course, unless you're totally mad you will already have the uncooked pastries shaped and frozen uncooked in your freezer. When you get up, take them out of the freezer and allow to defrost at room temperature. When they have defrosted and proved, glaze them with a little beaten egg yolk and sprinkle with seeds or herbs as desired (Pain au Chocolat and Pain aux Raisins will need to be decorated again after they have been cooked).

All the Yeasted Pastries served at the Beaujolais Breakfast can be made from the same basic Croissant Dough (see page 219). Roll out the croissant dough into a rectangle and divide it into three lengthways strips. Use one strip for each kind of pastry.

Croissants

Makes 8 small or 4 normal size croissants

⅓ of Croissant Dough (page 219) rolled out as described above
beaten egg yolk

1. Lay the dough strip on a lightly floured surface and trim the edges to form a perfect square. Cut an X shape into the square to make 4 perfect triangles. Cover with clingfilm and allow to rest in the fridge. While they are resting you can be preparing the other pastries.

2. When they have rested for about 20 minutes, shape the triangles one at a time. Place one apex of the triangle towards you and roll up the pastry from the opposite end. When it is

completely rolled up, make sure that the apex is tucked under the croissant, then twist the corners round towards you to form a crescent.

3. Arrange the croissants, with the other pastries, on a lightly oiled baking sheet.

4. Cover with a damp tea towel or clingfilm and prove in a warm place for 2 hours or until desirable size.

5. Brush with beaten egg yolk and bake in a hot oven at 230°C/450°F/Gas Mark 8 for 15 minutes.

To serve: Ideally serve straight from the oven. If not, allow to cool on a wire rack and reheat if necessary later. Present in an attractive basket lined with crisp white linen. Eat with French butter and a good apricot conserve or continental-style jam. If you're feeling really outrageous, dunk into your large cup of coffee.

Pain au Chocolat

Makes 8 small or 4 normal size pains au chocolat

$\frac{1}{3}$ of Croissant Dough (page 219) rolled out as described above
4 or 8 small pieces dark Belgian chocolate
beaten egg yolk
warmed strained apricot jam to glaze
a little extra chocolate, melted, to decorate

Do use the best quality dark chocolate for these pastries.

1. Lay the dough strip on a lightly floured surface and trim the edges to form a perfect rectangle. Cut this into four or eight rectangles. Cover with clingfilm and allow to rest in the fridge for 20 minutes.

2. Place a piece of dark chocolate on each rectangle, then fold the dough over it to make a tube containing the chocolate.

3. Arrange on a lightly oiled baking tray. Brush with egg yolk. Cover with a teatowel or clingfilm and leave to prove in a warm place for 2 hours or until desirable size.

4. Bake in a hot oven at 230°/450°F/Gas Mark 8 for 15–17 minutes.

5. While they are still hot glaze with a little hot apricot jam and decorate with a trickle of melted chocolate.

Pain aux Raisins

Makes 4 large rolls

$\frac{1}{3}$ of Croissant Dough (page 219) rolled out as described above

warmed honey, apricot jam or sugar syrup to glaze

Filling

50 g (2 oz) soft unsalted butter

50 g (2 oz) brown sugar

2 teaspoons cinnamon

50 g (2 oz) raisins (or more if you prefer)

Here's an alternative filling for croissants.

1. Beat together the butter, sugar and cinnamon. Fold the raisins in when the mixture is creamy.

2. Spread this on the dough rectangle, leaving a border around the edges.

3. Roll the dough up as tightly as possible, then cut across into four pieces. Place these on an oiled baking tray, cover with clingfilm and leave to prove in a warm place for 2 hours.

4. Bake in a hot oven at 230°C/450°F/Gas Mark 8 for 15 minutes.

5. Glaze with warmed honey, apricot jam or sugar syrup. Experiment with different fillings.

Important time saver

If you are really short of time, prepare and cook the pastries well in advance. Freeze, then reheat in a hot oven for 10 minutes.

These are not quite so wonderful as the freshly baked ones, but are still so good nobody else need know the truth. The quality of the butter used to make the Croissants is all-important when using this technique.

To make up for taking such an outrageous short-cut you could consider curling or shaping the butter. You could even make a sweet flavoured butter such as Orange-blossom Honey Butter, Maple Syrup Butter or even Malt Extract Butter.

To make these butters simply beat the butter with the chosen flavouring, wrap in greaseproof paper and chill well or freeze.

Walnut Bread

This wholesome bread is the perfect accompaniment to soups and cheese. It is best served hot and fresh or toasted, but it is also unusual in that it will improve in flavour with age up to 3 days.

Makes 1 loaf

1 oz (30 g) fresh yeast
1 pint (600 ml) milk, warmed
2 oz (50 g) unsalted butter, plus
    extra for greasing the tins
1 lb (450 g) organic wholewheat
    bread flour
a little salt
2 oz (50 g) demerara sugar
1 oz (30 g) walnut quarters
milk to glaze

Walnut Bread makes wonderful toast – the deep nutty flavour develops miraculously in the toaster.

1. Cream the yeast with a little milk.

2. Heat the butter carefully in a pan until it turns a nutty brown colour. Then add to the remaining milk.

3. Add the milk and butter to the yeast mix.

4. Mix the flour, salt and sugar, make a well in the centre and stir in the milk mix gradually.

5. Fold in the chopped walnuts.

6. Cover with a damp cloth and allow to prove in a warm place for about 1 hour. Heat the oven to 220°C/425°F/Gas Mark 7.

7. When the dough has doubled in volume knock it back by kneading lightly and either shape it by plaiting it or else just roll it up and place it in a well buttered loaf tin. Cover with clingfilm and leave in a warm place to rise again for at least 45 minutes. When it is ready to bake, brush a little milk over the surface to glaze.

8. Bake for 35 minutes. Turn out onto a wire rack to cool – or eat immediately.

9. If you wish to freeze walnut bread, allow it to cool, wrap in clingfilm and freeze immediately.

Poached Eggs

G *Makes as many as you like*

The key to a good poached egg is its freshness. Only good fresh eggs keep their white attached closely to the yolk. Fresh eggs make the whole procedure neat and tidy. If you can't get really fresh eggs, poach them in a cheat's poacher – one of those contraptions that look a bit like a frying pan with indentations in an insert for the eggs.

Choose white or brown, so long as they're free-range. When they are cooked, poached eggs should be runny inside with a thin coating of egg white on the outside. To help this happen, always use acidulated water (i.e. water with a few spoonfuls of vinegar in) to cook them. Make sure it is boiling vigorously. Then add the eggs, one at a time, breaking them first into a large tablespoon then gently dropping them into the water. Keep the water boiling gently and cook the eggs for 3 minutes. When ready, the eggs should be retrieved using a spoon with holes in and eaten immediately.

Deep Fried Brie

Serves 4

12 oz (325 g) Brie de Meaux
1 egg, beaten
2 oz (50 g) fresh wholewheat
    breadcrumbs
1 oz (30 g) sesame seeds
fine sea salt
freshly ground black pepper
oil for deep frying

Brie is a cows' milk cheese of 45% fat. A good Brie is neither too firm nor too soft. For this dish choose a Brie de Meaux for its mild creamy flavour. Allow 3 oz (75 g) of Brie per person – more if you want seconds. This recipe serves 4, so double the quantities if there are 8 of you.

1. Cut the Brie into 4 or 8 wedges.

2. Dip in the egg, then in a mixture of breadcrumbs and sesame seeds, seasoned with salt and pepper.

3. Heat the oil and deep fry the wedges of Brie until the breadcrumbs are golden brown. Serve immediately.

VARIATIONS

- Try different cheeses: Camembert, Mozzarella, Limburger, Caerphilly, Gouda, goat's cheese and Bel Paese would all be good.

- Change the coating – it could be other seeds or it could be batter.

Madeira Mushrooms

 Serves 8

4 oz (100 g) unsalted butter
2¼ lb (1 kg) organic chestnut
  mushrooms
fine sea salt
freshly ground black pepper
4 fl oz (120 ml) Madeira
8 fl oz (250 ml) sour cream (or
  crème fraîche)
2 tablespoons chopped parsley

Mushrooms are best picked fresh and wild. Failing that, choose chunky ones to slice or buttons cooked whole. Some supermarkets now stock organic brown chestnut mushrooms that have a lovely close texture and nutty flavour. Whatever you choose, they'll taste wonderful in this recipe.

1. Melt the butter in a large frying pan until it is hot.

2. Add the mushrooms and seasoning and sauté until they are turning brown.

3. Add the Madeira and bring it to the boil. Continue to boil until it has reduced by half.

4. Add the sour cream and bring the mixture back to the boil, then simmer quickly until the mixture has reduced by half and thickened naturally.

5. Season again and sprinkle each portion with parsley as you serve it.

VARIATIONS

Madeira Mushrooms make a great snack at any time of day, on toast, in an omelette or with a pancake. Try substituting brandy, sherry, port or Calvados for the Madeira.

Roasted Cherry Tomatoes

V G *Serves 8*

24 cherry tomatoes
1 tablespoon olive oil
salt and freshly ground black pepper

For this simple accompaniment choose plump sweet cherry tomatoes, with their stalks in place. They will provide a great edge to the cheese and colour to the plate as a whole.

Place tomatoes in a small, oiled roasting tin, baste with olive oil and season, then roast for about 30 minutes at 190°C/375°F/Gas Mark 5.

BUSINESS BREAKFAST

Entertaining a client or colleague for breakfast on home territory is a fairly new concept, but it makes a lot of sense especially if the client has had a very early start and has had to travel a fair distance. It may be that your home is nearer to where you both want to go than your office. Whatever the reason, a business breakfast should taste good and above all give the client the right impression about you and your company. Equally, if entertaining business colleagues, you not only want their impression of you enhanced but also to have a jolly good start to the day.

So here it is – the no-nonsense, stylish and effective business breakfast.

MENU

A BUSINESS BREAKFAST

SERVES 4

Fresh Grapefruit Juice
Dried Fruit Compote with Homemade Muesli, Greek
Yoghurt and Acacia Honey

— . —

Spinach and Mozzarella Scramble with Sesame and
Potato Croquettes

— . —

Organic Wholewheat Toast with Butter and
Marmalade

— . —

Coffee and Tea

COUNTDOWN

Day before
• Stew the dried fruits, cool and chill. • Make the muesli. • Make the croquettes. • Prepare the spinach and Mozzarella for the scramble. • Make a Perfect Toasting Loaf. • Curl the butter.

On the day
0–15 minutes before • Squeeze the grapefruit juice. • Heat the plates. • Make the coffee and/or tea. • Make the scramble. • Fry the croquettes. • Make the toast.

Freshly Squeezed Grapefruit Juice

V G Allow 2 grapefruit per person. Grapefruit are full of goodness and extremely low in calories. They contain vitamin C, potassium and folic acid. In addition they are full of pectin which is great for the digestion. To make sure you retain all the goodness squeeze grapefruit freshly and drink immediately. For sweetness, choose pink grapefruit with a good even colour and heavy weight. Serve cold.

Dried Fruit Compote

V G *Serves 4*

4 oz (100 g) dried peaches
4 oz (100 g) dried mango
4 oz (100 g) Lexia raisins
4 oz (100 g) pitted prunes
2 tablespoons honey (optional)
apple juice to cover
1 cinnamon stick
1 mace blade
a little sliced fresh ginger

A well prepared dried fruit compote can look just as attractive as a fresh fruit salad. Serve it warm or cold depending on the weather or your inclination. Choose any selection of dried fruits you can find or prefer. If you're feeling really adventurous add a touch of alcohol like Calvados or eau-de-vie de marc.

Place all the ingredients in a pan over a low heat and bring to the boil. If you are short of time, poach the fruit for 30 minutes to 1 hour, until soft. If you are well organised, once it has boiled leave the compote to soak overnight.

To serve: Remove the spices. Serve the compote on its own or

11

with thick creamy Greek yoghurt or fromage frais. Use as an accompaniment to muesli or other cereals.

VARIATIONS

- Try different fruits and spices.
- Add roasted cashews or macadamia nuts just before serving.

Home-made Muesli

V *Makes 5½ lb (2.5 kg)*

7 oz (200 g) organic regular oats
7 oz (200 g) organic jumbo oats
7 oz (200 g) rye flakes
7 oz (200 g) wheat flakes
7 oz (200 g) barley flakes
7 oz (200 g) fine desiccated coconut
7 oz (200 g) sunflower seeds
    (toasted)
7 oz (200 g) nibbed almonds
7 oz (200 g) roasted hazelnuts
7 oz (200 g) roasted cashews
7 oz (200 g) raisins
7 oz (200 g) sultanas
7 oz (200 g) dried apricots, chopped

Why do people buy muesli in little packets when it's the simplest breakfast item of all to make at home? Make enough for several breakfasts but not so much that it will go off before you've had time to use it. Bear in mind that, as most humans don't have the digestive tract of a horse, you will have to soak it overnight before eating. Alternatively, for a crunchy type of muesli, you can toast the grains in a hot oven until they are starting to brown. Granola is similar except the grains, nuts and seeds are roasted with demerara sugar or honey and a little oil at a lower temperature for a longer time with frequent stirrings.

A typical muesli will provide you with protein, dietary fibre, calcium, iron, thiamin, riboflavin and niacin before you lubricate it with milk, yoghurt, soya milk, cream, sour cream, fromage frais or crème fraîche.

The quantities given here will provide enough muesli for a while (depending on how much you eat). For this breakfast, allow about 3½ oz (90 g) of dry ingredients per person.

1. Mix together the grains and coconut and store in an airtight container. Mix the nuts, seeds and dried fruit and store separately.

2. Soak enough oats and flakes overnight in water or apple juice.

3. Combine with enough nuts and dried fruit the next day before eating.

4. Spoon Greek yoghurt over and add acacia honey to taste.

To serve: Serve with Dried Fruit Compote (see page 11) or any fresh fruit. Chopped dessert apple is traditional but berries are good, as too would be sweet plums or seedless grapes.

The permutations and combinations are endless – just use your own favourite ingredients but try to sweeten naturally with dried fruit rather than sugar.

Spinach and Mozzarella Scramble

G *Serves 4*

8 eggs
4 oz (100 g) unsalted butter
8 oz (225 g) spinach (washed, dried and chopped)
8 oz (225 g) Mozzarella (cut into small dice or grated)
fine sea salt
freshly ground black pepper

Allow two very fresh free-range eggs per person, size 3 or larger. You can check their freshness in a bowl with cold water. If they sink they're fresh, if they attempt to float they're not. The secret of a good scramble is to use plenty of butter, I'm afraid, and to cook as slowly as you can.

1. Beat the eggs energetically with a whisk.

2. Melt the butter in a deep heavy frying pan or a saucepan on a low heat.

3. Give the eggs a final beat then add to the butter. Using a wooden spoon, stir the eggs frequently, scraping the bottom and sides of the pan.

4. After about 2 minutes add the Mozzarella and continue to stir.

5. Cook for a further minute, then add the spinach and cook for a final 1 minute. Season and serve immediately onto hot plates with your accompaniments.

VARIATIONS

Scrambles are of course limitless. Try other raw and cooked vegetables, nuts, herbs, other cheeses, cream, crème fraîche or even Greek yoghurt.

Sesame and Potato Croquettes

G *Makes 8*

2 lb (900 g) potatoes, peeled and
   roughly chopped
fine sea salt
freshly ground black pepper
3 oz (75 g) unsalted butter
pinch freshly grated nutmeg
1 free-range egg, beaten
4 oz (100 g) sesame seeds
4 tablespoons vegetable oil

These croquettes are best made the night before and chilled in
the fridge before cooking. Choose a white floury potato such as
Pentland Crown.

1. Cook the potatoes until tender.

2. Season, add the butter and mash well.

3. Add the nutmeg and adjust the seasoning. Allow to cool before
handling.

4. Form the mixture into 8 sausage shapes.

5. Brush with egg and roll in sesame seeds.

6. Allow to chill overnight in the fridge.

7. Heat the oil in a frying pan and sauté the croquettes on a
medium heat, turning several times, until golden brown, for
about 6 minutes.

VARIATION

Garlic addicts may wish to add 4 crushed cloves of garlic to the
potato mixture. Add chillis or herbs to give the potato some extra
bite and colour.

The Perfect Toasting Loaf

Makes 2 × 2 lb (900 g) loaves

$\frac{1}{2}$ teaspoon demerara sugar
1–1$\frac{1}{4}$ pints (600–750 ml) tepid water
   (38°–46°C)
1 oz (30 g) fresh yeast
2 lb (900 g) organic wholemeal flour
$\frac{1}{2}$ oz (15 g) fine sea salt
$\frac{1}{2}$ oz (15 g) butter or vegan
   margarine or a dash of vegetable
   oil
a little milk or soya milk
poppy seeds for sprinkling

A good toasting loaf need not necessarily be fresh, but must be
inherently moist. The best way to ensure a loaf retains water is to
enrich the dough with oil or fat. Fat can mean butter or vegetable
margarine – so vegans can have moist bread too. I also like seeds
on toasted bread: they add a warm fragrance and nutty flavour.

   Non-vegans can substitute milk for all or some of the water in
this recipe.

1. Dissolve the sugar in 4 fl oz (120 ml) of the water in a small
bowl and then crumble in the yeast. Cover and set aside in a

warm draught-free place for 15 minutes or until it is foaming.

2. Mix most of the flour with the salt in a large bowl.

3. When the yeast is ready, add it to the flour with the rest of the water.

4. Add the butter and work the mixture into a sticky dough.

5. Work the dough on a clean surface, using the flour you retained to stop it sticking.

6. When the dough is smooth and firm but springy (rather like your ear lobe) you've done enough work. It'll probably take 15 minutes by hand – be careful not to overwork it.

7. Grease a large bowl with a little vegetable oil, place the dough in it and cover with a damp tea towel or clingfilm.

8. Allow to rise in a warm draught-free place at 24°C until it has doubled in volume – usually $2\frac{1}{2}$–3 hours.

9. When it is risen, put the dough on a lightly floured surface and knock it back to push the air out of it. Knead it once again for a minute and divide it in half.

10. Grease 2×2 lb (900 g) loaf tins and put dough into each one. Cover and allow to prove for an hour in a warm draught-free place or until doubled in volume again. Pre-heat the oven to 200°C/400°F/Gas 6.

11. Brush the tops of the loaves with milk or soya milk and scatter poppy seeds over the surface.

12. Bake the loaves for 45 minutes to 1 hour until they sound hollow when rapped with your knuckle on their base.

13. Allow to cool on a wire rack.

This of course is wonderful eaten fresh. It also freezes successfully. For toast it will keep for up to 4 days.

To serve: Toast must be hot when eaten – many people seem to ignore that salient fact. Equally butter or margarine must be soft. So the time taken to remove the toast from the toaster or grill and spread it with what you want must be so short that when the toast goes into your mouth it is still hot, buttery and succulent.

Try unsweetened jams and marmalade – you'll never notice the difference.

WEEK-END BRUNCH

Invite close friends or family round with their children for a brunch party. Like a breakfast party, brunch should be organised well in advance and as much preparation as possible done so that on the day your duties are minimal.

The brunch I've chosen will appeal to children and adults alike. There are no courses as such – everyone can just dive in as the feeling takes them. Fritata is good hot or cold and if you cook it in a heavy iron pan it will stay warm for quite a while. Brioche is a luxury – toast will suffice, but Brioche is better. The recipe is on page 220.

Choose a good, fresh, preferably organic apple juice. I prefer the cloudy ones made with English apples. Smoothies are a healthy alternative to milk-shakes, using no milk or dairy produce. Cream or yoghurt can be stirred in after they have been blended.

---

*M*ENU

WEEK-END BRUNCH

SERVES 8 (4 Adults and 4 Children)

Fresh Apple Juice or Banana Smoothies
Succulent Fruit Salad or Granola

— . —

Honey Sultana Muffins with Fruit Preserves and Butter
Spanish Fritata with Sun-dried Tomato Sauce and Brioche

— . —

Coffee and Tea

COUNTDOWN

3 days before
• Prepare the Granola, cool and store in an airtight container.

Day before
• Prepare the Muffins, cool and freeze. • Make the Brioche and place in fridge overnight. • Prepare the vegetables for the Fritata. • Prepare the Sun-dried Tomato Sauce. • Lay the table. • Remove the Muffins from the freezer.

On the day
• Prepare the Succulent Fruit Salad and chill. • Prepare the brioche. • Heat the oven. • Prepare the Banana Smoothie and chill.

30 minutes before • Prepare the Fritata and put it into the oven. • Reheat the Sun-dried Tomato Sauce.

0 minutes • Serve with the Brioche fresh from the oven.

Banana Smoothies

V G *Makes 4 large glasses*

$1\frac{3}{4}$ pints (1 l) apple juice
4 bananas
1 tablespoon peanut butter

Serve this chilled. If you don't have time to chill it, add some ice before you blend the ingredients (check your blender can take ice).

Put all the ingredients in a blender and blend on full speed until smooth.

VARIATION

Use different juices and fruits. Grape, orange and pineapple are good base juices whilst peaches, nectarines, berries, dates, mangoes, and any other sweet fruit make good partners. Dates are a good natural sweetener for any smoothie that is a bit tart.

Succulent Fruit Salad

V G *Serves 8*

4 nectarines, halved, stoned and
    sectioned
8 oz (225 g) strawberries, hulled and
    halved
2 Charentais melons cut into bite-
    size chunks
1 large pineapple
8 oz (225 g) seedless grapes
sprigs of mint
juice of 1 lime or lemon
some small rose petals

Unfortunately you can't get away from the fact that any fruit salad has to be prepared freshly so you will have some laborious work on the morning of your brunch. What you can do, however, to ease the chore is to choose fruits that are easy to prepare. Of course much will depend on your budget and what fruits are in season, but the list on the left is a suggestion.

Mix all the fruits in an attractive glass bowl, then garnish with mint and lime and some fresh rose petals from the garden.

'Food for friends' Granola

V *Makes about $2\frac{1}{2}$ lb (1.1 kg)*

12 oz (325 g) regular oats
8 oz (225 g) mixed chopped nuts
8 oz (225 g) sunflower seeds
5 oz (150 g) wheatgerm, toasted
2 oz (50 g) fine desiccated coconut
8 fl oz (250 ml) sunflower oil
4 fl oz (120 ml) malt extract
4 fl oz (120 ml) maple syrup
$\frac{1}{2}$ teaspoon real almond essence
1 tablespoon real vanilla essence
$1\frac{1}{2}$ tablespoons cinnamon
$1\frac{1}{2}$ teaspoons fine sea salt
3 oz (75 g) sultanas
3 oz (75 g) dates (cut into small
    pieces the same size as the
    sultanas)

We mentioned Granola before in the muesli section but I think it deserves a recipe of its own. Like muesli, it's always good to have a reserve of Granola. It keeps well, the children love it, and this recipe is exceedingly healthy.

Our longest serving Head Chef at *Food for friends*, Phil Taylor, used to volunteer to make it and as you will see it's quite a labour of love. Keep Granola crunchy at home in an airtight jar in a dark place. You can substitute honey or demerara sugar for maple syrup, and use whatever dried fruits are your favourites.

1. Put the first five ingredients in a bowl.

2. Heat the oil in a pan with the rest of the ingredients except the dried fruit, until it becomes watery.

3. Pour the liquid over the dry mix and stir to make sure it is well coated throughout.

4. Heat the oven to 170°C/325°F/Gas Mark 3.

5. Spread the mix over a large baking sheet or roasting dish.

6. Place in the oven and roast for 20 minutes, stirring every 5 minutes until the mix is golden throughout.

7. Transfer to a bowl and stir occasionally until the mix is cool and dry. Add the dried fruit.

8. Serve with milk and yoghurt and honey or maple syrup to taste.

Honey Sultana Muffins

Makes 12

10 oz (275 g) organic wholewheat flour
10 oz (275 g) unbleached plain flour
2 teaspoons salt
8 oz (225 g) sultanas (or mix sultanas with chopped apple)
$\frac{3}{4}$ pint (450 ml) milk or buttermilk
1 free-range egg
4 oz (100 g) unsalted butter, melted
4 oz (100 g) runny honey

Muffins are another simple comforting food that you can adjust to suit your larder. In other words, don't be ruled by ingredients, put in what you fancy or what you have left. They are very simple to make and children adore them.

1. Preheat the oven to 200°C/400°F/Gas Mark 6.

2. Grease 12 muffin tins with hard vegetable fat or line with silicone paper cases.

3. Sift the wholewheat flour and retain the bran. Mix the sifted flour, plain flour, salt and sultanas together in a bowl.

4. Put the bran in a separate bowl with some of the buttermilk, egg and melted butter. Allow the bran to soften, then add the honey.

5. Using a fork, stir the flour mix into the bran mix until you have a thick lumpy batter. Do not overstir.

6. Spoon into the muffin tins and bake until lightly browned – about 25 minutes.

Muffins can be frozen and you may wish to do that to avoid extra work on the morning of the party.

Spanish Fritata

G *Serves 8*

4 oz (100 g) unsalted butter
2 cloves garlic, crushed or chopped
3 shallots, finely sliced
1 large red pepper, deseeded and
  finely sliced
1 large green pepper, deseeded and
  finely sliced
1 large yellow pepper, deseeded and
  finely sliced
1 large orange pepper, deseeded and
  finely sliced
12 free-range eggs (size 3), beaten
1 medium potato, cooked and diced
1 bunch chives, finely chopped
fine sea salt and freshly ground
  pepper
2 oz (50 g) grated Pecorino cheese

You'll need quite a large ovenproof frying pan for this dish. Heavy metal ones are best. Failing that, use a large, well greased flan tin or deep-dish pizza tin. For smaller quantities, Fritata may be cooked on top of the stove.

1. Heat the oven to 180°C/350°F/Gas Mark 4.

2. Melt half the butter in your chosen dish.

3. Add the shallots and garlic and cook gently.

4. After 2 minutes, add the peppers and continue to cook until they are starting to soften. If you like them crunchy, leave them crunchy. If you like them soft, cook them until they are soft. They will not cook appreciably in the egg mix.

5. Give the eggs a final beat and stir in the pepper mixture along with the potato, chives and some seasoning.

6. While the frying pan is empty quickly wipe it clean with some kitchen paper in case bits of onion or pepper have burnt on the bottom.

7. Put the rest of the butter into the pan and melt. Make sure the entire bottom of the pan is well coated with butter.

8. Pour in the egg mix and place the frying pan in the oven for about 30 minutes or until set.

9. Turn on your grill, remove the Fritata from the oven and sprinkle it with the Pecorino. Pop it under the grill to brown.

10. Use a palette knife to ease the Fritata out of the pan and slip it onto a dish where it can be cut into wedges and served.

VARIATION

The pepper and potato mix may be replaced with any of your favourite combinations of vegetables. Always bear in mind that the filling must be cooked before it is mixed into the eggs.

Sun-dried Tomato Sauce

V G *Serves 8*

4 tablespoons olive oil, from the
    sun-dried tomatoes if possible
4–6 shallots, peeled and chopped
3 cloves garlic, crushed or minced
6 fl oz (180 ml) dry white wine (e.g.
    Frascati)
1 lb (450 g) fresh tomato purée
    (page 223)
1 tablespoon commercial tomato
    purée
6 oz (175 g) sun-dried tomatoes,
    drained and sliced
1 oz (30 g) fresh basil leaves,
    chopped
3 oz (75 g) black olives, stoned and
    chopped
freshly ground black pepper

Sun-dried tomatoes are great – far too expensive, but great.

They have an intense flavour that is unique. The best ones to use in sauces are the American vacuum-packed variety (by Sunoman). They are best because they're not salty or oily, which of course does affect any sauce you are making. However they are by no means commonly available and so this recipe uses the salty, oily variety and still achieves the most sumptuous sauce you will ever have tasted. Its clean edge goes well with rich dishes like Fritata but will be equally good in a lasagne or with a roast. It is excellent served hot with pasta or cold with salads and cold pastries. This sauce will keep well in the fridge and is probably best made at least the day before to allow its flavour to develop.

1. Heat the oil in a heavy saucepan.

2. Add the shallots and garlic. Cook gently until softening.

3. Turn up the heat and pour in the white wine. Cook until reduced by half.

4. Add the tomato purées and sun-dried tomatoes and bring back to the boil. Simmer for 10 minutes.

5. Stir in the basil and olives.

6. Adjust the seasoning, mostly with pepper as the sauce will already be quite salty.

Note: If you have time, allow the sauce to simmer on a very low heat for an hour so that the flavour of the sun-dried tomatoes is fully imparted. Always retain some fresh basil to stir in right at the end.

Chapter two

INFORMAL MEALS

Usually these informal meals are the best meals. Both guests and host are relaxed. Often ingredients are just what happens to be there. Best of all – the number of people eating is usually small. Fresh crusty bread with good mature Cheddar and pickles is a meal I never tire of, but it's not the sort of dish you need to be told about. So in this section of the book is a selection of recipes that have proved popular at the restaurant. They are generally quick and easy to make but are also a little out of the ordinary and therefore bound to impress your guests. Feel free to embellish them with side salads, bread and favourite condiments.

Nothing more complicated than cheese or fruit is all that's needed to round off a relaxed meal. But for the times when you would like to offer more than this, the second half of this chapter contains a selection of desserts. You can mix and match the main courses and desserts to make up complete meals; here are just some suggestions:

- Biryani followed by Coconut Custard Creams

- Port and Mushroom Linguini followed by Tiramisu

- Hot Chanterelle Salad followed by Blackberry and Almond Tart

- Moroccan Couscous followed by Fresh Figs with Blueberries and Greek Yoghurt

- Rösti with Tomato and Garlic Sauce and Red Med Salad followed by Rhubarb and Strawberry Cheesecake

I've also slipped in two excellent recipes for cakes – one for a rich a fruity Guinness cake, and the other a Vegan Date and Walnut Bread. Both are ideal for entertaining and wonderfully versatile. For example the Date and Walnut Bread is delicious on its own or spread with a little vegan margarine and served at breakfast or afternoon tea. Delicate, thin slices make the perfect partner to cheese, and it's ideal for picnics and lunchboxes too.

SAVOURY DISHES

Port and Mushroom Linguini

Serves 4–6

3 oz (75 g) butter (or 1½ oz (40 g)
   butter and 1 tablespoon olive oil)
2 medium onions, finely sliced
1 red pepper, cut into strips
1 green pepper, cut into strips
1 yellow pepper, cut into strips
1 lb (450 g) organic brown or
   chestnut mushrooms, sliced
1 tablespoon Dijon mustard
½ tablespoon soya sauce (optional)
1 wineglass port
1 pint (600 ml) whipping cream (or
   sour cream or fromage frais)
1 bunch chives, snipped
fine garlic sea salt
freshly ground black pepper
1 lb (450 g) dry linguini
freshly grated Parmesan or Pecorino
   cheese

This is one of my favourite pasta dishes. It's quick, simple and incredibly tasty. Any pasta goes well – I like spinach tagliatelle or linguini, as here.

Do try to use the brown or chestnut mushrooms as they do not release lots of water like cultivated flat or cup mushrooms.

1. Melt the butter slowly in a deep heavy pan, taking care not to burn it. You may wish to mix the quantity 50/50 with good virgin olive oil.

2. Add the onions and cook gently until starting to soften, then stir in the peppers and cook for a further 3 minutes before adding the mushrooms.

3. Stir in the mustard and soya. Then add the port. Increase the heat and reduce the liquid by half, stirring frequently.

4. Finally add the cream and bring to the boil. Boil the mixture vigorously until it has reduced by at least a third and thickened to a good consistency. Take care not to burn the sauce in your haste to reduce it. Stir in the chives and adjust the seasoning just before serving. Garlic lovers may like to dose it heavily with the revered bulb at this stage, using a garlic crusher.

5. Cook the pasta in plenty of boiling salted water to which a little olive oil has been added. Drain and toss it in the sauce. Serve with freshly grated Parmesan or Pecorino cheese.

VARIATIONS

- Add a spoonful of tomato purée to the sauce before the cream is added.

- Substitute Madeira, sherry or vermouth for the port. Brandy is good too but use half the quantity.

Biryani

V G *Serves 4–6*

Pilau

1 lb (450 g) basmati rice

5 tablespoons melted butter or ghee or vegetable oil

1 large onion, finely sliced

pinch saffron strands

3 cloves garlic, crushed

½ teaspoon finely grated fresh ginger

1¾ pints (1 l) spicy vegetable stock (see page 225)

½ teaspoon garam masala

½ teaspoon ground cardamom

3 tablespoons rosewater (if unavailable lemon juice is nice)

2 oz (50 g) sultanas

6 oz (175 g) frozen peas

4 oz (100 g) frozen sweetcorn

1 oz (30 g) toasted flaked almonds

Vegetables

3 oz (75 g) butter or ghee

3 large onions, sliced

5 cloves garlic, crushed and chopped

1 tablespoon fresh ginger, finely chopped

1 large aubergine, cut into bite-size pieces

2 red peppers, cut into 2 in (5 cm) strips

2 green peppers, cut into 2 in (5 cm) strips

8 oz (225 g) organic brown chestnut mushrooms, sliced

3 tablespoons mild curry paste

2 teaspoons salt

2 teaspoons lemon juice

½ teaspoon garam masala

½ teaspoon ground cardamom

1 fresh red chilli, halved, deseeded and finely chopped

This is an incredibly simple dish, nourishing, satisfying and at the same time very healthy. The ingredients are not rigid; choose your favourite vegetables or see what needs using up before deciding on the ultimate combination. A biryani as we make it is essentially spicy cooked vegetables layered with pilau rice and finished off in the oven. There are two distinct sections to the preparation. The pilau can be made well in advance if necessary. Don't be put off by the long list of ingredients.

To cook the rice

1. Wash the rice thoroughly and drain. Allow to dry if possible.

2. Heat the butter, ghee or oil in a deep pan and add the onions. Cook until starting to colour. Then add the saffron, garlic and ginger and cook for a further minute. Add the rice and cook for a further 5 minutes.

3. Add stock, garam masala, rosewater, cardamom and sultanas.

4. Cover the pan and cook over a low heat for a further 20 minutes. Do not lift the lid during cooking.

5. When the rice is cooked, stir in the peas and sweetcorn. Remove from heat and stand, covered, for 5 minutes, then sprinkle with almonds.

To cook the vegetables

1. Melt the butter or ghee in a pan. Sauté the sliced onions, garlic and ginger until they start to soften.

2. Add the aubergine, peppers and mushrooms and stir to coat them evenly with the mixture. Cook for a further 5 minutes.

3. Add the curry paste and continue to cook for 1 minute more, then stir in the salt and the lemon juice.

4. Finally add the rest of the ingredients except the chopped coriander. Cover and bring back to the boil, turn the heat down and simmer gently for 30 minutes to allow the flavours to mingle. The mixture should be very thick, almost dry. Sprinkle it with the fresh coriander.

1 tablespoon chopped fresh mint or
  1 tablespoon dried
2 tomatoes, peeled, deseeded and
  chopped
2 tablespoons chopped fresh
  coriander

To finish
1 oz (30 g) butter, melted, or ghee
chopped fresh coriander
roasted pistachio nuts
lemon slices

To assemble

1. Heat the extra butter or ghee in a large casserole dish. Make sure the bottom is well coated. Add extra garlic if you're a fan.

2. Spoon in about one third of the pilau. Cover that with about half the vegetable mix. Then repeat the procedure, ending with a final layer of pilau. Pat it down gently.

3. Cover the casserole and place in a preheated oven at 200°C/400°F/Gas Mark 6 for 20 minutes – double the reheating time if the pilau is stone cold.

4. Drizzle over the butter or ghee and garnish with chopped fresh coriander, roast pistachio nuts and slices of lemon.

To serve: Serve with an onion salad, poppadoms, pickle and raitas.

Autumn Vegetable Soup

V G *Serves 4–6*

2 tablespoons olive oil
1 onion, chopped
1 lb (450 g) leeks, chopped
1 large carrot, chopped
1 large potato, chopped
1 turnip, chopped
1 parsnip, chopped
2 sticks celery, chopped
$2\frac{1}{2}$ teaspoons chopped thyme
1 teaspoon chopped marjoram
1 teaspoon chopped basil
4 cloves garlic, crushed
2 tablespoons tomato purée
juice of 1 lemon
1 tablespoon soya sauce
4 oz (100 g) sweetcorn
4 oz (100 g) flageolet beans, cooked

This soup could easily be winter, spring or summer vegetable soup. Just use whatever vegetables you have or can easily get. There's no better sight for hungry guests than to see a steaming tureen of soup appear accompanied by hot flavoured bread or croutons.

1. Heat the oil and sauté the onions until softening.

2. Add the rest of the vegetables and herbs and cook with the lid on for 15–20 minutes on a lowish heat, stirring occasionally.

3. Stir in the garlic, tomato purée, lemon juice and soya sauce. Cover generously with water and bring to the boil.

4. Simmer for another 15 minutes or until all the vegetables are tender.

5. Remove a good third of the soup and blend in a blender. Pour back into the soup along with the sweetcorn and the flageolet beans. Bring back to the boil and adjust the seasoning and consistency (if too thick add a little water – if too thin reduce on a high heat).

Serving suggestion: Serve with a dollop of sour cream or yoghurt and plenty of cheese croutons (or garlic croutons if vegan).

Indonesian Layer Bake

V *Serves 4–6*

6 oz (175 g) medium bulghar wheat
1 pint (600 ml) water
juice and zest of 1 lemon
1 teaspoon fine sea salt
2 tablespoons peanut or sesame oil
1 large onion, finely sliced
1 large carrot, finely diced
3 cloves garlic, crushed or chopped
1 tablespoon finely chopped fresh
    ginger
2 courgettes cut on a slant into bite-
    sized pieces
1 large red pepper, cut into strips
2 sticks celery, cut into matchsticks
4 oz (100 g) mushrooms, sliced
6 baby sweetcorn, whole or halved
    lengthways
2 oz (50 g) fine beans, top and tailed
    and halved if too long
2 oz (50 g) mung bean sprouts
1 tablespoon soya sauce

Sauce
peanut oil or sesame oil or butter
1 medium onion, chopped
$\frac{1}{2}$ teaspoon chilli powder (more or
    less depending on your taste)
2 cloves garlic, crushed or chopped
8 oz (225 g) peanut butter (use an
    unadulterated chunky variety)
1 tablespoon tomato purée
1 tablespoon honey or sugar
1 tablespoon soya sauce

To finish
1 oz (30 g) whole roasted peanuts
1 oz (30 g) whole roasted sunflower
    seeds
lemon slices for garnish

This is incredibly more-ish and surprisingly quick to make. The joy in eating it comes from the contrasting textures and flavours. The lemony bulghar wheat sidles up to the simply cooked vegetables and then . . . Whoosh, the whole lot is suddenly immersed in tangy peanut sauce.

1. Put the bulghar wheat in a large, heat-resistant dish and cover it with boiling water. Add the lemon juice and stir it well. Season. Allow it to stand for at least 15 minutes, then drain.

2. Heat the oil in a large deep pan. Add the onion and carrots. Where the onions start to soften, stir in the garlic and ginger.

3. Add the rest of the ingredients and stir-fry. The bean sprouts must be added last and only just heated through before the soya sauce is added. Remove from the heat. All the vegetables should be cooked but crunchy. Adjust the seasoning.

4. Oil a large baking dish with a little peanut or sesame oil. Spoon in the cooked bulghar wheat and top with the vegetables.

To make the sauce

1. Heat a little oil in a saucepan. Add the onion and cook until translucent. Stir in the chilli powder and garlic. Continue to cook for 1 more minute.

2. Spoon in the peanut butter, the tomato purée and the honey or sugar. The mix will now be incredibly dry.

3. Add water, stirring in a little at first, rather like making a béchamel sauce. Gradually add more and more, until you have achieved a thick but fluid consistency. Remove from the heat. Season with soya sauce.

To finish

Pour the sauce over the vegetables in the baking dish, ensuring they are well covered. Scatter peanuts and sunflower seeds over the top and then bake in a preheated oven at 220°C/425°F/Gas Mark 7 for 30–40 minutes or until bubbling. Serve garnished with lemon slices. Enjoy.

Moroccan Couscous

V *Serves 4–6*

The couscous
8 oz (225 g) couscous
pinch of saffron
1 tablespoon chopped fresh
    coriander

The sauce
1 tablespoon olive oil
1 leek, sliced
2 cloves garlic, crushed
1 teaspoon chopped fresh mint
2 teaspoons ground cumin
1 teaspoon chilli powder
1 teaspoon crushed coriander seed
2 teaspoons chopped fresh coriander
1 pint (600 ml) fresh tomato purée
    (see page 223)
½ pint (275 ml) water

The vegetables
1 tablespoon olive oil
1 aubergine, chopped
6 button onions
6 button mushrooms
6 baby sweetcorn
6 okra
1 carrot, chopped
2 sticks celery, cut into fingers
2 courgettes, roughly chopped
12 mangetout (or sugar snap peas)

Couscous is the national dish in most North African countries. Couscous itself is a special type of semolina and is usually served as an accompaniment to a savoury stew, though in Egypt it is served as a dessert. We shall be cooking the savoury version, which is traditionally served with a spicy sauce. You will need a couscousière or a steamer, or more simply a wire sieve that will fit into a saucepan above a sauce. Preparation is simple but must be done in stages.

1. Soak the saffron for 5 minutes in enough warm water to cover the couscous.

2. Cover the couscous with this water and soak for 20 minutes.

3. While the couscous is soaking make the sauce. Heat the oil in a deep heavy pan and add the leek and seasonings. Stir-fry for 3 minutes, then add the tomato purée and water and bring to the boil. Allow to simmer for 15 minutes – you may wish to strain it at this point but I don't.

4. Pour off any liquid from the couscous and put the couscous in a sieve to steam above the bubbling tomato sauce. Cover with a pan lid. Steam it for 20 minutes above the sauce, forking through occasionally to break up any lumps.

5. In a frying pan stir-fry the vegetables in a little olive oil. Add the aubergine and onion first as they will take longest to cook. When you are satisfied all the vegetables have become well heated through, remove the steamer with the couscous temporarily and add the vegetables, except the mangetout, to the tomato sauce. Replace the couscous and simmer the vegetables for 8 minutes. Add the mangetout or sugar snap peas and continue to cook for a further 2 minutes.

6. Spread the couscous over a large warmed dish.

7. Strain the vegetables through a sieve and arrange nicely on the couscous. Pour a little of the sauce over them but retain the rest to serve separately. Sprinkle with freshly chopped coriander.

Note: This dish can be made with any baby vegetables you can get. Tiny courgettes, aubergines, carrots and turnips are good.

Chinese Stir-Fried Vegetables and Tofu with Lemon Grass-Scented Rice

V G *Serves 4*

Rice

1 oz (30 g) butter or oil
1 tablespoon dried lemon grass, finely chopped, and tied in a muslin bag
12 oz (325 g) rice
1½ pints (900 ml) water
fine sea salt

Stir-fry

2 tablespoons sesame oil
½ teaspoon chilli powder
1 medium carrot, peeled, halved and thinly sliced
1 bunch spring onions, trimmed and sliced
1 tablespoon dried black beans
3 cloves garlic, crushed or chopped
1 small yellow pepper, cut into strips 1½ in (3 cm) long
1 small red pepper, cut into strips 1½ in (3 cm) long
2 oz (50 g) broccoli, sliced into small florets
8 oz (225 g) extra firm tofu, drained and cut into ½ in (1 cm) chunks
1 oz (30 g) cashew nuts
2 large mushrooms, sliced or 2 oz (50 g) Chinese mushrooms, soaked
6 oz (175 g) choy sum (or Chinese leaf), roughly chopped
7 oz (200 g) water chestnuts
1 tablespoon balsamic vinegar (or mirin)
1 tablespoon brown sugar
1 tablespoon soya sauce
3 oz (75 g) bean sprouts
salt and black pepper
a little arrowroot to thicken, if desired

Choose succulent vegetables for this dish. Prepare and cook them quickly but before you do anything put the rice on. This will give you 30 minutes to prepare and cook the vegetables and tofu.

To cook the rice

1. Melt the butter or oil in a deep pan.

2. Add the lemon grass and stir-fry gently for 2 minutes. Add the rice, cook for 3 minutes, then pour on the water.

3. Bring to the boil, then simmer gently with the lid on for 20 minutes. Under no circumstances remove the lid. When 20 minutes is up, turn the heat off but keep the lid on.

To cook the stir-fry

As soon as you have covered the rice start to prepare the stir-fry.

1. Heat the sesame oil with the chilli powder in a large heavy frying pan or wok. When it is hot add the carrot and stir-fry for 1 minute. Season with black pepper.

2. Add the spring onion, black beans and garlic and continue to cook for another minute.

3. Add the peppers and broccoli and cook for another 3 minutes.

4. Add the tofu and cashew nuts. Fry for another minute.

5. Stir in the mushrooms, choy sum and water chestnuts and continue to cook for another 3 minutes or until very hot.

6. When it is positively sizzling, add the vinegar, bring to the boil and reduce by half before adding the sugar and the soya sauce, then once again bring to the boil. Reduce again before tossing in the bean sprouts.

7. Cook the bean sprouts thoroughly for about a minute and then, if desired, thicken the sauce with a little arrowroot. Adjust the seasoning and serve on or beside the rice on a hot plate.

OPTIONAL EXTRAS

- Add the juice and zest of 1 lemon to the rice.

- Marinate the tofu in soya sauce, ginger, garlic and chilli, deep fry, then add to the rest of the mixture.

Hot Chanterelle Salad

V   *Serves 4–6*

1 lb (450 g) mixed salad (choose from frisée, mache, lollo rosso, radicchio, oak leaf, chicory, rocket, young spinach leaves, fresh snipped chives)
2 red onions, finely sliced
5 tablespoons hazelnut, walnut or olive oil
4 tablespoons pine nuts
3 slices organic brown bread, cubed
3 cloves garlic, crushed and sliced
8 oz (450 g) chanterelles, whole or halved
3 tablespoons raspberry vinegar
1 teaspoon brown sugar
1 teaspoon Dijon mustard
fine sea salt
freshly ground black pepper
chopped chives to garnish

Hot salads are a quick, unusual, but very tasty way of feeding a few friends casually. Hot mushroom salads are best in autumn when you can gather all types of different edible fungi. A neat way of avoiding the seasonal limitations of this delicacy is to preserve the mushrooms you have gathered in olive oil. To do this, simply plunge them into a boiling liquid made of half cider vinegar and half salted water for 5 minutes. Then drain them and allow them to dry in a cloth for at least 6 hours. Next, spoon them into a sterile kilner jar together with whole coriander seeds, black peppercorns, garlic cloves, a bay leaf, thyme and rosemary. When the jar is three-quarters full, cover generously with olive oil, making sure all the mushrooms are submerged, and seal. Store for 1 month before using.

Whether you use preserved mushrooms or fresh, a hot mushroom salad will only take minutes to prepare so have everything ready.

Try to find creamy chanterelle mushrooms for this recipe. Wipe and brush them clean – do not wash. They will stay fresh for up to a week in the refrigerator. If you cannot find chanterelles (they grow in oak or beech woods mainly) use cultivated oyster mushrooms or organic brown caps.

1. Rub a salad bowl with a clove of garlic.

2. Put the salad leaves into the bowl with the onion. Tear any leaves that are too big.

3. Using a large heavy frying pan heat $1\frac{1}{2}$ tablespoons of oil. When it's hot, add the pine nuts and heat for 1 minute, stirring constantly. When the kernels are golden brown, remove them from the oil and allow to drain on some kitchen paper.

4. Add the bread cubes to the pan, season and cook until crisp and golden, then transfer to some kitchen paper. Keep the pine kernels and croutons warm in the oven.

5. Add more oil to the pan and cook the garlic and mushrooms together for about 4–5 minutes or until tender. Chanterelles prefer longer gentler cooking to other mushrooms – they also exude a lot of liquid so it is necessary to remove them from the liquid and reduce it by at least two-thirds. When this is done, return them and add the rest of the oil with the vinegar, sugar, mustard, salt and pepper. Heat briefly and stir well before pouring the lot over the salad leaves.

6. Sprinkle with hot pine nuts, croutons and chopped chives and eat immediately.

Rösti

V G *Serves 4–6*

2 lb (900 g) baking potatoes
6 oz (175 g) unsalted butter, vegan
    margarine or olive oil
2 teaspoons chopped fresh rosemary
fine sea salt
freshly ground black pepper
pinch grated nutmeg

God I love rösti – a nicely prepared rösti, a rösti that is crisp outside, soft inside, plain or delicately flavoured.

Rösti can go with just about anything, and yet how often do you see this most simple of simple dishes? Even children love it. Also it's not only cheap, it is simple and versatile.

We've been known to add a few grated carrots to the potato mix for colour and sweetness, or celeriac for its delicious nutty flavour. Rösti can be prepared in advance and reheated in the oven when it is needed. If you can't find old floury potatoes, simply parboil and use the potatoes you have.

It's equally good as a starter or main course. Next time a few friends drop round, try this on them, you can't go wrong. Here's a good way of doing individual rösti – allow 2 per person.

1. Parboil then cool, peel and coarsely grate the potatoes.

2. Mix the potatoes with rosemary, nutmeg, seasoning and 2 oz (50 g) of the melted butter. Divide into 6 equal portions.

3. Heat 2 oz (50 g) of butter in a deep frying pan. Place two 4 in (10 cm) muffin rings in the pan and when the butter has melted and is bubbling put a portion of the mixture into each ring. Cook on a medium flame until the underside is slightly honey coloured. Remove the rings and turn the rösti. Cook until the other side is the same colour. Keep the rösti warm while you repeat the process to use up the rest of the mixture.

To serve: Serve with one or two substantial sauces such as Food for friends Cauliflower Cheese Sauce or Fresh Tomato and Garlic Sauce (pages 106 and 80). Fresh Horseradish Dip (page 153) is also an excellent partner. Rösti is very adaptable. It even goes well with curry. Or try it with a sharp fruit sauce and a blob of sour cream or crème fraîche.

VARIATIONS

- Add to the mixture 1 large Spanish onion, finely sliced and cooked until soft but without colour. A welcome addition can be 4 oz (100 g) grated Gruyère or Cheddar cheese.

- Rather than cook the rösti in rings which can be a bit fiddly, simply cook in the base of a 10 in (25 cm) frying pan with a heavy bottom. When the underside is cooked (about 20–25 minutes), cover with a large plate and invert the whole rösti on the plate. Melt a little more butter in the pan. Slip the rösti back into the pan to cook the other side for 10 minutes. Serve the rösti cut into wedges on an attractive flat dish.

Red Med Salad

V G *Enough for 6*

1 lb (450 g) tomatoes, peeled, deseeded and finely chopped

8 oz (225 g) red onions, finely chopped

4 large red peppers, deseeded and cut into $\frac{1}{2}$ in (1 cm) dice

1 bunch fresh English radishes, cut to match the other vegetables

fine sea salt and freshly ground black pepper

a few attractive salad leaves

fresh coriander to garnish (optional)

This salad is an excellent accompaniment to rösti. It needs no dressing apart from salt and pepper. Somehow it dresses itself and the combination of flavours and colour is irresistible. The most important thing is the chopping of the vegetables; try to make them all the same size.

Mix all the vegetables well with the seasoning. Line a bowl with some attractive leaves and pour the salad on top. If desired sprinkle with chopped fresh coriander.

VARIATION

- Add a favourite vinaigrette – it's still a good combination.

31

Geordie Mushroom and Ale Pies

V *Serves 4–6*

8 oz (225 g) barley

2 tablespoons butter or vegetable oil

2 large onions, thinly sliced

1 large carrot, finely diced

3 stalks celery, finely diced

1 large parsnip, finely diced

1 small swede, finely diced

2 teaspoons thyme

3 bay leaves

8 oz (225 g) flat mushrooms, thickly sliced

2 oz (50 g) butter or vegan margarine

2 oz (50 g) organic white flour

1 tablespoon soy sauce (optional)

1 tablespoon vegetarian Worcestershire sauce (optional)

1¼ pints (750 ml) vegetable stock (see page 225)

1 pint (600 ml) ale (Newcastle Brown is good)

1 bunch parsley, chopped

fine sea salt

freshly ground black pepper

puff pastry (see page 221)

1 egg, beaten, or a little soya milk if vegan

Here's a hearty meal that is eminently suitable for a cold winter's day or evening when you've got a few friends coming round. The pie filling is best made the day before to allow its flavour to develop. Serve with baked potatoes filled with sour cream, and lightly cooked mangetout. Instead of individual pies you can cook the pie in a large dish, using a pastry duck to support the centre.

1. Heat the oven to 220°C/425°F/Gas Mark 7.

2. First cook the barley. Put it in a saucepan together with 1¼ pints (750 ml) of cold water. Add a little salt, then bring to the boil. Cover and simmer for 45 minutes or until tender. Drain, and run under the cold tap to cool. Put aside.

3. Melt the butter or oil in a deep heavy pan. Add the onions and cook for 5 minutes. Then add the rest of the root vegetables and the herbs. Sauté, stirring occasionally, for at least 10 minutes.

4. Add the mushrooms and cook for a further 5 minutes with the lid on, then remove from the heat.

5. In another saucepan, melt the butter or margarine and stir in the flour to make a roux. Cook it well to a dark biscuit colour without burning. Allow it to cool if you have time.

6. If the vegetable stock is a bit weak, pep it up with soy and Worcestershire sauce. Bring the vegetable stock to the boil, then add it gradually to the roux over a medium heat to make a very thick sauce. Now gradually stir in the beer, being careful not to boil it too much. Boiling beer seems to make it unnecessarily bitter. Finally, throw in the parsley, adjust the seasoning and remove from the heat. The sauce should be fairly thick.

7. Combine the sauce, barley and vegetables to form a fairly liquid casserole. Adjust the seasoning. Remember the barley will absorb some of the sauce in the final cooking.

8. Divide the vegetable and barley mix among 4–6 ovenproof bowls. Roll out the pastry and cut out circles to fit the bowls. Place the pastry lids on and press round the edges. Brush with beaten egg or soya milk. Then bake for 30 minutes or until the pastry has risen and is golden brown.

VARIATIONS

Instead of pastry, top the casserole with herby dumplings, mashed potato or slices of boiled potato brushed with melted butter or vegetable oil.

Chimichangas

Serves 4

4 large soft flour tortillas

Refried beans (Refritos)

1 lb (450 g) uncooked kidney or
    pinto beans
$1\frac{1}{2}$ teaspoons salt
3 tablespoons olive oil
1 large onion, chopped
3 cloves garlic, crushed
2 teaspoons ground cumin
1 medium green pepper, chopped
$\frac{1}{2}$ teaspoon black pepper

Mexican chilli sauce

2 tablespoons olive oil
1 medium onion, chopped
2 cloves garlic, crushed
1 teaspoon ground cumin
$\frac{1}{2}$ teaspoon ground coriander seeds
2 fresh red chillies, chopped
$1\frac{1}{2}$ lb (550 g) tomatoes, skinned,
    deseeded and chopped
$\frac{1}{4}$ pint (150 ml) water
red wine
2 tablespoons tomato purée
$\frac{1}{4}$ teaspoon black pepper

One of the great things about chimichangas is that once you've made them you can pop them in the fridge and forget about them till it's time for cooking. When eventually they are set before your guests they should bring gasps of delight as they can look extremely attractive.

As you will see you have to make at least four things to construct this dish – do not be daunted as all four are simple and it's well worth the effort!

To make the refried beans

Cook the beans in salted water until soft (allow around 2 hours). Drain well and mash with a potato masher. It is very much a case of personal preference how much you mash them – I prefer them only semi-mashed.

Heat the oil in a deep heavy-bottomed pan and then add the onions, garlic and cumin. Cook on a low heat until the onions are softening. Add the chopped green pepper, cover and simmer gently for 10 minutes. Stir the mixture into the beans, season and set aside to cool.

To make the Mexican Chilli Sauce

Heat the oil in the pan you just used for the refried beans. Add the onions and garlic and cook until softening. Add the spices and chillies. Stir in the tomatoes, water, wine and tomato purée and then season. Bring back to the boil and allow to simmer for as long as possible – at least 30 minutes, although 2 hours is best.

You may wish to leave the sauce as it is, or you can purée all or part of it.

Guacamole
2 ripe medium avocados, mashed
juice of 1 lemon
3 cloves garlic
salt and pepper

Sour cream, sweetcorn and chives
1 pint (600 ml) sour cream
4 oz (100 g) tinned or frozen
    sweetcorn
1 bunch chives

To finish
8 oz (225 g) grated Mozzarella
lime wedges

To make the Guacamole

Simply combine the ingredients and either mash or purée together. Adjust seasoning.

To make the Sour Cream, Sweetcorn and Chive Sauce

Simply stir the ingredients together and season. Keep well chilled until use.

To assemble

Take the large flour tortillas and fill with the bean mixture. Place on a large well oiled tray. Sprinkle with Mozzarella. Cook in the oven at 190°C/375°F/Gas Mark 5 for approximately 45 minutes or until the cheese is brown and bubbly.

Heat the chilli sauce if you have allowed it to cool.

Serve on plates decorated with lime wedges. Either alternate the sauces over the chimichangas to give contrasting coloured effects, or serve the sauces separately.

VARIATION

Use Roasted Red Pepper and Chilli Sauce (see page 227) instead of Mexican Chilli Sauce.

SWEET DISHES

Coconut Custard Creams

G *Serves 4–6*

12 fl oz (325 ml) unsweetened
  coconut milk
1 teaspoon vanilla essence or $\frac{1}{2}$ vanilla
  pod
8 oz (225 g) soft brown sugar or
  palm sugar
5 medium-sized free-range eggs,
  beaten

This is a simple dish to make and will store well overnight in the fridge if you wish. You will need 6 custard cream cups or ramekins.

1. Heat the coconut milk gently with the vanilla essence or pod. When it starts to boil remove it from the heat immediately. Remove the vanilla pod if used.

2. Add about half the sugar to the eggs and beat until they are creamy.

3. Gradually add the hot coconut milk to the egg and sugar mixture, beating continually.

4. Put the rest of the sugar in a heavy saucepan and heat gently over a low flame. Allow the sugar to caramelise – it should melt and turn a dark brown colour. Be careful not to let it burn. Pour a little into the bottom of each custard cream cup or ramekin.

5. Pour the custard through a fine strainer equally into the cups.

6. Place the cups in a deep baking tin, then pour hot water into the tin carefully around the cups, so that they are semi-submerged.

7. Place the pan in the oven (preheated to 170°C/325°F/Gas Mark 4) and bake for 30 minutes, or until just set (test with the tip of a knife).

8. Allow to cool, then chill before running a small knife around the edges of the cups and inverting them onto a plate. If you are not using until the next day let the creams remain in their cups in the fridge, covered with clingfilm.

VARIATIONS

For a slight kick to your Custard Cream, add a tablespoon of light rum, Kahlua or Malibu to the cup instead of caramelised sugar before pouring in the egg mix.

Peach and Cinnamon Strudel

V   *Serves 4–6*

Enough filo pastry to form a sturdy
   20 in (50 cm) square.
1½ oz (40 g) butter or vegan
   margarine, melted
1½ oz (40 g) fine organic wholewheat
   breadcrumbs
1½ lb (675 g) ripe but firm peaches,
   peeled, stoned and cut into thick
   slices
lemon juice
1½ oz (40 g) demerara sugar or
   honey
1½ oz (40 g) nibbed almonds,
   toasted
1½ oz (40 g) chopped prunes, soaked
   in Kirsch if you like
1 teaspoon ground cinnamon
icing sugar
Greek yoghurt to serve

We've been making different types of strudel in the restaurant for years, but peach has always been a favourite. In the early days we made our own strudel pastry, but as demand increased we were forced to use filo, which is a good substitute but never as good as home-made strudel pastry. For a casual lunch, though, filo is fine.

1. Preheat the oven to 200°C/400°F/Gas Mark 6.

2. Lay the filo pastry out and brush with some of the melted butter. If using two layers, repeat the process.

3. Sprinkle the pastry with breadcrumbs, leaving a 3 in (7.5 cm) border all the way round.

4. Mix the peaches with a little of the lemon juice, the sugar, almonds, prunes and cinnamon. Spread on top of the bread-crumbs.

5. Fold the border in, partially enclosing the filling. Then roll the pastry up to form a tightly packed log. Brush with the rest of the butter.

6. Bake for about 40 minutes or until the pastry is brown and crisp.

7. While still hot, sprinkle with icing sugar.

To serve: Serve hot with thick Greek yoghurt.

Tiramisu

Serves 4–6

3 tablespoons dark rum
2 tablespoons brandy
4 fl oz (120 ml) strong black coffee
20 sponge fingers
14 oz (400 g) Mascarpone cheese
¾ pint (450 ml) fresh double cream
4 tablespoons icing sugar
1 tablespoon Amaretto (optional)
6 oz (175 g) grated bitter chocolate
cocoa powder for decoration

Tiramisu means 'pick-me-up' and one thing's for certain – you won't be able to resist doing just that once you have made this delicious Italian dessert. It's best made at least two days in advance. Mascarpone is an unsalted cows' milk cheese with a soft buttery consistency. Do try your hardest to get it, but if everything fails use cream cheese or low-fat cream cheese instead.

1. Mix together the rum, brandy and coffee.

2. Line the bottom of an attractive serving dish with 7 sponge fingers and brush them generously with the alcohol/coffee mixture.

3. Beat the Mascarpone, cream and sugar together until smooth and light. Then carefully fold in the Amaretto.

4. Cover the fingers with one-third of the cream cheese mix and sprinkle with 2 oz (50 g) of chocolate. Then repeat the procedure twice, finishing with a sprinkle of chocolate.

5. Cover and store in the fridge for 2 days.

6. Sprinkle a little cocoa powder over the surface before serving.

Tropical Fruit Tango

G *Serves 6*

1 medium-sized pineapple, cut into
  ½ in (1 cm) cubes
3 medium-sized bananas, chopped
  into similar sized pieces
6 tablespoons golden rum
6 oz (175 g) lightly toasted fine
  desiccated coconut
1 pint (600 ml) Greek yoghurt or
  double cream
4 tablespoons honey, optional

This quick and delightful dessert involves no real cooking – a little toasting and tasting perhaps. Choose your favourite tropical fruits but try to contrast textures for all-round mouthfeel. I've chosen pineapple and banana but you could equally use mango and melon, fresh fig and papaya, or nectarine and strawberry. The only thing that is compulsory is that the fruit is perfectly ripe.

1. Divide the fruit equally into 6 individual bowls. Add about a tablespoon of rum to each bowl.

2. Sprinkle the fruit with about half the coconut, then cover with yoghurt or cream.

3. Finally trickle honey over the surface, if desired, and sprinkle with the remaining coconut.

4. Chill for at least 1 hour.

Blackberry and Almond Tart

Serves 4

11 oz (300 g) sweet pastry (see page
  222)
1 oz (30 g) unsalted butter
1 oz (30 g) soft brown sugar
1 lb 2 oz (500 g) fresh blackberries
2 tablespoons blackberry liqueur (or
  Crème de Cassis)
4 oz (100 g) unsalted butter
4 oz (100 g) demerara sugar
1 free-range egg, beaten
4 oz (100 g) ground almonds
1 oz (30 g) plain wholewheat flour
1 tablespoon milk
cream or crème fraîche to serve

This recipe requires an 8 in (20 cm) flan tin. It's best made with fresh blackberries in September or October, though frozen ones will work too.

1. Preheat the oven to 190°C/375°F/Gas Mark 5.

2. Roll the pastry out and line a greased tin with it. Allow it to rest in the fridge while you make the filling.

3. In a deep heavy pan melt the first quantity of butter. Add the sugar and cook gently until the sugar melts.

4. Pour in the blackberries and liqueur and cook for a few minutes. Allow to cool.

5. Cream together thoroughly the second quantity of sugar and butter. When it is light in colour fold in the rest of the ingredients to form a smooth creamy mixture.

6. Spread the almond mixture smoothly over the pastry. Pour the blackberries over the top. Bake in the preheated oven for 35 minutes.

To serve: Serve hot or cold with fresh cream or crème fraîche.

Nutty Pear and Lemon Crumble

 Serves 4

2 lemons, juice and zest

2 lb (900 g) pears, peeled, cored and chopped

3 tablespoons honey or demerara sugar

1 teaspoon powdered ginger

5 oz (150 g) butter or vegan margarine, melted

6 oz (175 g) wholewheat flour or pinhead oatmeal

2 oz (50 g) demerara sugar

pinch of salt

3 oz (75 g) nibbed hazelnuts

Crumbles have never ceased to feature on the menu at *Food for friends*. They are warm and comforting, doing as much for your psyche as your stomach. Try your own favourite combination of fruit. Serve with Real Custard (see page 228).

1. Preheat the oven to 200°C/400°F/Gas Mark 6.

2. Prepare the pears and coat with lemon juice, zest, honey and ginger. Place in an ovenproof dish.

3. Mix the melted butter with the flour to form a breadcrumb-like texture. Mix in the sugar, salt and the hazelnuts.

4. Pour the crumble mix over the pears. Bake for 50 minutes or until slightly browned on top.

White Chocolate Mousse with Passion Fruit Coulis

Sounds grand ... doesn't it? But this dish can be prepared well in advance and only takes a few minutes to make anyway. Once again, the quality of the ingredients is essential. Eggless chocolate mousses only work when the chocolate is of the highest quality. The mousse 'sets' when the chocolate solidifies after it has amalgamated with the cream to form a rich creamy mousse. Low quality chocolate will never reset and so neither will the mousse.

39

G Serves 4–6

For the mousse
½ pint (275 ml) double cream
3 oz (75 g) white chocolate

For the passion fruit coulis
12 passion fruit, cut in half and
    scooped out
juice of 1 orange
1½ oz (40 g) demerara sugar
4 tablespoons water

This cool smooth, chocolatey chocolate dish is especially good after a hot chilli.

Any soft fruit may be turned into a sauce by the method given here for Passion Fruit Coulis. A suitable alcohol may be added in place of water, and sugar should only be used to taste. Sweet fruits like raspberries and ripe strawberries do not need any sugar but may need a little lemon juice to preserve their colour.

1. Whip the cream until thick but still soft – not fully whipped.

2. Melt the chocolate over steam. Allow to cool but do not allow to reset.

3. Beat the cool liquid chocolate into the cream and pour into individual ramekins. Store in a cool place to set.

4. Purée the ingredients for the sauce together in a blender.

5. Bring to the boil in a small saucepan and simmer for 2 minutes.

6. Force through a fine strainer with a small ladle. Cover and chill. Coulis can be kept for several days in the fridge.

7. Turn out the mousses onto individual plates and pour a little coulis round each one. Serve.

Note: The mousses are nice served on thin discs of chocolate sponge cake soaked in Kirsch or rum.

Pineapple and Banana Sponge Pudding with Apricot Sauce

On certain days there's no pudding quite like a sponge pudding. Perhaps they are days of insecurity, cold days or simply empty days. A good sponge pudding and the best company can be all that is needed to lift the spirit, revitalise the body and firm the resolve. Choose any fruit that is available. Some fruits may need a little pre-cooking and will give you the chance to add other flavours that should enhance rather than dominate the dish. Sauces too can reinforce the main dish and should vary in consistency from a thick vanilla custard through a sabayon to a light coulis.

This dish requires a 10–12 in (25–30 cm) iron casserole dish.

Serves 4–6

For the fruit

1 medium pineapple, cut into
    chunks
3 bananas, cut into similar sized
    chunks
2 tablespoons honey or demerara
    sugar
½ pint (275 ml) pineapple juice
a generous dash of dark rum
    (optional)
juice and rind of 1 lemon

For the sponge

8 oz (225 g) unsalted butter
8 oz (225 g) demerara sugar
6 free-range eggs, beaten
½ teaspoon vanilla essence
8 oz (225 g) wholewheat pastry
    flour
½ teaspoon baking powder
2 oz (50 g) nibbed roasted hazelnuts
1½ oz (40 g) dessicated coconut

Apricot sauce

1 lb 2 oz (500 g) fresh sweet apricots
    or 8 oz (225 g) dried apricots
    (soaked overnight)
½ pint (275 ml) sugar syrup (see page
    228)
sugar
lemon juice
1 tablespoon Kirsch (optional)

To prepare the fruit

1. Simply bring all the ingredients except the bananas to the boil and boil vigorously for 5 minutes, then stir in the bananas and remove from the heat.

2. Pour into a greased casserole dish. The fruit should stick out of the liquid. If it is submerged or semi-submerged you will need to cook the liquid to reduce it further.

To make the sponge

1. Preheat the oven to 180°C/350°F/Gas Mark 4.

2. Put the butter and sugar into a bowl and beat until light in colour and texture.

3. Beat the egg mixture gradually into the sugar and butter with the vanilla.

4. Sieve the flour and baking powder and retain the bran separately. Fold the flour, nuts and coconut into the mixture, then fold in the bran.

5. Pour the sponge batter over the fruit, spreading it gently to the edges, and bake in the preheated oven for about 1 hour plus 10–20 minutes.

6. While the pudding is in the oven, prepare the sauce.

To make the Apricot Sauce

1. Wash, stone and chop the apricots.

2. Bring the apricots to the boil with the sugar syrup. Reduce the heat and allow to simmer until the apricots are cooked. If the apricots are ripe this will only be 5 minutes.

3. Let the mixture cool, then push it through a fine sieve. Adjust the taste with more sugar and lemon juice and finally add the Kirsch if desired.

4. Reheat to serve with the pudding.

Note: The sauce is equally good served cold.

Fresh Figs with Blueberries and Greek Yoghurt

G *Serves 4–6*

8–12 ripe figs (allow 2 per person)

8 oz (225 g) fresh or frozen blueberries

$\frac{3}{4}$ pint (450 ml) Greek yoghurt

a little Greek mountain honey to taste

fresh blueberries to decorate

Figs for this recipe must be perfectly ripe. Quite often the figs that are available are bruised and under-ripe, so choose them carefully. They are best and cheapest in August and September when French and Spanish figs become available. Fresh blueberries are best, but you could use the more commonly found frozen ones. Don't use the tinned variety for this dish as they will be too sweet.

1. Liquidise the blueberries with a little water, then push through a strainer. Taste, and sweeten with honey if necessary.

2. Pour the blueberries onto one half of each serving plate and Greek yoghurt onto the other half.

3. Decorate with the figs and garnish with blueberries.

Rhubarb and Strawberry Cheesecake

V *Serves 4–6*

Compote (for both versions)

1 lb (450 g) rhubarb, finely chopped

8 oz (225 g) strawberries, hulled and halved

honey or sugar to taste (about 3–4 oz (75–100 g))

4 oz (100 g) good strawberries for decoration (optional)

Those of you who read *The Reluctant Vegetarian* will already know that I'm rather fond of the rhubarb–strawberry combination. For a cheesecake they have the perfect blend of acidity and sweetness to cut across the richness of the cheese mixture. For vegans I've included a cheese- and egg-free alternative that we've made in the restaurant to wide acclaim.

Ask your greengrocer if he has any strawberries that need using quickly as these are ideal for the compote.

To make the compote

Poach the rhubarb in just enough water with sugar or honey to taste. When the rhubarb is starting to soften, add the strawberries and turn up the heat to reduce the water content. The resulting compote should be of 'loose' jam consistency. Cool and then chill.

V **Vegan**

7 fl oz (200 ml) soya milk

1¼ lb (550 g) firm tofu

8 tablespoons vegetable oil

1 teaspoon vanilla essence

juice of 1 lemon

2 teaspoons arrowroot

8 oz (225 g) vegan sweet pastry (see page 222)

Vegan method

1. Allow plenty of time to make the pastry and to allow to rest in the refrigerator for at least 2 hours.

2. Heat the oven to 180°C/350°C/Gas Mark 4.

3. Oil an 8 in (20 cm) flan tin (preferably loose-bottomed). Push the pastry into the tin, making it as even as possible. Chill.

4. Blend together the soya milk, tofu, oil, vanilla, lemon and arrowroot.

5. Bake the pastry blind for 10 minutes, then pour in the filling and continue to cook for a further 30 minutes (maximum) or until the filling is firm to the touch. Allow to cool.

6. Top with compote, decorate with halved strawberries if liked and chill well before serving.

Non-Vegan

1¼ lb (550 g) low-fat cream cheese

¼ pint (150 ml) sour cream

3 oz (75 g) demerara sugar or honey

3 fresh free-range eggs

½ teaspoon vanilla essence

1 tablespoon cornflour

juice of 1 lemon

10 oz (275 g) sweet pastry (see page 222)

Non-vegan method

1. Make the pastry and allow to rest in the refrigerator for at least 2 hours.

2. Heat the oven to 200°C/400°F/Gas Mark 6.

3. Oil an 8 in (20 cm) flan tin, preferably loose-bottomed. Roll out the sweet pastry on a lightly floured surface to line the flan tin and extend 1 in (2.5 cm) up the sides. Chill while making the filling.

4. Blend the cream cheese, sour cream, sugar or honey, eggs, vanilla, cornflour and lemon juice together.

5. Pour the dairy cheesecake mix into the pastry case and bake for 40 minutes or until firm to touch. Remove from the oven and allow to cool before adding the rhubarb and strawberry topping. Decorate with halved strawberries if liked. Chill well before serving.

Other good combinations are: blackberry and lemon, blueberry and vanilla, chocolate and banana, gooseberry and lime, raspberry and orange.

Guinness Cake

Makes 1 × 8 in (20 cm) cake, enough for 14 slices

1 lb (450 g) sultanas (or any combination of glacé cherries, raisins, dates, prunes etc. Make sure they are well washed. Nuts may be included too.)

14 oz (400 g) currants

zest of 1 lemon

1½ teaspoons mixed spice

15 fl oz (450 ml) Guinness (draught is best)

6 oz (175 g) slightly salted butter

6 oz (175 g) muscovado sugar

3 large free-range eggs, beaten lightly

12 oz (325 g) strong organic wholewheat flour

This lovely rich cake is ideal for entertaining. It actually improves with age and should be kept for at least 2–3 days before eating. Here are a few tips to guarantee success with fruit cakes of all descriptions.

- The weight of fruit and nuts should equal the weight of sugar + eggs + flour + butter.

- Always use slightly salted butter to bring out the flavour of the fruit.

- Wash the fruit at least three times before use to remove stickiness.

- Always soak the fruit in the alcohol you are using.

- If using nuts, choose fresh sweet ones and toast them slightly beforehand to bring out their flavour.

- It is best to use warm ingredients for the batter.

- Always use dark brown (muscovado) sugar for the batter.

- Once the cake has browned, cover it with greaseproof paper to prevent it burning.

1. Heat the oven to 170°C/325°F/Gas Mark 3.

2. Put the fruit, lemon zest, spice and Guinness in a bowl. Mix well and leave to soak overnight.

3. Grease a deep 8 in (20 cm) cake tin and line the sides with greaseproof paper.

4. Cream the butter and sugar together until light and creamy.

5. Gradually add the eggs, then the fruit, and finally fold in the flour.

6. Pour into the prepared tin, then place in the preheated oven and bake for 2½–3 hours or until a small skewer inserted in the centre comes out clean.

7. Turn out onto a wire rack and allow to cool before wrapping in brown paper or greaseproof paper. Store in an airtight tin for 2–3 days before eating.

Vegan Date and Walnut Bread

V *Makes 1×2 lb (900 g) loaf*

8 oz (225 g) dates, chopped
12 fl oz (325 ml) water
1 teaspoon bicarbonate of soda
2 oz (50 g) walnuts, chopped
1 oz (30 g) vegan margarine
8 oz (225 g) demerara sugar
8 oz (225 g) soft wholewheat flour
8 oz (225 g) strong wholewheat
  flour

Yes, I've heard all those vegans saying 'What about us?' And here at last is almost the perfect vegan cake. It's moist but not overly heavy. It lasts well and – most important – it tastes delicious.

1. Heat oven to 170°C/325°F/Gas Mark 3.

2. Bring the dates, water and bicarbonate of soda to the boil in a pan.

3. Mix the rest of the ingredients together until uniformly crumbly.

4. Add the water and date mixture to the crumble mix and beat together thoroughly.

5. Pour the mixture into a well oiled loaf tin and bake for 1 hour or until a skewer inserted into the centre comes out clean.

6. Remove from the oven and turn out onto a wire rack. Allow to cool.

Chapter three

LUNCH AND DINNER

PARTIES

A few years ago, when Phil Taylor was the Head Chef at the restaurant, my partner Jerry and I decided to do a season of gastronomic evenings. Each evening was a gastronomic success but a fiscal disaster. Many of the recipes in this section of the book were tried and tested at the gourmet evenings to great acclaim. One thing the gastronomic evenings brought home to us was that when food is the main entertainment for the evening it not only has to taste good, but it should also smell good and look good too. One of the great joys of most of our dishes is the natural vivid colours and a variety of textures. Equally important is that the wine drunk with the food bolsters its flavour rather than dominates it and vice versa – it is important to choose wine that will not be totally dominated by the flavour of the food.

Choosing wines to go with vegetarian food can be slightly tricky. Quite often vegetarian dishes have more flavours within them than dishes based on meat and fish. However I do believe that most people worry too much about matching food with wine. There are certain obvious combinations that do not go well with each other; if you have any doubts choose lower priced wines so that mistakes will not cost you dear. Don't forget, too, that in some areas of uncertainty a fortified wine like sherry, port, madeira, pineau or marsala may be the answer and, at the end of

the day, good quality sparkling wines will go with just about any vegetarian dish.

The setting of the table will be enhanced with crisp starched linen, shiny stout cutlery and cut glass or the lovely pale green recycled glass from Spain. I always try to make sure the room is adorned with flowers, preferably wild ones in the summer. Depending on the size of your table, a vast vase on the table is not always practical and a tiny container of violets, snowdrops, pansies, sweetpeas or freesias could be just as effective.

For dinner, lighting must be candlelight, with at least one on the table. Candelabra look good but take up a lot of room, generate heat and create barriers between people. Choose a couple of single or double candle holders with a background light of wall mounted candles. If it's still too dark, position a side light judiciously close to the action without dominating it. There should always be just enough light to see the food clearly on the table – you wouldn't want all the hard work going unnoticed would you?

Every recipe in this section comes with a guide to preparation so that whether it be lunch or dinner you've got plenty of time to relax, make yourself feel lovely and then confidently finish off the dishes.

All the menus in this chapter are suitable for both lunch and dinner parties. Do not feel bound to keep them exactly as I have written them.

MENU

LUNCH PARTY 1

SERVES 4

Tam's Tarragon Tofu served with Satay Sauce

—·—

Avocado, Red Pepper and Tomato Filled Crespolini
with Leek and Vermouth Sauce
Steamed Broccoli with Lemon Butter
Potato and Onion Roast
garnished with lambs' lettuce, toasted pine nuts and
lemon wedges

—·—

Hazelnut and Blackcurrant Trifle

COUNTDOWN

3 days ahead
• Make the pancake filling and freeze it (omit the avocado if freezing).

2 days ahead
• Make the pancake mix. • Make the hazelnut sponge for the trifle.
• Make the blackcurrant mixture for the trifle.

Day before
• Make the Satay Sauce. • Fry the pancakes. • Make the Leek and Vermouth Sauce and keep, covered with buttered greaseproof paper, in the fridge. • Par-cook the potatoes. • Make the custard for the trifle. • Assemble the trifle but do not decorate.

On the day
• Slice and marinate the tofu at least 4 hours ahead. • Remove lemon butter from freezer at least 2 hours beforehand. • Prepare the

garnishes. • Add the avocado to the pancake filling (if frozen beforehand). • Fill the pancakes, coat for frying and chill in the fridge. • Prepare the broccoli for steaming.

1 hour before serving • Put the potatoes and onions in the oven. • Garnish the plates for the first course.

30 minutes before • Gently start to warm the Satay Sauce and the Leek and Vermouth Sauce. • Slice the lemon butter. • Garnish the trifle. • Heat the oil for deep frying if you have an electric fryer.

0–5 minutes before • Sauté the tofu and arrange on plate with garnish and serve. • Heat the main course plates. • Steam the broccoli and deep fry the crespolini. • Arrange crespolini, broccoli, potatoes, sauce, lemon butter and garnish on the plates or serving dishes.

Tam's Tarragon Tofu served with Satay Sauce

V G *Serves 4*

1 packet of fresh Shanghia tofu (not silken)
2 tablespoons finely chopped fresh tarragon
4 or 5 bay leaves
2 oz (50 g) cornflour
1 teaspoon sea salt
$\frac{1}{3}$ teaspoon ground black pepper
2 tablespoons olive oil
sprigs of tarragon for garnish
$\frac{1}{2}$ quantity Satay Sauce (see page 146)

My partner's Chinese wife, Tammy, first served this dish at a memorable dinner party. It's so good it completely changed my views on tofu.

This dish is best if the tofu is soaked for at least 4 hours before preparation.

1. Drain off the water in which the tofu was originally stored.

2. Fill with fresh cold water the bowl in which the ingredients are to be soaked. Place the tofu in the bowl, piling the pieces on top of each other. Add the finely chopped tarragon and bay leaves. Place in the fridge and allow to soak for approximately 4 hours.

3. Drain off the water, remove the tofu and cut it into 4 triangular shapes about $\frac{1}{2}$ in (1 cm) thick.

4. Mix the cornflour with salt and pepper and place in a flat-bottomed bowl. Gently lift the tofu, pat dry on a piece of kitchen paper, then coat each piece with the flour mixture.

5. Heat the olive oil in a pan, then fry the tofu until golden brown in colour (3–4 minutes) over a medium high heat. Turn occasionally so that both sides become crispy.

6. Garnish with small sprigs of tarragon. You can also quickly fry the bay leaves for a few seconds and place one on each slice of tofu.

7. Serve immediately with Satay Sauce.

Avocado, Red Pepper and Tomato Filled Crespolini

Serves 4–6

Pancakes

4 oz (100 g) organic wholewheat pastry flour

2 large free-range eggs

$\frac{1}{4}$ pint (150 ml) milk

$\frac{1}{4}$ pint (150 ml) water

3 tablespoons butter

Filling

2 tablespoons olive oil

1 onion, chopped

1 lb (450 g) red peppers, roasted, skinned, deseeded and cut into $\frac{1}{2}$ in (1 cm) cubes

$2\frac{1}{4}$ lb (1 kg) fresh tomatoes, blanched, skinned, deseeded and cut into $\frac{1}{2}$ in (1 cm) chunks

2 large avocados, stoned, peeled, chopped and soaked in lemon juice

2 tablespoons chopped fresh basil

3 cloves garlic, crushed

fine sea salt and freshly ground pepper

Coating

1 egg, beaten

$\frac{1}{4}$ pint (150 ml) milk

4 oz (100 g) wholewheat breadcrumbs

1 oz (30 g) sesame seeds

(ingredients continued overleaf)

These delicious filled pancakes are coated in breadcrumbs and sesame seeds, then fried.

To make the pancakes

1. Whizz all the ingredients together except the butter. Melt half the butter and add it to the pancake mix. Retain the rest for cooking. Ideally allow the batter to rest for 2 hours or overnight in a fridge to let the individual grains of flour expand. Add a little water if the batter is too stiff the next day.

2. Heat a little of the butter in a heavy frying pan. When it's hot pour off any excess. Quickly stir the batter with a tablespoon then measure two good tablespoons into the frying pan, depending on its size. Run the batter evenly over the bottom of the pan and cook for about 30–45 seconds, then flip the pancake over to cook the other side – usually for only 20–30 seconds. Crespolini pancakes are best slightly undercooked because they are going to be cooked again. As each pancake is made, remove it to a plate, cover it with a square of greaseproof and put the next pancake on top of this. Make at least 12 – more if you think your guests might want seconds.

3. Allow to cool, then store in the fridge.

To make the filling

1. Heat the oil in a deep heavy casserole dish. Add the onions and cook until softening. Pour in the peppers and tomatoes and cook without a lid for at least 40 minutes or until the mixture is fairly thick.

For deep frying
lots of vegetable oil

For garnish
lambs' lettuce (mache)
toasted pine nuts
lemon wedges

2. Stir in the avocado, basil and garlic and cook for a further 5 minutes. Season with salt and pepper and remove from the heat. Allow to cool before use.

To assemble

1. Put a good tablespoonful of the filling into each pancake, fold in the edges and roll up.

2. Beat together the egg and milk. Brush each pancake with this, then coat in breadcrumbs and sesame seeds. Deep or shallow fry in oil until golden brown all over.

Alternatively: Omit the egg-and-breadcrumbing, sprinkle with grated Cheddar or Parmesan cheese and bake in the oven.

To serve: Serve garnished with lambs' lettuce, toasted pine nuts, lemon wedges and, of course, Leek and Vermouth Sauce.

Leek and Vermouth Sauce

G *Serves 4–6*

1 oz (30 g) butter
8 oz (225 g) leeks, topped, tailed, trimmed, washed and finely chopped
1 pint (600 ml) double cream
$\frac{1}{4}$ pint (150 ml) dry vermouth
fine sea salt and freshly ground black pepper

This sauce may be made a day in advance and reheated in a bowl over a pan of simmering water. When storing in the fridge, make sure it is covered with buttered greaseproof paper to stop a skin forming.

1. Melt the butter in a deep pan, then sauté the leeks until softening.

2. Add the cream and cook until reduced in volume by half, to make it thick and slightly biscuit coloured. Be careful not to burn it during the reduction.

3. In a separate pan, cook the vermouth to reduce it to a tablespoonful and then add it to the cream. Adjust the seasoning.

Steamed Broccoli with Lemon Butter

V G *Serves 4–6*

1 lb (450 g) broccoli, cut into 3 in (7.5 cm) long florets (save any waste for stock)
1 pint (600 ml) boiling salted water
1 quantity Lemon Butter (see page 179)

For this part of the menu there is no real work; the lemon butter can be made well in advance. If it is frozen, remember to remove it in time to saw enough sections off for each guest.

1. Choose a colander that will fit over a large saucepan. Place the broccoli in the colander so that the heads are closest to the steam. Put the colander over the saucepan filled with boiling water. Cover with tinfoil to help prevent steam escaping. Steam like this for 12 minutes.

To serve: Serve immediately with $\frac{1}{2}$–1 oz (15–30 g) of lemon butter per portion.

Potato and Onion Roast

V G *Serves 4–6*

2 oz (50 g) butter or 2 tablespoons oil
1 large onion, finely chopped
1 teaspoon paprika
$\frac{1}{2}$ teaspoon cumin
$\frac{1}{2}$ teaspoon chilli powder
2 cloves garlic, crushed or chopped
$1\frac{1}{2}$ lb (675 g) potatoes, peeled and cut into 1 in (2.5 cm) chunks

Imagine your plate. The pancake is issuing a succulent tomato mixture which is mingling with that rich leek sauce, the broccoli is sitting there all holier than thou apart from the knob of lemon butter melting into its perfectly cooked florets. What you really need now is something to mop it all up with. A humble baked potato would be adequate. But why not enhance the experience with this dish?

1. Heat the butter or oil in a casserole dish and gently cook the onion and spices.

2. Add the garlic and potato, coat well in butter or oil and continue to cook in the oven at 200°C/400°F/Gas Mark 6 until done – about 45 minutes to 1 hour.

Hazelnut and Blackcurrant Trifle

Serves 4–6

Hazelnut Sponge

4 oz (100 g) ground hazelnuts
8 oz (225 g) demerara sugar
5 oz (150 g) unsalted butter
3 small eggs
4 fl oz (120 ml) sour cream
1 teaspoon vanilla essence
$\frac{1}{2}$ teaspoon almond essence
6 oz (175 g) unbleached white flour
$\frac{3}{4}$ teaspoon baking powder
$\frac{1}{2}$ teaspoon bicarbonate of soda
pinch of salt

Blackcurrant mixture

4 oz (100 g) demerara sugar
zest and juice of 1 lemon
1 wineglass Crème de Cassis
14 oz (400 g) fresh or frozen
   blackcurrants

To assemble

1 × quantity Real Custard (see page
   228)
$\frac{1}{2}$ pint (275 ml) double cream, softly
   whipped
rose petals
chocolate shavings

Every part of this recipe can be prepared ahead and assembled at the last minute, or you can put the dish together well in advance and let the flavours mingle.

To make the Hazelnut Sponge

1. Preheat the oven to 170°C/325°F/Gas Mark 3.

2. Use 1 oz (30 g) of the butter to grease shallow rectangular baking trays.

3. Beat the nuts and sugar together in a mixing machine, then add the remaining butter.

4. Add the eggs, one at a time. Finally add the sour cream and flavourings. Transfer to a bowl.

5. Sift the flour with the baking agents and salt. Fold a third of the flour into the mixture. When it is absorbed, add a further third and repeat.

6. Pour the batter into the rectangular trays and bake in the centre of the oven for 30–35 minutes or until springy to the touch and golden in colour. Remove, turn out and cool. Cut into finger shapes.

To make the blackcurrant mixture

1. Dissolve the sugar with a little water, the lemon zest and juice and the Crème de Cassis. Bring to the boil.

2. Add the blackcurrants and cook for 3 minutes. Add more sugar to taste, remove from the heat and cool.

To assemble

Place at least 2 hazel sponge fingers in each individual bowl, cover with blackcurrant mixture, coat with custard and top with whipped cream. Chill, and just before serving decorate with rose petals and chocolate shavings.

DRINKS

Here are a few suggestions – and remember they are only suggestions. With the tofu, try a dry pungent white like Alsace Pinot Gris. Alternatively serve a fino sherry. The main course deserves something more substantial like a Rioja or an Australian Shiraz. For dessert try any sweet wine like Sauternes or Muscat de Rivesaltes or a fortified wine such as madeira.

$\mathcal{M}$ENU

LUNCH PARTY 2

SERVES 4–6

Cheesy Mushroom and Spinach Toasts

—·—

Broccoli and Cauliflower Coulibiac with Red Wine
and Mustard Cream Sauce
Glazed Courgettes and Celeriac with Ginger
Peppered Beetroot and Mangetout

—·—

Very Lemon Tart

COUNTDOWN

3 days before
• Make the Lemon Tart and freeze.

2 days before
• Prepare the brioche dough. Wrap and store in fridge. • Cook the beetroot.

Day before
• Prepare the coulibiac and store, uncooked, in the fridge. • Prepare the wine and cream sauce separately and store, covered with buttered greaseproof paper, in the fridge. • Prepare the courgettes and celeriac and marinate in the fridge overnight. • Prepare the mangetout, peel and slice the beetroot, allow to marinate overnight. • Prepare the topping for the spinach and mushroom toasts.

On the day
• Prepare the garnishes. • Remove the Lemon Tart from the freezer.

40 minutes before • Garnish the Lemon Tart and replace in fridge.

30 minutes before • Place the coulibiac in the oven.

20 minutes before • Toast the bread on one side. Spread the other with the spinach.

10 minutes before • Combine the cream and tomato and reheat gently in a bain-marie. Warm the plates.

5 minutes before • Grill the toasts, garnish and serve on warm plates. Put the main course plates into the oven to warm.

After 1st course • Remove coulibiac from oven immediately. Set aside. • Completely dress the beetroot salad. • Stir-fry the courgettes and celeriac. • Slice the coulibiac. • Serve on a warm plate with the garnish and sauce. Serve the vegetables separately.

Cheesy Mushroom and Spinach Toasts

Serves 4–6

2 oz (50 g) unsalted butter
2 shallots, peeled and finely chopped
8 oz (225 g) organic brown cap
    mushrooms, finely chopped
pinch of grated nutmeg
1 teaspoon chopped fresh tarragon
8 oz (225 g) fresh spinach, stalked
    and finely chopped
3 tablespoons white wine
6 tablespoons sour cream
salt and freshly ground black pepper
6 slices organic wholewheat bread
10 oz (275 g) Gruyère cheese, sliced
6 sun-dried tomatoes
snipped chives to garnish

The mix for these is easy to prepare in advance. Use wild mushrooms instead of organic brown caps if they are available.

1. Melt the butter in a deep frying pan. Add the shallots and cook for a few minutes.

2. Stir in the mushrooms, nutmeg and tarragon and turn up the heat for 2 minutes before adding the spinach. Continue to cook over a high heat for a further 3 minutes.

3. Pour in the wine and the cream and continue cooking until the mixture is almost dry. Season with salt and pepper.

The recipe up to this point can be done a day in advance. The rest is easy.

4. Toast the slices of bread on one side and spread the spinach and mushroom mixture evenly on to the other side. You may have enough for a couple of extra slices – I'm sure they won't go begging.

5. Cover the mixture with slices of Gruyère and top with sun-dried tomato. Place under a hot grill until bubbling. Garnish with snipped chives and serve.

Broccoli and Cauliflower Coulibiac

Serves 4–6

The rice layer
olive oil
2 shallots, finely chopped
5 oz (150 g) organic long-grain
    brown rice
1 oz (30 g) wild rice
1 bay leaf
7 fl oz (200 ml) vegetable stock or
    water
4 fl oz (120 ml) dry white wine
8 fl oz (250 ml) double cream
freshly ground pepper and sea salt
2 tablespoons chopped fresh parsley

The mushroom layer
1 tablespoon olive oil
8 oz (225 g) organic brown cap or
    wild mushrooms
1 teaspoon dried thyme
3 fl oz (90 ml) dry white wine
freshly ground black pepper and sea
    salt

The cheese layer
8 oz (225 g) grated Cheddar,
    Gruyère or Emmental cheese

The vegetable and egg layer
6 eggs, lightly hard-boiled and sliced
12 oz (325 g) cauliflower, cut into
    florets and steamed
12 oz (325 g) broccoli, cut into
    florets and steamed

The dough
1½ lb (675 g) brioche dough (see
    page 220)
1 egg yolk, beaten

This dish is a particularly successful way of using up any succulent vegetables you have a glut of. The coulibiac can be made the day before and stored uncooked in the fridge. At the restaurant we use brioche dough for the pastry but you can use puff equally successfully.

To cook the rice

1. Heat the olive oil in a deep heavy pan. Sauté the shallots for 3 minutes, then add the brown and wild rice.

2. Continue to stir-fry until all the grains are well coated with oil, add the bay leaf and when the whole mixture is very hot pour in the vegetable stock or water and wine. Put a lid on the pan and cook the rice without removing the lid for 25 minutes.

3. Meanwhile, in a separate small saucepan, reduce the cream in volume by one-third to a half, season and stir in the parsley.

4. When the rice is cooked, fold in the cream and set to one side to cool.

To cook the mushrooms

1. Heat the oil in a deep frying pan, add the mushrooms and thyme. When the whole mixture is very hot add the wine and continue to cook until the wine has been absorbed. Adjust the seasoning and set aside to cool.

The assembly

1. Heat the oven to 190°C/375°F/Gas Mark 5. Roll out one-third of the brioche dough into a rectangle ⅛ in (2 mm) thick. Make sure your baking tray is big enough to hold a coulibiac this size.

2. Sprinkle the dough with one third of the cheese, then spread one-third of the rice over the dough, leaving a border of about 1½ in (3 cm) all the way round. Top with one-third of the mushroom mix, then one-third of the egg slices, then one-third of the steamed vegetables (make sure they are well seasoned). Then repeat this layering twice more.

3. Roll out the rest of the brioche dough to form a rectangle approximately $1\frac{1}{2}$ times bigger than the original rectangle. Brush the edges of the original rectangle with beaten egg yolk, then lower the larger brioche rectangle over the whole assembly. Trim away any excess dough and crimp or flute the edges together decoratively.

4. Brush the entire surface of the coulibiac with beaten egg yolk and decorate with leftover pieces of dough.

5. Bake in the oven for 40–45 minutes until golden.

Red Wine and Mustard Cream Sauce

G | *Serves 4–6*

$\frac{1}{2}$ oz (15 g) unsalted butter or vegan margarine or $\frac{1}{2}$ tablespoon olive oil
4 shallots, finely chopped
1 tablespoon red wine vinegar
8 fl oz (250 ml) red wine (Bordeaux will do)
1 teaspoon dried thyme
2 teaspoons chopped chervil
3 fl oz (100 ml) vegetable stock
2 tablespoons fresh tomato purée (see page 223)
1 tablespoon Dijon mustard
fine sea salt and freshly ground black pepper
$\frac{1}{2}$ pint (275 ml) double cream

This sauce is best made a day in advance, though the tomato and cream mixture should be kept separate.

1. Choose a deep saucepan. Melt the butter and sauté the shallots for 5 minutes without colouring.

2. Add the red wine vinegar and reduce by two-thirds.

3. Add the red wine, thyme and chervil and reduce by half.

4. Add the stock and reduce by half again.

5. Stir in the tomato purée and mustard, whisking continuously. Bring back to the boil and reduce further, if necessary, to a good coating consistency. Adjust seasoning and set to one side.
     Up to this point the sauce is vegan.

6. In a small pan, reduce the cream by half and set aside.

7. If desired, pass the tomato and mustard sauce through a fine sieve, then reheat. Stir in the cream before serving and adjust the seasoning once more.

57

Glazed Courgettes and Celeriac with Ginger

V G *Serves 4–6 easily*

12 oz (350 g) courgettes, coarsely grated
1 lb (450 g) celeriac, coarsely grated
2 cloves garlic, crushed
1 oz (30 g) preserved ginger, finely chopped
juice of 1 lemon
2 tablespoons olive oil
1 oz (30 g) butter or vegan margarine
fine sea salt and freshly ground black pepper

1. Toss the vegetables with the garlic, ginger and lemon juice and allow to marinate for several hours.

2. Just before serving, heat the oil and butter or margarine together in a large frying pan. Add the vegetables and marinade and stir-fry for 5 minutes or until *al dente*. Adjust seasoning and serve.

Peppered Beetroot and Mangetout

V G *Serves 4–6*

6 oz (175 g) mangetout, topped and tailed
1 tablespoon Szechuan peppercorns
1 tablespoon balsamic vinegar
3 tablespoons light sesame oil
freshly ground black pepper
8 oz (225 g) cooked beetroot, skinned, trimmed and sliced into wedges
1 bunch spring onions, finely copped, chive flowers or borage flowers, for garnish

Here is a salad that will add colour and texture to your plate. Keep any flowers from the chives used in the first course to decorate this dish.

1. Pour boiling water over the mangetout and leave for 1 minute. This makes them bright green. Rinse in cold water and drain thoroughly.

2. Heat the peppercorns in a small heavy frying pan over a low heat until they begin to smoke. Remove and grind.

3. Whizz together the vinegar and oil and add the ground pepper with a few twists of ordinary black pepper too.

4. Allow the beetroot and mangetout to marinate in half the dressing for a couple of hours and add the rest of the dressing just before serving. Decorate with chive flowers, borage flowers or chopped spring onions.

Very Lemon Tart

Serves 6 with second helpings

The base

4 oz (100 g) butter or margarine, softened

3 tablespoons sunflower oil

2 oz (50 g) demerara sugar

8 oz (225 g) organic wholewheat pastry flour

$\frac{1}{2}$ teaspoon baking powder

The topping

4 oz (100 g) butter or margarine

4 oz (100 g) demerara sugar

finely grated zest and juice of 3 lemons

4 egg yolks

4 oz (100 g) ground almonds

4 fl oz (120 ml) double cream

Although this dish has a pastry base, it's so lemony it clears the palate perfectly. Try flavouring the sugar used for this dish by adding a split vanilla pod to the jar for a few days.

The base

1. Beat the butter or margarine, oil and sugar together until light and creamy. Sift together the flour and baking powder and fold into the mixture.

2. The resultant pastry will be very crumbly. Push it into a 10 in (25 cm) greased flan dish lightly with your fingertips.

3. Bake in the oven at 180°C/350°F/Gas Mark 4 for 8 minutes. Remove and cool.

The topping

1. Beat the butter or margarine, sugar and lemon zest together well.

2. Gradually add the egg yolks, beating all the time.

3. Fold in the ground almonds and lemon juice and mix in well.

4. Finally, stir in the double cream.

The assembly

1. Pour the lemon mixture over the pastry base and bake for 15 minutes in the oven. Then turn the temperature down to 170°C/325°F/Gas Mark 3 and cook for a further 10–20 minutes or until golden brown and firm to touch.

To serve: Serve hot with plenty of whipped cream, sour cream or crème fraîche.

DRINKS

Try any dry sparkling Cava to cut through the toasted flavour of the cheesy spinach and mushroom starter. A Barbera d'Alba would suit the coulibiac and would have sufficient tannin to fend off the tomato and mustard sauce. The lemon tart is too strong for most wines but might be enjoyed with a liqueur like Cointreau.

MENU

LUNCH PARTY 3

SERVES 4–6

Blinis with Roasted Peppers and Sour Cream

—·—

Lentil Kiev with Sweet and Sour Broad Beans
Tagliatelle of Root Vegetables
Potatoes with Quark

—·—

Blackberry and Apple Pavlova

COUNTDOWN

2–3 days before
• Make the Garlic and Lemon Butter (or vegan margarine) for the Kievs and freeze. • Make the Pavlova base and store it in a rigid box in the freezer. • Make the fruit filling for the Pavlova and freeze. • Make the Kievs and freeze.

Day before
• Roast the peppers and marinate in the fridge overnight • Make the blinis, cool and freeze (only do this if you are very short of time). • Make the Sweet and Sour Broad Beans and store in the fridge. • Prepare and par-cook the Tagliatelle of Root Vegetables. Allow to cool and refrigerate.

On the day
• Remove the Kievs from the freezer and store in the fridge. • Remove the blinis from the freezer and store in the fridge. • Prepare the garnishes and accompaniments. • Prepare the potato dish. • Remove the Pavlova base from the freezer. • Remove the fruit filling from the freezer. • Heat oven to 170°C/325°F/Gas Mark 3.

1 hour before • Put the potatoes into the oven. • Whip the cream for decorating the Pavlova and store in a piping bag in the fridge.

20 minutes before • Heat the oil in your deep fryer.

15 minutes before • Cover the blinis with tinfoil and heat in the oven with starter plates. • Put the Sweet and Sour Broad Beans in a heatproof glass dish over a saucepan of water. Bring the water to the boil. Cover the beans and reheat gently, keeping the water at a simmer. • Sauté the Tagliatelle of Vegetables until *al dente*. Keep warm over simmering water.

5 minutes before • Gently heat the peppers in their marinade.

Just before eating • Place a blini or two on each plate and top with sour cream and peppers. Garnish. Heat plates for main course.

After the first course • Remove the Kievs from the fridge and, if you wish, egg and breadcrumb them. Deep fry whilst they are still very cold. • Serve immediately with the rest of the vegetables. Assemble the Pavlova. Garnish with cream and blackberries and serve.

Blinis with Roasted Peppers and Sour Cream

Serves 4–6

2 medium red peppers
2 medium yellow peppers
2 tablespoons olive oil
1 pinch saffron
1 bunch fresh basil
1 egg, separated
$\frac{1}{2}$ teaspoon salt
$\frac{1}{4}$ pint (150 ml) warm water
$\frac{1}{2}$ sachet easy blend yeast or $\frac{1}{4}$ oz (7 g) fresh yeast
6 oz (150 g) strong organic wholewheat flour
$\frac{1}{4}$ pint (150 ml) milk
butter or oil for frying
$\frac{1}{2}$ pint (275 ml) sour cream
parsley sprigs or basil leaves for garnish

1. First prepare the peppers as they will improve in flavour the longer they are left. Roast the peppers in a hot oven or under the grill until their skins are blackening.

2. Cut in half and remove the seeds. Cut into small squares.

3. Warm the olive oil, add the saffron, peppers and basil. Allow to marinate in a cool place overnight (or longer).

4. Whisk the egg yolk and salt with $\frac{1}{4}$ pint (150 ml) warm water.

5. Mix the yeast and flour together in a bowl and form a well in the centre.

6. Gradually add the water and egg mix to the flour, whisking until it forms a smooth batter.

7. Whisk the egg white until stiff and fold into the batter.

8. Cover with a damp cloth or clingfilm and leave in a warm place for 30 minutes or until doubled in size.

9. In a saucepan, heat the milk with 4 tablespoons of water until almost boiling. Fold into the batter, cover and allow to rise again.

10. To cook the blinis, heat a little butter or oil in a frying pan. Stir the batter gently, then add 1 tablespoon to the hot batter. Cook until small bubbles rise to the top of each blini, then turn to cook the other side.

11. If you are eating immediately, wrap the blinis in a napkin and store in a warm place. For a dinner party, however, it is more advisable to allow them to cool and freeze them in rigid containers. To reheat, simply cover with tinfoil and heat directly in a warm oven.

To serve: Serve with a dollop of sour cream topped with the roasted pepper mixture which can be heated. Garnish with parsley sprigs or a little basil.

VARIATION

Use marinated mushrooms or sun-dried tomatoes (or both) as an alternative topping.

Lentil Kiev

I've always like the idea of self-lubricating food, it's both fun and practical. Vegetarian dishes using lentils, nuts, beans and grains can tend to be on the heavy side, but not Lentil Kievs. These succulent rissoles have at their centre a core of frozen Garlic and Lemon Butter, which on cooking melts and waits for the unsuspecting diner's knife to penetrate. Vegans can of course use vegan margarine instead of butter for their Garlic and Lemon Butter.

V G *Serves 4–6*

Garlic and lemon butter

4 cloves garlic, crushed or minced
juice and zest of 1 lemon
8 oz (225 g) unsalted butter or
vegan margarine
fine sea salt and freshly ground black
pepper

Lentil mixture

6 oz (175 g) brown lentils
4 oz (100 g) split red lentils
2 bay leaves
2 tablespoons olive oil
1 medium onion, finely chopped
4 oz (100 g) flat mushrooms, finely
chopped
1 tablespoon lemon juice
1 tablespoon soya sauce
2 oz (50 g) wholewheat
breadcrumbs or pinhead oatmeal
2 tablespoons chopped fresh parsley
fine sea salt and freshly ground black
pepper
4 oz (100 g) grated Cheddar cheese
or tofu (optional)
oil for frying
beaten egg and breadcrumbs for
coating (optional)
lemon twists for garnish

1. First make the lemon garlic butter by beating the garlic, lemon juice and zest, butter and seasoning together either by hand (very tiring) or in a food processor (simple). The quantity specified will make more than enough but this flavoured butter is always useful to have around. In fact it's quite a good idea to do double the amount and freeze half.

2. When the butter is completely blended, divide it into 12 to 16 pieces and roll each into a little ball, then place in a plastic tray, cover and freeze.

3. In separate saucepans cook the lentils in water until soft, with a bayleaf in each to add flavour.

4. Heat the olive oil in a large heavy casserole and sauté the onion until softening, then add the mushrooms and cook for 8 minutes.

5. Pour in the lemon juice and soya sauce and bring to the boil.

6. Add the lentils and breadcrumbs and mix together well. Remove two-thirds of the mixture and roughly blend it, then add back to the unblended mix.

7. Fold in the parsley and adjust the seasoning. Add the cheese or tofu if desired and beat in well. The mixture should be stiff.

8. Remove the frozen butter from the fridge. Using floured hands, shape the lentil mixture into balls around each nugget of butter. Each Kiev should weigh about 4–5 oz (100–150 g).

9. If desired you can now egg and breadcrumb the Kievs.

10. If the Kievs have been prepared well in advance it may be wise to freeze them. If only a couple of days before, simply chill them. They are best if very cold when cooked.

11. Deep frying is the best method; slower cooking may result in your buttery surprise disappearing (although the flavour remains). Deep-fry for 5–6 minutes or until golden brown.

12. Serve garnished with twists of lemon.

VARIATIONS

- Chopped roast nuts may be added to the mixture.

- Try different types of flavoured butter – eg chopped herbs.

- Try flavoured cream cheese instead of butter.

Sweet and Sour Broad Beans

V G *Serves 4–6*

1 lb (450 g) broad beans
1 tablespoon soya sauce
1 tablespoon dry sherry
3 tablespoons tomato purée (see page 223)
2 tablespoons white wine vinegar
2 tablespoons demerara sugar (or honey)
2 tablespoons peanut oil
2 cloves garlic, crushed
pinch of fresh grated ginger
1 bunch spring onions, finely chopped
1 red pepper, cut into squares
1 tablespoon cornflour
1 tablespoon water

Broad beans are delicious fresh or frozen, whatever way you cook them. I've included them here in a sweet and sour sauce as a cross between a vegetable dish and a sauce for the Lentil Kievs.

1. Poach the broad beans in salted water until tender. Drain and retain 6 fl oz (180 ml) of this water for the sauce.

2. Heat the soya, sherry, tomato purée, vinegar, bean stock, sugar or honey together in a saucepan. Stir occasionally and make certain the sugar or honey has dissolved.

3. Heat the oil in a deep pan. Add the garlic, ginger, onion and peppers. Sauté for 2 minutes.

4. Add the liquid and bring to the boil. Make a paste of the cornflour and cold water, stir in a little hot liquid, then pour this into the saucepan and stir to thicken the sauce. Stir in the broad beans. Serve immediately or allow to cool and marinate overnight in the fridge. Be careful not to overcook the beans if doing this as they will continue to cook in the sauce when it is cooling down.

Tagliatelle of Root Vegetables

V G *Serves 4–6*

8 oz (225 g) carrots, topped, tailed and cut into long thin strips
8 oz (225 g) leeks, topped, tailed and cut into long thin strips
8 oz (225 g) daikon radish, topped, tailed and cut into long thin strips
2 oz (50 g) butter or 2 tablespoons vegetable oil
$\frac{1}{2}$ teaspoon grated nutmeg
fine sea salt and freshly ground black pepper
squeeze of lemon juice

This is a very simple dish that requires a little skill with the knife and not much else. It is probably best to prepare it and par-cook it in advance, then just quickly finish off the cooking on the day.

1. Poach the vegetables in boiling salted water until crisper than *al dente*. Add the carrot first, then the leek and then the radish. Cool if finishing off later.

2. Heat the butter or oil in a large pan. Throw in the vegetables and seasonings. Sauté gently until all the vegetables are hot. Add a squeeze of lemon and serve immediately.

Potatoes with Quark

G *Serves 4–6*

1 oz (30 g) butter or 1 tablespoon
    olive oil
2 medium onions, finely sliced
2 cloves garlic, crushed or chopped
12 oz (325 g) quark
$\frac{1}{4}$ pint (150 ml) skimmed milk
butter and garlic to flavour the dish
2 lb (900 g) white floury potatoes
    such as Pentland Crown, peeled
    and finely sliced
fine sea salt and freshly ground black
    pepper

Quark is a sharp soft skimmed milk cheese. It is low in fat and easy to digest.

1. Heat the oven to 170°C/325°F/Gas Mark 3.

2. Melt the butter in a deep frying pan and cook the onions and garlic gently together until soft but not coloured.

3. Beat the Quark and milk together to loosen it up.

4. Rub a baking dish with butter and garlic.

5. Layer the potatoes, Quark and onions in that order, finishing with a layer of Quark. Season.

6. Bake for 1 hour 20 minutes or until the potatoes are tender.

Blackberry and Apple Pavlova

G *Serves 4–6*

4 free-range egg whites
pinch of salt
8 oz (225 g) caster sugar
1 teaspoon cornflour or arrowroot
1 teaspoon vanilla essence
2 teaspoons white wine vinegar
2 tablespoons blackberry liqueur
    (Crème de Mûre) or Calvados
1 oz (30 g) unsalted butter
8 oz (225 g) soft brown sugar
2 lb (900 g) cooking apples, peeled,
    cored and cut into chunks
$\frac{1}{2}$ pint (275 ml) double cream,
    whipped
8 oz (225 g) punnet of blackberries

Once you've made your Pavlova base you can freeze it and store it in a box, then fill it with any seasonal fruit.

1. Heat the oven to 140°C/275°F/Gas Mark 1.

2. Put a sheet of silicone paper on a baking sheet.

3. Whisk the egg whites with the salt until they are starting to form peaks.

4. Gradually beat in the sugar, a little at a time, until the mix is so stiff a wooden spoon will stand in it.

5. Fold in the cornflour, vanilla and vinegar and whisk thoroughly together.

6. Using a large spoon, transfer the mix to the silicone paper, shaping it into a rough circle. Try to create a rough bowl shape about $1\frac{1}{2}$ in (3 cm) thick at the centre. The mix will spread in the oven.

7. Place in the oven and cook for 1 hour. Then turn the oven off and leave the meringue inside to cool.

8. While the meringue is cooking, prepare the apple purée. Melt the butter in a saucepan and add the sugar, apples and blackberry liqueur (or Calvados) and soft brown sugar. Cook with the lid on for about 30 minutes or until the apples are soft and there is no liquid. Remove from the heat and pass through a sieve. Allow to cool.

9. Keep the meringue and fruit separate until just before serving otherwise your carefully cooked meringue will go soggy. It's quite easy if you have the purée, meringue base, prepared and washed blackberries and a piping bag with a star nozzle full of whipped double cream ready in the fridge.

To serve: When you are ready to serve the Pavlova, quickly spoon the purée onto the meringue and decorate with cream and black-berries. Serve in wedges.

VARIATIONS

Choose any of these fruits or combinations of these fruits: peaches, nectarines, cherries, apricots, greengages, plums, black, red or white currants, cranberries, gooseberries, raspberries, strawberries, kumquats, clementines, pears, quinces, seedless grapes, mango, papaya, pineapple, passion fruit, kiwi fruit, guava, star fruit, fresh figs, bananas, rhubarb. You could even try flav-oured compote of dried fruit.

DRINKS

A lunch party like this begs to be started with some ice cold glasses of good vodka or schnapps that has been stored in the freezer. Put the glasses in the freezer too. Try not to have more than one glass yourself, though, or you'll never assemble the Pavlova.

With the main course the Sweet and Sour Broad Beans are the problem – try a medium dry Sauvignon Blanc.

The dessert is flavoured with Crème de Mûre or Calvados so it might be best to miss the alcohol altogether with this course or just linger on your Sauvignon Blanc.

---

*M*ENU

SUNDAY LUNCH

SERVES 4–6

Semolina Gnocchi with Pesto and Rich Tomato Sauce

—·—

Tofu-stuffed Mushrooms with Green Peppercorn Sauce
Brussels Sprouts with Chestnuts
Roast Fanned Potatoes
Honeyed Swede and Carrot Purée

—·—

Two-Berry Summer Pudding

COUNTDOWN

3 days before
• Make the Two-Berry Summer Pudding and natural fruit sauce.

2 days before
• Prepare the potatoes and store in an airtight container in the fridge.
• Prepare the Rich Tomato Sauce. • Prepare the Green Peppercorn Sauce. Cover with buttered greaseproof paper and refrigerate.

Day before
• Prepare the gnocchi. • Prepare the julienne of vegetables for the gnocchi. • Prepare the Tofu-stuffed Mushrooms. Cover with tin foil and refrigerate. • Prepare the Brussels sprouts and chestnuts. Refrigerate. • Prepare the swede and carrot purée. Cover and refrigerate.

On the day
• Combine the tomato sauce with the vegetable julienne; spread over the bottom of a deep baking dish. • Cut the gnocchi into circles as instructed and place on top of the julienne and tomato mixture.

- Refrigerate. • Prepare the garnishes and accompaniments.

1 hour before • Put the potatoes in the oven.

30 minutes before • Brush the top of the gnocchi with olive oil or melted butter and put into the oven.

20 minutes before • Put the stuffed mushrooms into the oven. Start to reheat the peppercorn sauce in a bain-marie.

10 minutes before • Warm the plates for the gnocchi.

0 minutes before • Serve the gnocchi with garnish. Put the main course plates in the oven and the swede purée. • Cook the brussels sprouts and chestnuts. Decant the cooked roast potatoes into a serving dish followed by the stuffed mushrooms. • Serve the main course. • Turn out the pudding and serve with fruit sauce and cream.

Semolina Gnocchi

Serves 4–6

The gnocchi

1¾ pints (1 litre) milk

1 onion, sliced

1 bay leaf

pinch of freshly grated nutmeg

1½ teaspoons salt and freshly ground black pepper

8 oz (225 g) semolina

3 eggs

2 oz (50 g) Parmesan cheese, grated

2 oz (50 g) Cheddar cheese, grated

1 oz (30 g) butter, melted

The pesto

1 oz (30 g) pine nuts (substitute almonds or walnuts if pine nuts unavailable)

4 cloves garlic (more or less depending on your own taste)

2 bunches fresh basil (ideally leaves only) and/or fresh coriander leaves

8 tablespoons grated Parmesan cheese

I suggest when you tell your guests about this dish you refer to semolina as ground durum wheat. Most people still have a horror of semolina dating back to their school days. In actual fact semolina is a beautiful word meaning flower of flour – and is a valuable source of carbohydrate that is easily used by the human body. This dish is one we've used at the restaurant and I've used at home on countless occasions – as they say, 'Once bitten forever smitten'. Unlike potato gnocchi, semolina gnocchi are simplicity itself to prepare. Everything should be done a day in advance to allow the flavour to develop fully.

To make the Gnocchi

1. Combine the milk with the onion, bay leaf, nutmeg and seasoning in a saucepan. Gradually bring the mixture to the boil, then set aside for 10 minutes for the flavours to infuse. Strain into another saucepan and bring back to the boil.

2. Remove from the heat again and sprinkle in the semolina a little at a time, beating continuously with a wooden spoon.

3. When all the semolina has been added, return the pan to the heat and continue to cook uncovered for 10–15 minutes, stirring, if not continuously, very frequently. Be careful not to burn or allow the mixture to stick. The semolina is cooked when your spoon stands unaided in the mixture.

$\frac{1}{4}$ pint (150 ml) pure virgin olive oil
fine sea salt and freshly ground black
    pepper

Rich tomato sauce
2 tablespoons extra virgin olive oil
1 large onion, finely sliced
1 clove garlic, crushed or chopped
2 lb (900 g) fresh ripe tomatoes,
    skinned, deseeded and chopped
2 teaspoons chopped fresh oregano
1 bunch fresh basil, chopped
2 tablespoons tomato purée (see
    page 223)
4 fl oz (120 ml) water or red wine
1 tablespoon demerara sugar
fine sea salt and freshly ground black
    pepper

Julienne of vegetables
1 tablespoon olive oil
1 large onion, finely sliced
1 large leek, cut into fine strips
1 large carrot, cut into fine strips
4 oz (100 g) mushrooms, finely
    sliced
2 stalks celery, cut into fine strips

4. Remove the semolina from the heat and allow to cool for 5 minutes. Then beat in the eggs, cheeses and melted butter and adjust the seasoning.

5. Oil a rectangular baking dish (rub it with garlic too if you're an addict). Pour in the semolina mixture and smooth over to an even thickness – about $\frac{1}{2}$ in (1 cm) is good. Allow to cool, then refrigerate overnight or for at least 3 hours until the semolina is firm to touch. Cover with greased greaseproof paper to prevent a skin forming.

To make the pesto

1. If you use pine nuts, toast them in the oven or under a grill.

2. Put all the ingredients in a blender and whizz. Store overnight in the fridge to allow the flavour to develop.

To make the Rich Tomato Sauce

1. Heat the oil in a saucepan. Add the onion and garlic and cook gently until softening.

2. Add the rest of the ingredients, bring to the boil and simmer for about 1 hour.

3. Remove from the heat and purée if you like. Adjust seasoning and allow to cool. Refrigerate overnight to allow flavour to develop.

To make the julienne of vegetables

1. Heat the oil in a saucepan and sauté the vegetables until *al dente*. Season.

2. Set aside to cool.

To assemble

1. Combine the tomato sauce with the julienne of vegetables and cover the bottom of a baking dish with this mix.

2. Spread the pesto over the surface of the semolina.

3. Use a $1\frac{1}{2}$ in (3 cm) round, plain or fluted pastry cutter to cut out circles of pesto-covered semolina.

4. Any leftover bits of semolina should be dotted judiciously about the vegetable julienne and tomato sauce mixture – waste not, want not.

5. Carefully place the semolina circles on top of the julienne and tomato sauce mix. Ideally they should overlap.

6. Brush with a little warm olive oil or melted butter, then bake for 15–20 minutes until golden green in an oven preheated to 220°C/425°F/Gas Mark 7.

Serve hot and bubbling.

Tofu-stuffed Mushrooms

V G *Serves 4–6*

2 tablespoons vegetable oil
4 shallots, finely chopped
3 sticks celery, finely chopped
1½ lb (675 g) firm tofu, mashed
4 oz (100 g) regular oats
2 tablespoons soya sauce
1 teaspoon celery salt
1 teaspoon chopped thyme
1 clove garlic, crushed or minced
2 tablespoons olive oil
freshly ground black pepper
6 horse or large field mushrooms,
    thoroughly brushed, stalks
    removed and reserved
salt and freshly ground black pepper

At Sunday lunch, especially, it's nice to have a centrepiece around which you serve some more traditionally cooked vegetables. Large mushrooms make a tasty and pleasing receptacle for countless stuffings. This one uses tofu and is vegan to boot. The recipe is only lightly spiced to allow children to eat it too.

1. Heat the oven to 220°C/425°F/Gas Mark 7.

2. Heat the oil in a deep heavy pan. Add the shallots and celery and cook gently until softening and slightly browned.

3. Mix the tofu, oats, soya sauce and celery salt together in a bowl, then combine with the onion and celery. Remove half the mixture and blend in a blender with the mushroom stalks. Add it back to the rest of the mix and beat in thoroughly.

4. Mix the thyme, garlic, oil and seasoning together and brush this onto the gills of the mushrooms. Now divide the stuffing into six and spoon it into the mushrooms, making certain to cover the gills properly.

5. Brush the outside of the mushrooms with any remaining flavoured oil. Grease a baking sheet and put the mushrooms on it. Cook in the oven for 30 minutes.

6. Serve piping hot, garnished with chopped herbs and radish roses.

Green Peppercorn Sauce

V   *Serves 4–6*

2 tablespoons olive oil

4 oz (100 g) onions, roughly
    chopped

4 oz (100 g) carrots, roughly
    chopped

4 oz (100 g) celery, roughly
    chopped

4 oz (100 g) mushrooms, roughly
    chopped

1 tablespoon chopped mixed herbs

3 oz (75 g) vegan margarine or
    butter

3 oz (75 g) organic wholewheat
    flour

2 tablespoons tomato purée (see
    page 223)

1 tablespoon French mustard

schooner of dry sherry

2 pints (1.2 l) vegetable stock or
    water mixed with wine, hot

1 oz (30 g) green peppercorns

salt and freshly ground black pepper

This sauce must be made one if not two days in advance. It's well worth the effort to make such a great sauce with no meat.

1. Heat the oil in a deep heavy saucepan.

2. Add the vegetables and herbs and cook for 30–40 minutes until browning.

3. In another saucepan, melt the vegan margarine. Add the flour, stir to make a roux and cook until brown. Transfer the cooked vegetables to the roux and add the tomato paste and mustard.

4. Return the saucepan that used to have the vegetables in it to the heat and pour in the sherry. Stir vigorously to remove all the flavours from the bottom of the pan, then pour into the roux.

5. Gradually add the hot stock to this mixture, stirring all the time.

6. When all the stock has been combined with the roux pass through a sieve into the first saucepan and add the green peppercorns. Partially cover and allow to simmer for up to 2 hours or until the desired consistency has been reached.

7. Adjust the seasoning, pour into a plastic container, cover with buttered greaseproof paper and allow to cool before refrigerating. To reheat, place in a bowl above boiling water or cover and microwave.

VARIATIONS

Instead of green peppercorns try a reduction of your favourite alcohol, 4 oz (100 g) chopped pitted black cherries or more tomato purée.

Brussels Sprouts with Chestnuts

V G *Serves 4–6*

1 lb (450 g) Brussels sprouts (the smaller the better), any damaged outer leaves removed

8 oz organic Italian dried chestnuts, cooked until tender

1 oz (30 g) butter or vegan margarine

1 tablespoon sesame oil

1 tablespoon soya sauce

1 teaspoon grated fresh ginger

zest of $\frac{1}{2}$ lemon

This 'old chestnut' is one of my favourite combinations as a side dish – somehow the two foods complement each other perfectly.

1. Cook the Brussels sprouts in boiling salted water for 3 minutes – longer if large. Refresh in cold water and allow to drain. This can be done the day before.

2. Heat the butter or margarine and oil in a frying pan. Add the sprouts and chestnuts and stir-fry for 3–4 minutes until very hot. Add the soya sauce, ginger and lemon. Serve immediately.

VARIATION

Omit the sesame oil (add more butter), ginger and lemon, and add $\frac{1}{2}$ pint (275 ml) of cream or sour cream.

Roast Fanned Potatoes

V G *Serves 4–6*

2 lb (900 g) waxy potatoes (choose King Edward, Craig Royal or Pentland Squire)

4 tablespoons vegetable oil

fine sea salt

This is my favourite way of cooking roast potatoes. They take a little extra time but the extra crispness is worth it.

1. Heat the oven to 190°C/375°F/Gas Mark 5.

2. I don't like parboiling my roast potatoes but if you're in a hurry by all means do.

3. Peel, eye and cut the potatoes into evenly sized pieces, approximately $1\frac{1}{2}$ oz (40 g) each in weight. Keep them submerged in salted water to stop them going black.

4. Take each section of potato and, with its flat surface against the chopping board, make a series of slices approximately halfway through the depth of the potato.

5. Place the potatoes in a large clean tea towel and gather up the ends to form a pouch. Holding the pouch tightly, bash the potatoes violently onto the work surface two or three times (don't go mad otherwise you will end up with potato pieces). This roughens the surfaces of the potatoes and dries them.

6. Take your largest roasting pan and heat the oil in it on the stove. The oil should just cover the entire base of your pan. When the oil is really hot, add the potatoes, sprinkle with salt and make sure each piece of potato is well covered with hot oil. Place in the oven and roast for $1-1\frac{1}{4}$ hours until brown and crisp.

VARIATION

Before placing in the oven, brush a little flavoured oil like garlic or chilli over the incisions in the potatoes.

Honeyed Swede and Carrot Purée

G *Serves 4–6*

1 lb (450 g) swedes
2 large carrots
2 oz (50 g) butter
1 tablespoon clear honey

This is a lovely comforting dish especially when everything else on the plate is very savoury.

1. Top, tail and peel the swedes and carrots. Cut into rough, even-sized pieces and place in a suitable saucepan.

2. Cover with boiling salted water and cook until tender.

3. Drain and roughly mash with a potato masher, first with the butter and then with the honey. ON NO ACCOUNT liquidise.

4. Serve immediately or allow to cool, cover and refrigerate, then reheat above steam or in a microwave.

VARIATIONS

• At a dinner party, you may wish to add an egg or two to the cooled mixture and pipe the purée onto a buttered baking sheet in attractive cone shapes. Then simply brush with melted butter and reheat in the oven.

• V Vegans can substitute maple syrup for the honey.

Two-Berry Summer Pudding

Serves 4–6

1 lb (450 g) blackcurrants or
  blueberries
1 lb (450 g) raspberries or
  strawberries
2 tablespoons water
1 vanilla pod, split
3 oz (75 g) demerara sugar
6–9 slices stale unbleached white
  bread
whipped double cream or crème
  fraîche to serve

Choose just two varieties of summer berry for this version of a classic dessert.

1. Heat the blackcurrants, raspberries, water, vanilla and sugar together gently for about 10 minutes. Be careful not to make the fruit mushy.

2. Strain the berries and remove the juice and the vanilla pod.

3. Dip the bread into the juice and use it to line a $2\frac{1}{2}$ pint (1.5 l) pudding basin. Retain 1 or 2 pieces for the top.

4. Quickly pour the fruit into the bread-lined basin and cover with the slice or two of juice-soaked bread.

5. Cover with a plate that will fit snugly inside the pudding bowl and onto this put a 1 lb (450 g) weight. Leave in the fridge overnight but remove it in time to bring it to room temperature the next day before eating.

6. If you have any fruit juice left over after the bread dipping, reduce it by boiling to make a nice natural fruit sauce.

7. To serve, run a palette knife carefully around the edge of the bread. Place a serving plate over the top and invert the whole dish. Serve with the fruit sauce and whipped double cream or crème fraîche.

DRINKS

The gnocchi certainly deserves a Barbera or a New Zealand Sauvignon Blanc. The warming green peppercorn sauce is certainly not fiery and poses a slight dilemma as to what to drink. Try a young Côtes du Rhône or a Cabernet. The summer pudding certainly demands a Monbazillac or Sauternes.

MENU

A SPRING MEAL

SERVES 4–6

*Globe Artichoke Mousse with Rhubarb and Date
Relish*

—.—

*Asparagus-filled Buckwheat Crèpes with Fresh Tomato
and Garlic Sauce*
Chicory, Orange and Pistachio Salad
Hoffnung's Sautéed Potatoes

—.—

Iced Gooseberry and Lime Soufflé

The trouble with spring in Britain is that as far as vegetables and fruit go it doesn't really happen till early summer. So if you are planning a spring menu in March or April, you'll find there's not much in the shops that you haven't seen all winter. What is different, though, is the mood, the temperature and the feeling of freedom and growth. Let your inspiration guide your cooking, for the most important ingredient is love.

COUNTDOWN

3 days before
• Make the Fresh Tomato and Garlic Sauce.

2 days before
• Prepare the Rhubarb and Date Relish.　• Prepare the batter for the crèpes.

Day before
• Prepare the Globe Artichoke Mousse and store, covered, in the

fridge. • Cook the crèpes. • Make the filling for the crèpes. Cool, cover and refrigerate. • Make the iced soufflé. • Make the fruit sauce for the soufflé.

On the day

• Prepare the garnishes and accompaniments. Do some butter curls for the toast. • Fill the pancakes, roll up and place in a buttered baking dish. Store in the fridge until needed, then follow the recipe. • Prepare the potato dish. • Prepare the salad and salad dressing.

4 hours before • If serving red wine, remove cork and allow it to come to room temperature. Chill white wine.

3 hours before • If serving cheese, remove it from the fridge and put it in the dining room covered with a tea towel.

30 minutes before • Start cooking the potato dish or reheating in the oven.

15 minutes before • Turn out the mousses, garnish and glaze. Put the crèpes in the oven. Start heating the Tomato and Garlic Sauce in a *bain-marie*. Put main course plates in the oven.

5 minutes before • Toast the bread and keep warm in the oven.

0 minutes before • Serve the mousse with its appropriate garnish, the relish and the toast. • Put the salad in a bowl, dress and garnish with hot pistachios. • Put the potatoes in a serving dish in the oven. Steam the asparagus tips. • Serve the main course. • Serve the cheese. • Turn the individual iced soufflés out onto cold plates. If you have trouble getting them out, briefly immerse the ramekins in hot water, being careful not to get any on the souffle. • Carefully pour a little of the sauce onto each plate and serve the rest in a sauceboat.

Globe Artichoke Mousse

Artichokes come into season in France in March and September. You know it's artichoke season because everywhere you look everyone has a large bag or basket of artichokes in their hands. In England, artichokes are mainly imported from France so it is between those two times of the year that they are usually available at a reasonable price. Essentially artichokes will grow year round if the weather is mild – they cannot stand frost unprotected.

G *Serves 4–6*

8 large globe artichokes

4 oz (100 g) Mascarpone cheese

¼ pint (150 ml) Greek yoghurt (or low fat if you prefer)

fine sea salt and freshly ground pepper

pinch cayenne pepper

juice of 1 lemon

2 teaspoons agar-agar

¼ pint (150 ml) cooking liquor from the artichokes

capers to garnish

1 oz (30 g) clarified butter

1. Break the stalks off the artichokes. Place in 1, 2 or 3 large pans of salted water – depending how large your pans are!

2. Bring to the boil and boil for 45 minutes or until a leaf can easily be pulled. Drain and cool. Retain the cooking liquor.

3. Remove the leaves from the artichoke. Separate the chokes from the hearts. Trim the hearts so that only succulent flesh remains and place in a blender. If you have time, scrape the flesh from the leaves into the blender as well. Blend to a smooth consistency.

4. Grease a soufflé dish or at least 8 individual ramekins.

5. Spoon the artichoke purée into a bowl and fold in the Mascarpone and yoghurt. Season and add the cayenne pepper and lemon juice.

6. Follow the instructions on the type of agar-agar you are using, substituting artichoke cooking stock for water. Agar-agar usually needs to be gently heated for up to 20 minutes, then boiled for 1 minute prior to use, but there are some more instant varieties on the market now.

7. Pour the agar-agar and stock onto the artichoke mixture and mix in carefully.

8. Pour this mixture into the prepared moulds and refrigerate until set.

9. When the mousse is set, cover the soufflé dish with a large attractive plate and turn upside down. It should slip out immediately, but if it doesn't give it a sharp tap.

10. Decorate the top with a few capers and perhaps some sprigs of parsley and glaze with the clarified butter.

To serve: Serve on its own with hot buttered organic wholewheat toast, or with a fresh leafy salad. A little sharp pickle, chutney or relish is a good accompaniment as the mousse is quite rich. Alternatively try a tasty vinaigrette flavoured with mustard, tomato or chilli.

Rhubarb and Date Relish

V G *Makes 1 lb (450 g)*

8 oz (225 g) rhubarb
8 oz (225 g) demerara sugar
4 oz (100 g) chopped dates
3 cloves garlic, crushed
1 shallot, finely chopped
2 teaspoons freshly grated ginger
4 fl oz (120 ml) white wine vinegar
pinch cayenne
zest and juice of $\frac{1}{2}$ lemon or lime

This is a deliciously incisive relish that will cut through the richest of hot or cold dishes and cheeses. Its vivid colour is a useful addition to any plate.

1. Put all the ingredients in a deep heavy pan. Bring to the boil and simmer until thickening – up to 20 minutes.

2. Allow to cool before use. If you want to keep this relish, simply pour it into a sterilised jar and seal.

Asparagus-filled Buckwheat Crèpes

Makes 8–12 crèpes

The Crèpes
3 large free-range eggs
4 oz (100 g) buckwheat flour
4 oz (100 g) organic wholewheat
  flour, sifted
fine sea salt
$\frac{1}{2}$ pint (275 ml) milk
$\frac{1}{2}$ pint (275 ml) water
2 oz (50 g) melted butter or
  $2\frac{1}{2}$ tablespoons vegetable oil
3 oz (75 g) butter for frying

The filling
1 lb 2 oz (500 g) fresh asparagus,
  tips cut off at $1\frac{1}{2}$ in (3 cm), the
  rest cut into $\frac{1}{2}$ in (1 cm) pieces
1 oz (30 g) butter
2 shallots, finely chopped
1 sherry glass of Calvados
1 pint (600 ml) double cream (or
  $\frac{1}{2}$ pint (275 ml) béchamel sauce)

Asparagus is synonomous with English springtime. For this dish choose best English green asparagus, available in April. If money is tight, substitute leeks for half the quantity of asparagus. It is very important to cook asparagus correctly, for once overcooked it is never the same. We produced this dish originally at one of our gourmet evenings but, as you will see, it is not difficult and can be prepared to some extent in advance.

To make the crèpes

1. In a bowl, mix the eggs and flours together with the salt.

2. Beat in the milk and water, a little at a time, to form a smooth batter. Stir in the melted butter or oil. Allow the batter to rest at room temperature for at least 2 hours before use. Just before using the batter, add a little water to lubricate it.

3. Melt a knob of butter in a frying pan. Be careful not to burn it. Using a ladle, pour enough batter into the pan to scantily cover the bottom. Cook until the pancake slides easily when shaken, then turn over and cook the other side for up to 2 minutes. Be careful not to overcook as you want to be able to roll them up later on.

½ pint (275 ml) sour cream
1 clove garlic, crushed or chopped
12 oz (325 g) Brie, skin removed
    and cut into pieces
melted butter
4 oz (100 g) Gruyère cheese, grated
chopped chives and parsley, and
    cherry tomatoes, for garnish

4. As each pancake is cooked, turn it out onto a plate and cover it with a square of greaseproof paper ready to receive the next pancake. This will help keep the pancakes moist yet easy to separate. Cook at least 8 large pancakes or 12 smaller ones.

To make the filling

1. Blanch the chopped asparagus stems in boiling salted water for no more than 1 minute. Drain and set aside.

2. Melt the butter in a saucepan, add the shallots and cook until golden brown. Add the Calvados and reduce by two-thirds.

3. Pour in the creams, bring back to the boil and then gently reduce by half. Stir frequently to avoid burning.

4. Add the asparagus and the garlic and cook gently for a further 2 minutes.

5. Adjust the seasoning and set aside to cool if the pancakes are going to be assembled later or the next day.

To assemble

1. Butter an attractive baking dish.

2. Take a pancake and spoon the asparagus mixture on to it, then add some of the Brie.

3. Roll the pancake up and stow it neatly, seam side down, in your baking dish. Continue this process until all the mix has been used. Try to make enough for seconds if possible! Push them tightly together.

4. Brush with melted butter, then sprinkle evenly with the grated Gruyère. Season and decorate with chopped fresh chives and parsley. Whole cherry tomatoes are good too.

5. Bake (if making from cold) for 40 minutes in an oven preheated to 180°C/350°F/Gas Mark 4 or until the cheese is golden brown and bubbly.

6. Just before serving, steam the asparagus tips then toss in melted butter and use for garnish.

To serve: Serve really hot with a simple sauce (see page 80) that can counteract the richness of the filling. Use the asparagus tips dipped in melted butter to adorn the top of the pancakes.

VARIATIONS

Stuffed pancakes cooked this way are hugely popular even with ardent meat-eaters. Try other vegetables: leeks, mushrooms, spinach, broccoli, cauliflower, peppers, aubergines, tomatoes, avocados, squash, sweetcorn – all are good.

Other cheeses too can be used, like Roquefort, Devonshire blue, Stilton or Camembert.

Do try to counterbalance a rich filling with a simple sauce.

Fresh Tomato and Garlic Sauce

Makes about ½ pint (275 ml)

6 medium tomatoes, skinned, deseeded and chopped
2 tablespoons olive oil
2 shallots, chopped
4 or more cloves garlic, crushed or chopped
1 tablespoon demerara sugar
4 tablespoons red wine vinegar
2 tablespoons tomato purée
2 tablespoons water
2 teaspoons soya sauce
fine sea salt and ground black pepper

Here's a tomato sauce that relies on good ingredients for its flavour. If fresh ripe tomatoes are completely impossible to come by, substitute good tinned plum tomatoes. The sauce can be made well in advance – at least 4 days – and will improve in flavour.

1. Heat the oil in a saucepan. Add the shallots and cook gently for 5 minutes.

2. Add the rest of the ingredients and bring to the boil. Put the lid on and simmer for 15 minutes.

3. Blend the sauce and pass through a sieve. Allow to cool. Store covered in a fridge.

To serve: Simply reheat and adjust seasoning if necessary.

VARIATION

Add one bunch of chopped fresh parsley at stage 2, and reduce the amount of garlic, for a more herby sauce.

Hoffnung's Sautéed Potatoes

V G *Serves 4–6*

1½ lb (675 g) potatoes, peeled and
   cut into pieces 1 in (2.5 cm)
   square and ¼ in (5 mm) thick
1 oz (30 g) butter or 1 tablespoon
   vegetable oil or olive oil
8 oz (225 g) leeks, topped, tailed,
   washed and finely chopped
½ teaspoon chopped thyme
8 oz (225 g) tinned flageolet beans,
   drained and rinsed
3 oz (75 g) butter or 3 tablespoons
   vegetable oil or olive oil
2 oz (50 g) tiny button mushrooms
   (optional), brushed and trimmed
salt and freshly ground black pepper

My Aunt June introduced Kate and me to this dish when we
were visiting her in France once. Kate immediately fell in love
with it and we've been cooking it at home and at the restaurant
ever since. It's good as a meal in its own right, but equally forms
an interesting accompaniment to other dishes. The children like
it too. To avoid last-minute panics, cook it in advance and reheat
in the oven.

1. Par-cook the potatoes in boiling salted water. When done,
drain and cool under running water. Place near some heat to dry
off. Sprinkle with 1 tablespoon of salt and season with freshly
ground black pepper.

2. While the potatoes are par-boiling, heat the 1 oz (30 g) of
butter or oil in a saucepan and add the leeks and thyme. Sauté
gently for 5 minutes or until the leeks are softening. Add the
flageolet beans and continue to cook for another 5 minutes.
Remove from heat.

3. Heat the rest of the butter or oil in a large frying pan. Add
the potatoes and cook gently for up to 40 minutes, turning
occasionally. When the potatoes are golden brown add the leeks,
flageolet beans and button mushrooms. Mix in well. Continue
to cook for a further 5 minutes.

4. Serve immediately, or allow to cool and then reheat alongside
the main dishes in the oven for no more than 30 minutes.

VARIATION

Add a few whole or halved cooked chestnuts with the leeks.

Chicory, Orange and Pistachio Salad

V G *Serves 4–6*

1 head of curly endive (half a head
will do if you can buy one),
washed and trimmed

2 chicory bulbs, base removed,
leaves washed

1 head gem lettuce (or any other leaf
for colour), washed and pulled
apart

3 sweet oranges, segmented (but
retain as much juice as possible)

juice of 1 lime

6 tablespoons olive oil

3 teaspoons demerara sugar or
honey

fine sea salt and freshly ground black
pepper

2 oz (50 g) shelled unsalted
pistachio nuts

Here we use two types of chicory – the curly frenetic one which
is more akin to a leaf than anything else (sometimes known as
curly endive) and the prim elegant, pale yellow tipped bulb that
is most commonly called chicory. The combination of orange,
pistachio and chicory is unique and if served with a succulent,
cheesy, creamy dish like Asparagus-filled Buckwheat Crèpes the
result will be sensational.

1. Prepare all the leaves and place in a bowl with the orange
segments.

2. Combine the orange juice, lime juice, oil and sugar to make a
dressing. Season it to taste.

3. Toast the pistachio nuts and add them to the leaves.

4. Dress the salad just before serving, if possible with the pistachios still warm.

VARIATIONS

Substitute pine nuts or walnuts or hazelnuts for pistachios. Add
slices of mango or paw-paw. Try Parmesan cheese, croutons or
goat's cheese crumbled over.

Iced Gooseberry and Lime Soufflé

G *Serves 4–6*

12 oz (325 g) fresh or frozen
    gooseberries
a little sugar (to taste)
juice and zest of 2 limes
4 oz (100 g) demerara sugar
$\frac{1}{4}$ pint (150 ml) water
2 egg whites
pinch fine sea salt
$\frac{1}{4}$ pint (150 ml) double cream

After any large filling meal, something cool and refreshing is always welcome. I know gooseberries tend to be in the shops in late spring/early summer but here's a dessert that will be perfect at any time of year.

1. Poach the gooseberries with a little sugar until soft. Add the lime juice and zest and leave to cool.

2. Heat the sugar and water together until the sugar dissolves. Boil vigorously for 5 minutes.

3. Whisk the egg whites with the salt in a clean metal bowl until they form peaks. Add the boiling sugar to the egg whites in a steady stream, whisking all the time, until the mixture is thick and shiny. Stand the bowl of meringue on ice in some cold water. Whisk occasionally.

4. Whip the cream until thick but not stiff.

5. Purée the cool poached gooseberries and fold into the cream, then fold the cream into the meringue.

6. Pour the mixture into a mould or ramekins. Chill, then freeze.

To serve: Serve on plates or in individual ramekins, turned out, with a fruit sauce such as Raspberry Coulis (see recipe for Passion Fruit Coulis on page 39).

DRINKS

With the mousse, try a Sauvignon de Touraine. With the crêpes, how about a spicy Shiraz? While with the iced soufflé you must try a Moscato d'Asti.

---

*M*ENU

A SUMMER MEAL

SERVES 4–6

*Marinated Baby Vegetables with Poached Quails' Eggs
and Hot Walnut Bread*

— · —

*Fresh Spinach and Goat's Cheese Ravioli with
Coriander and Mint Sauce
Preserved Peppers
Grilled Aubergines with Fresh Tomato Salsa
Nearly Caesar Salad*

— · —

Wild Strawberry Tartlets

Summer dinner parties, especially *al fresco*, are the very stuff of dreams. Long cool drinks before sunset and then to your candlelit table for a light but lavish meal combining all the colours, scents and flavours of high summer. As the last rays linger, the mood is languorous and the food sumptuous.

The menu is simple like the clothes you are wearing. It's too hot to be complicated – they want white wine, ice cold, and food that just is!

COUNTDOWN

3 days before
• Make the Walnut Bread and freeze. • Make the preserved peppers.

2 days before
• Make the pasta dough. • Make the pasta filling. • Make the sauce for the pasta.

Day before

• Steam the baby vegetables. Make the marinade and marinate the vegetables, covered, in the fridge. • Make the pastry for the tartlets. • Make the ravioli. Store, covered, in the fridge. • Defrost the Walnut Bread, cut slices halfway through, butter and wrap in tinfoil. Refrigerate. • Make the Fresh Tomato Salsa. • Make the dressing for the salad. • Make some Real Custard, cover and refrigerate.

On the day

• Prepare the garnishes and accompaniments.

3 hours before • If serving cheese, remove from the fridge and place in the dining room. Open red wine and allow to come to room temperature. • Strain the vegetables from the marinade. Keep cold separately. Blend the marinade, adding a little oil if necessary, and adjust seasoning. It should have a coating consistency. • Bake the pastry cases for the tartlets. • Prepare the aubergines for grilling. • Prepare the salad leaves and croutons for the salad.

1 hour before • Finish the tartlets and stow in fridge.

30 minutes before • Assemble Nearly Caesar Salad but do not dress. Put the Walnut Bread in the oven.

5 minutes before • Poach the quails' eggs. Arrange the baby vegetables on plates with a slice of hot Walnut Bread. Serve as per recipe. Put a large pan of boiling salted water on the go. Eat your starter. • Poach the ravioli in the boiling salted water. Heat the pasta sauce in a pan and add cream if desired. Drain the ravioli and toss in hot sauce and cream. Grill the aubergines while the ravioli is poaching. • Dress the Caesar Salad. Arrange the Preserved Peppers attractively on a plate and drizzle a little oil on. • Serve the main course with plenty of Sbrinz or Parmesan. Eat your main course. • Serve cheese and remove tartlets from fridge. • Serve tartlets on attractive side plates accompanied by Real Custard. • Relax.

Marinated Baby Vegetables with Poached Quails' Eggs

Few starters could make a more perfect first course on a balmy summer evening. Succulent young vegetables, still crisp and full of goodness and flavour, contrast with the mellow softness of warm walnut bread and lightly cooked eggs. If you can't eat eggs, substitute lightly cooked tofu. Use a conventional domestic

Serves 4–6

The vegetables

6 baby carrots, scrubbed, with leaves intact but trimmed neatly

6 baby turnips, scrubbed, with leaves intact but trimmed neatly

6 button onions or spring onion bulbs, trimmed

6 baby courgettes, wiped carefully, with flower still intact (flower may need careful washing)

4 oz (100 g) green beans, topped and tailed

12 sugar snap peas (mangetout will do if you can't find these delightfully crisp pods of peas)

6 baby sweetcorn

The marinade

4 oz (100 g) raspberries (fresh, frozen or even tinned will do)

6 tablespoons white wine vinegar

juice and zest of 1 lemon

2 tablespoons demerara sugar or honey

2 cloves garlic, crushed

6 tablespoons walnut oil

fine sea salt and freshly ground black pepper

The eggs

12 quails' eggs

The bread

6–12 slices fresh walnut bread (see page 6) served as bread or toast

The garnish

fresh herbs, chopped or snipped

poacher rather than risk damaging them in boiling acidulated water. Not only will they be aesthetically pleasing, you will also be able to cook them just to perfection – i.e. still runny in the middle and firm but not hard on the outside.

1. First make the marinade by boiling the raspberries with the vinegar, lemon and sugar or honey for 5 minutes. Set aside to cool.

2. When the raspberry mix is cool put it into a blender and with the motor running add the garlic, then pour in the oil gradually to form a good liaison. Season with salt and pepper.

3. Steam the carrots, turnips and onions together for 7 minutes. They will still be crisp. Put to one side. Then briefly steam the courgettes, beans, sugar snaps and baby sweetcorn. Add them to the first lot of vegetables and, whilst still warm, cover with the marinade. After about 1 hour of marinating, strain off the marinade and reserve.

To assemble

1. Arrange the marinated vegetables on individual plates, leaving space in the centre of each for a piece of walnut bread or toast. Whizz the reserved marinade in the blender again.

2. Poach the quails' eggs when everyone is sitting at the table. Toast the walnut bread or heat it through, sliced and buttered, in tinfoil in the oven (like garlic bread).

3. Place the hot buttered walnut bread in the centre of the vegetables, slip a couple of quails' eggs onto each piece and drizzle a little extra raspberry dressing over the vegetables.

4. Sprinkle a good amount of chopped parsley, coriander or snipped chives over the whole. Serve with more of the raspberry vinaigrette.

VARIATIONS

There are many other vegetables that are suitable for this dish. Choose from: asparagus tips, baby or wild mushrooms, baby artichokes, celery batons, roasted pepper strips, cherry tomatoes, tiny new potatoes, little leeks, baby aubergines, cauliflower and broccoli florets, kohlrabi batons, celeriac matchsticks, Brussels sprouts, chestnuts, fennel, avocado strips (not cooked), baby parsnips, baby beetroots, okra and broad beans.

Fresh Spinach and Goat's Cheese Ravioli with Coriander and Mint Sauce

Serves 4–6

Organic wholewheat spinach pasta

2 oz (50 g) spinach

2 large free-range eggs, beaten

7 oz (200 g) organic wholewheat pastry flour

2 oz (50 g) semolina

1 teaspoon salt

2 tablespoons virgin olive oil

1 egg, beaten

The filling

2 tablespoons olive oil

3 cloves garlic, finely chopped

2 oz (50 g) shallots, finely chopped

6 oz (175 g) young spinach, stalks removed, leaves blanched

8 oz (225 g) St Christophe or Montrachet goat's cheese, crumbled (or even Bucheron)

2 oz (50 g) grated Sbrinz cheese or Parmesan (optional)

3 oz (75 g) cream cheese

1 tablespoon chopped fresh parsley

fine sea salt

freshly ground black pepper

pinch grated nutmeg

pinch chilli powder

The coriander and mint sauce

1 bunch fresh coriander, without stalks

1 bunch fresh mint, without stalks

3 cloves garlic

juice of $\frac{1}{2}$ lemon

(*ingredients continue on page 88*)

If your first course is a little bit on the complex side then a simple main course is the perfect answer both logistically and gastronomically. Fresh pasta is great fun to make. You only need a rolling pin, a pastry board and a cutter (a small biscuit cutter will do). If you intend to make it regularly you could invest in a pasta-rolling machine. Pasta dough must be made well in advance.

To make the pasta

1. Wash the spinach and blanch it in boiling salted water for 30 seconds. Cool immediately with ice-cold water to preserve the vivid green colour. Drain well.

2. Put the spinach in a blender with the eggs and zap to a fine purée.

3. Mix the wholewheat flour, semolina and salt together on a smooth surface (marble is ideal). Make a well in the centre and add the spinach and egg mixture and oil.

4. Knead together to make an elastic dough for about 10 minutes. If it's still sticky add a little more semolina.

5. Roll the dough into a ball and wrap it in tin foil. Allow to rest in a cool place (ideally not in the fridge, though) for 2 hours.

6. Divide into two. Use a rolling pin or pasta machine to roll the dough out very thinly, giving you two thin layers of pasta dough about the same shape.

To make the filling

1. Heat the olive oil in a saucepan.

2. Add the garlic and shallots and sauté until softening. Remove from the heat and cool.

3. Put the shallot and garlic mixture in a blender with the blanched spinach, add the goat's cheese and Sbrinz and blend to a fine purée.

4 tablespoons olive oil

4 tablespoons Sbrinz cheese (or Parmesan)

fine sea salt and freshly ground black pepper

2 tablespoons double cream (optional)

2–3 tablespoons pine nuts, toasted, to garnish

herb flowers, to garnish (optional)

4. Remove from the blender and beat well into the cream cheese along with the parsley and seasoning.

5. Put the mixture into a piping bag with a $\frac{1}{2}$ in (1 cm) plain nozzle and chill.

To make the sauce

Simply blend all the ingredients (except the optional cream, pine nuts and herb flowers) together in a food processor or blender.

To assemble

1. Brush one half of the rolled out pasta dough with egg.

2. Mark this half of the pasta with a round $2\frac{1}{2}$ in (6 cm) fluted cutter.

3. Pipe a walnut-sized amount of filling onto the centre of each lightly marked circle.

4. Cover with the other sheet of pasta, gently pushing the pasta over the filling. Then, using the cutter, cut the ravioli out.

5. Make sure each ravioli is sealed all the way round but try not to manhandle them. At this point, if you are making them the day before, place them on a well oiled tray, cover tightly with clingfilm and store in the fridge. If not, continue as follows:

6. On the stove, have a huge pan of boiling water on the go, well salted and oiled. Put the ravioli gently into the water and cook for 5 minutes.

To serve: Heat the sauce gently in a large pan. Add the cream, if desired. Add the cooked ravioli and heat gently. Have Sbrinz, Parmesan and more sauce available on the table.

VARIATIONS

Try different fillings for the ravioli. Mushroom, asparagus and tomato are all good. Ricotta is a nice cheese to use and of course try other types of pasta and sauce, including pesto.

OPPOSITE: *Toasted Haloumi with Fresh Figs and Walnut Vinaigrette (page 93)*

OPPOSITE PAGE 89: *Chinese Stir-fried Vegetables and Tofu with Lemon-grass-scented Rice (page 28)*

Preserved Peppers

V G *Serves 4–6*

2 red peppers
2 yellow peppers
3 tablespoons extra virgin olive oil
(or enough to cover the peppers)
1 pinch of saffron
3 cloves garlic, crushed
1 bunch fresh basil leaves
fine sea salt and freshly ground black
pepper

This dish is the perfect accompaniment to pasta. It's great for a dinner party as it involves barely any work on the evening.

1. Cut the peppers into quarters. Remove the stems, seeds and pith.

2. Grill the peppers skin side up until blistering all over. Allow to cool, then peel and cut into $\frac{1}{2}$ in (1 cm) wide strips.

3. Heat the olive oil with the saffron and garlic for 2 minutes, then allow to cool.

4. Tear the basil leaves and scatter over the peppers, then cover with the warm saffron, garlic and oil. Allow to marinate in a cool place overnight.

5. If you wish to keep your peppers longer, put them in a sterilised kilner jar and cover totally with oil. Make sure none of the peppers is exposed to air. Store in a cool dry place.

To serve: Simply remove from the oil and drain.

Grilled Aubergines with Fresh Tomato and Basil Salsa

V G *Serves 4–6*

2 medium sized aubergines, cut into
four lengthways and sprinkled
with salt and freshly ground black
pepper
virgin olive oil – or even better
would be the oil from the peppers
in the last recipe!
a little fresh Tomato and Basil Salsa
(page 156)

This is an extremely simple dish, again excellent as an accompaniment to pasta.

1. Cut each aubergine, depending on size, into slices $\frac{1}{4}-\frac{1}{2}$ in (5 mm–1 cm) thick, then salt and leave for about 1 hour. Rinse and dry.

2. Brush each slice of aubergine with olive oil, season and place under the grill for 5 minutes or until the flesh browns. Turn, season and repeat.

3. Serve immediately, garnished with a little fresh Tomato and Basil Salsa.

Nearly Caesar Salad

Serves 4–6

The salad

3 heads of cos lettuce or 4 heads of
  gem lettuce

3 tablespoons extra virgin olive oil

1 oz (30 g) butter

2 cloves garlic, crushed or chopped

4 slices organic wholewheat bread,
  preferably one-day-old, cut into
  small slices

3 oz (75 g) Parmesan cheese

10 chives, cut into thirds

The dressing

2 cloves garlic

¼ pint (150 ml) olive oil

4 tablespoons red wine vinegar

1 oz (30 g) Parmesan cheese (vegans
  may omit)

1 teaspoon fresh dill weed (or
  ⅓ teaspoon dried dill)

fine sea salt and freshly ground black
  pepper

6 tablespoons yoghurt

4 tablespoons mayonnaise (vegans
  may omit the yoghurt and
  mayonnaise and substitute
  butterbean mayonnaise)

1 dash vegetarian Worcestershire
  sauce

Why come up with a brilliant idea for a salad, then totally mask its flavour with tinned anchovies? For that matter, why render it a health risk with the inclusion of raw egg yolks? Essentially Caesar Salad is all about creamy, garlicky, cheesy and crunchy crisp mouth sensation. The raw egg yolks introduce an unwelcome clinginess while the tinned anchovies seem to vie with the Parmesan cheese for dominance, with neither winning the battle. So here it is – the 'Nearly Caesar Salad'.

I recommend it as an accompaniment to all pasta dishes or as a main dish in its own right. You may wish to reduce the Parmesan in any main course pasta dish, bearing in mind its presence in the salad.

1. Remove the outer leaves of the lettuce. Tear off the root end, then wash and dry each remaining lettuce leaf.

2. Heat the oil and butter in a frying pan, add the garlic and cook gently for 1 minute. Toss in the bread and fry, turning often, until crisp and golden.

3. Add 1 oz (30 g) of the Parmesan cheese and stir into the croutons, making sure they are all well coated.

4. Blend the first six ingredients of the dressing together. Pour into a bowl and stir in the remaining ingredients. You will now have a thick creamy garlicky dressing.

To assemble

1. Put the leaves in an attractive salad dish. Pour the dressing over them.

2. Sprinkle with the rest of the Parmesan, the croutons and the chives.

3. Serve while the croutons are still warm if possible.

Wild Strawberry Tartlets

Makes 12 tartlets

1 lb (450 g) rich organic sweet
   shortcrust pastry (see page 218)
1 lb (450 g) wild strawberries,
   hulled
2 tablespoons Pernod
$\frac{1}{2}$ pint (275 ml) double cream
2 tablespoons demerara sugar
$\frac{1}{4}$ pint (150 ml) fromage frais
redcurrant jelly
Some Real Custard, cold, to serve
   (optional; see page 228)

I can't, with my hand on my heart, honestly say that we use wild strawberries at the restaurant. The quantities involved would be impossible. At home, though, wild strawberries grow like weeds all over our garden throughout the summer, making this dessert quite possible. Frequently I get my elder children, Daisy and Hamish, to pick them for their pocket money. If you can't get wild strawberries use the smallest cultivated strawberries you can find – they're usually the tastiest.

1. Preheat the oven to 190°C/375°F/Gas Mark 5.

2. Make sure the pastry is well chilled. Roll it out thinly and cut out 12 (or more) $3\frac{1}{2}$ in (8 cm) rounds with a fluted pastry cutter.

3. Line well greased patty tins with pastry circles, prick the bases and chill for 15 minutes.

4. Bake blind in the oven (see page 217) for 10–15 minutes or until the pastry has cooked. Allow to cool.

5. Liquidise 4 oz (100 g) of wild strawberries with the Pernod.

6. Beat the double cream with the sugar until stiff.

7. Fold the strawberry and Pernod purée into the cream.

8. Gently stir the fromage frais into this mixture.

9. Spoon or pipe the cream into the tartlet cases. Decorate each tartlet with about 1 oz (50 g) of wild strawberries.

10. Melt the redcurrant jelly and brush the tops of the wild strawberries.

To serve: Serve on an attractive plate with a little cold Real Custard.

DRINKS

As an aperitif, try a good, ice-cold English wine. The quails' eggs would go well with a sparkling Saumur or a low-priced champagne. The pasta has a pungent salsa to go with it – try a hefty Barbera as accompaniment. For dessert, surprise your guests with a good red from Bordeaux or a sweet white like Monbazillac.

MENU

AN AUTUMN MEAL

SERVES 6

*Toasted Haloumi with Fresh Figs and Walnut
Vinaigrette*

———·———

*Wild Mushroom Filo Parcels with Grilled Tomato and
Coriander Sauce
Parsnip and Walnut Croquettes
Herby Sweetcorn Fritters
Two Pear Salad*

———·———

*Kirsch-flavoured Stuffed Peaches with Blackberry
Sauce*

Autumn is probably the most satisfying time of year from a vegetarian chef's point of view. In England, early autumn sees the grand fruition of not only the year's growth but also the summer's growth. It is harvest time, everything abounds in quantity and quality. Even winter vegetables are at their best, being young, small and tender. The abundance of produce is reflected at market – rarely in the course of the year is so much produce available at such a reasonable price. To add to this plethora of edible riches, all sorts of fungi suddenly start to appear and for the avid mushroom-picker and eater there is no time like the present. Dinner parties in the autumn should reflect still warm days while accepting that late evening can bring with it the chill forewarning of winter.

COUNTDOWN

3 days before
• Go mushroom hunting.

Day before
• Make the vinaigrette for the haloumi.   • Make the filling for the filo parcels.   • Make the tomato sauce. Cover and refrigerate.   • Make the croquettes. Chill in the fridge.   • Prepare the peaches. Fill and store in the fridge.   • Make the Blackberry Sauce. Chill.

On the day
• Prepare all garnishes and accompaniments. Squeeze the limes.
• Prepare the haloumi, accompanying salad and bread for toasting.
• Prepare the filo parcels. Tie and store in the fridge.

2 hours before   • Make the sweetcorn batter. Take cheese from the fridge (if serving) and uncork the red wine. Chill the white wine.

1 hour before   • Prepare the two pears in the Two Pear Salad – they are best prepared as fresh as possible. Arrange on the plate with the garnish, well covered in lime juice.

6 minutes before   • Toast the bread on one side. Put the tomato sauce in a saucepan over a *bain-marie.*

5 minutes before   • Put the haloumi on the untoasted side of the bread. Follow recipe and serve. Put the filo parcels in the oven. Put some main course plates in to heat up.   • Cook the croquettes and fritters. Keep the croquettes warm in the oven until you are ready to serve. The Two Pear Salad is already made so just go and eat.   • Serve cheese. Heat the Blackberry Sauce in a saucepan over a *bain-marie.*   • Toast the cob nuts. Place the peaches in glass bowls, cover with hot (or cold) Blackberry Sauce and finally the toasted cob nuts and flowers.

Toasted Haloumi with Fresh Figs and Walnut Vinaigrette

Haloumi is a semi-soft Cypriot goat's cheese. It's very mild and will offend no one's taste buds. Uncooked, it is quite rubbery, but cooked it lends itself particularly well to this dish. Sweet fresh figs and mellow walnut dressing work well with the silky cheese. Haloumi is available at most supermarkets these days.

Serves 6

6 slices organic wholewheat bread
6 slices haloumi, 1 in (2.5 cm) thick
garlic oil for brushing (see page 224)
6 sprigs of oregano
salt and freshly ground black pepper
6 fresh figs, cut partly into 4 and
    peeled back to reveal their flesh
1 head lollo rosso, washed well and
    dried
1 orange pepper, thinly sliced
    (roasted if you wish)
6 walnuts, toasted
12 mangetout, topped, tailed and
    blanched briefly in boiling water

The walnut vinaigrette
4 tablespoons walnut oil
1 tablespoon sherry vinegar
$\frac{1}{2}$ teaspoon Dijon mustard
$\frac{1}{2}$ teaspoon demerara sugar
fine sea salt and freshly ground black
    pepper

1. Toast the bread on one side only.

2. Place the haloumi on the untoasted side.

3. Brush the haloumi with plenty of garlic oil, decorate with oregano and season with salt and pepper. All this can be done well in advance.

4. Arrange the figs, lettuce, peppers, walnuts and mangetout attractively on plates, leaving space in the centre for the haloumi.

5. Toast the haloumi under a low grill until it is beginning to melt. Don't toast quickly or the bread will brown before the cheese has melted.

6. Combine the ingredients for the dressing in a blender. Spoon some of the walnut dressing over the cheese and salad and serve immediately.

VARIATIONS

Try other cheeses – especially goat's cheese. Try making a dressing with raspberry vinegar. Vegans can try it with pan-fried marinated tofu.

Wild Mushroom Filo Parcels

Wild mushrooms are of course special to autumn with the exception of girolles (or morels) which appear only in spring. Picking wild mushrooms yourself is fun and very rewarding. Start early to deny insects their share and, above all, learn which ones *not* to pick. It is easier to learn to recognise the few mushrooms that are inedible and dangerous than to know all the mushrooms that are good to eat. When cooking wild mushrooms think always of their delicate flavour before anything else.

It may seem like an awful lot of mushrooms but the chanterelles will reduce to about a third of their original volume when cooked. Chanterelles are hardly ever attacked by insects so simply wipe them clean and gently brush their gills to remove any dirt. Slice the larger ones lengthwise. Never chop chanterelles – it would be criminal to destroy their beautiful shape.

Serves 6

1½ lb (675 g) chanterelles

8 oz (225 g) button mushrooms, trimmed

3 cloves garlic, crushed or chopped

fine sea salt and freshly ground black pepper

4 oz (100 g) butter or 4 tablespoons olive oil

3 shallots, finely chopped

4 tablespoons vermouth

½ pint (275 ml) double cream

½ pint (275 ml) sour cream

3 teaspoons arrowroot blended with 6 teaspoons of cold water (optional)

juice of ½ lemon

2 tablespoons chopped fresh parsley

12 sheets filo pastry, each 13 × 8 in (32.5 × 20 cm)

2 oz (50 g) melted butter for brushing

2 spring onions for tying, cut into strips lengthwise

1. Heat the oven to 200°C/400°F/Gas Mark 6.

2. Mix the prepared chanterelles and button mushrooms with the garlic and season.

3. Heat the butter or oil in a large deep frying pan. When bubbling gently add the shallots and cook until softening. Add the chanterelles and continue to cook gently. Chanterelles give off a lot of liquid when cooking.

4. Cook the chanterelles for 5 minutes, then remove from the liquid with a slotted spoon. Add the vermouth and reduce the entire liquid by two-thirds. Stir in the cream and sour cream and reduce by half. Add the chanterelles back into the cream and if necessary thicken with arrowroot. The mix must be fairly thick.

5. Adjust the flavour of the sauce with lemon juice, salt and pepper, and stir in the parsley. Set aside to cool, then refrigerate.

6. Place a sheet of filo pastry on a flat surface and brush with melted butter, then place another crosswise over the first one to form a square with 'bites' taken out of the corner. Brush with melted butter.

7. Spoon one-sixth of the chanterelle mixture onto the centre of the filo square, gather up the edges and tie the filo with a strip of spring onion in the shape of a little old-fashioned purse. Repeat steps 6 and 7 until you have 6 parcels. The parcels may be stored in the fridge overnight.

8. Prior to cooking, brush the outside of the filo parcels with melted butter, then place on a buttered baking sheet and cook in the oven for 10–15 minutes or until piping hot and golden brown.

To serve: Serve on plates with a little Grilled Tomato and Coriander Sauce and a garnish of frisée leaves.

VARIATIONS

• Try any mushrooms you have available – but don't forget the recipe may cook in a slightly different way.

• Add another succulent vegetable like asparagus tips.

• If you can afford it, flavour the sauce with truffle.

Grilled Tomato and Coriander Sauce

V G *Serves 4–6*

1¼ lb (550 g) ripe tomatoes, washed and halved
2 oz (50 g) cold butter, cut into dice
1 tablespoon cold olive oil
1 bunch fresh coriander, chopped
2 cloves garlic, crushed or chopped
fine sea salt and freshly ground black pepper

Autumn is the only time when sun-ripened English tomatoes are plentiful and naturally sweet. At other times of the year they will need sweetening with sugar.

1. Grill the tomatoes, cut side uppermost, until well cooked.

2. Pass through a fine sieve.

3. Heat gently, taking care not to boil the purée.

4. Whisk in the butter, oil, coriander and garlic.

5. Taste and adjust the seasoning.

Parsnip and Walnut Croquettes

Serves 4–6

1 lb (450 g) young parsnips, topped, tailed and scrubbed, not peeled
1 oz (30 g) butter
1 egg
4 oz (100 g) walnuts, toasted and finely chopped
wholewheat flour
fine sea salt and freshly ground black pepper
1 teaspoon paprika
2 oz (50 g) breadcrumbs
2 oz (50 g) sesame seeds
1 egg, beaten
2 tablespoons vegetable oil
2 oz (50 g) butter
1 bunch parsley, chopped

Parsnips are grown year round but are best in autumn or winter. Choose small parsnips with no indication of woodiness, few blemishes and good firm flesh.

1. Cut the parsnips into similar sized pieces. Place in boiling water and cook until tender.

2. Drain and return to a low heat with the butter. Use a potato masher to mash them together. Add the egg and the walnuts and continue to mash thoroughly.

3. Mould the mixture into 6 sausages.

4. Mix the flour with the seasonings. Mix the paprika, breadcrumbs and sesame seeds together. Roll the sausages in the flour, then in the beaten egg, then in the sesame and breadcrumb mix. Make sure they are well coated.

5. Allow to chill overnight in the fridge before frying in the oil and butter for about 10 minutes. Garnish with chopped parsley.

Herby Sweetcorn Fritters

Makes 12 small fritters, enough for 6

5 oz (150 g) organic wholewheat
    pastry flour
pinch of salt
2 large free-range eggs, separated
2 tablespoons corn oil
8 fl oz (250 ml) milk
10 oz (275 g) cooked sweetcorn
    kernels
1 bunch chives, chopped
vegetable oil for frying

Autumn brings with it a glut of sweetcorn. While I enjoy corn on the cob, I do think people forget how easy it is to prepare fresh sweetcorn in other ways. For this recipe, if fresh sweetcorn isn't available, frozen or tinned will substitute. Sweetcorn should have a healthy husk intact, the kernels should be pale yellow, plump and full of milky liquid. To cook fresh corn *off* the cob, cut off the ends, scrape off the kernels with a sharp knife and cook in boiling unsalted water for about 25 minutes. After 15 minutes add a teaspoon of salt and a teaspoon of sugar.

1. Put the flour and salt in a bowl and make a well in the centre.

2. Add the egg yolks, corn oil and milk. Whisk together into a smooth batter. Allow to rest in the fridge for 2 hours.

3. While the batter's resting, prepare the sweetcorn.

4. Beat the egg whites until they form peaks.

5. Fold the sweetcorn into the batter, then fold in the egg whites and chopped chives.

6. Using a tablespoon to measure the batter, fry the fritters in hot oil on both sides until golden brown.

Drain on a piece of kitchen paper and keep warm in the oven until ready to serve.

Note: Herby Sweetcorn Fritters are best made fresh – they tend to go stodgy if allowed to cool.

To serve: If desired, serve with a dollop of sour cream or yoghurt or a flavoured butter – see page 179. They're also great with a relish or chutney.

VARIATIONS

Use chopped peppers, courgettes, cauliflower or even cooked potato as a substitute for sweetcorn or in addition. Change the herbs used to dill, marjoram, parsley, coriander or basil.

Two Pear Salad

V G   *Serves 6*

3 large ripe William pears
3 large ripe avocados
juice of 2 limes
2 bunches of watercress, washed
    well and trimmed
1 curly endive, pulled apart and
    washed
fine sea salt and freshly ground black
    pepper
pinch of paprika

The only difficult thing about this salad would be getting both types of pear exactly ripe on the same day.

1. Peel and cut the pears in half. Remove the stones from the avocados and the cores from the pears.

2. Thinly slice both types of pear and brush with lime juice.

3. Arrange in alternate slices on a plate garnished with watercress and curly endive. Brush more lime juice onto the pears and sprinkle with paprika. Season lightly.

VARIATIONS

Substitute other fruits such as papaya for pear. Substitute a fruity vinaigrette for lime juice. Crumble blue cheese over the pears.

Kirsch-flavoured Stuffed Peaches with Blackberry Sauce

Serves 6

6 large ripe yellow peaches
4 fl oz (120 ml) Kirsch
3 oz (75 g) demerara sugar
$\frac{1}{2}$ teaspoon cinnamon
finely grated rind and juice of
    1 lemon
5 oz (150 g) crème fraîche
2 oz (50 g) Mascarpone cheese
$\frac{1}{2}$ teaspoon vanilla essence
1 tablespoon icing sugar
1 lb (450 g) blackberries
2 oz (50 g) cob nuts, toasted
borage flowers for garnish

Peaches are still excellent in early autumn and some of the larger sweeter varieties are more readily available. Late autumn tends to bring spongy rejects, though, so be careful when selecting. Allow 1 large or 2 small peaches per person.

1. Peel the peaches.

2. Place the peaches in a saucepan with the Kirsch, 2 tablespoons of demerara sugar, cinnamon, lemon juice and rind and enough water to barely cover. Place a lid on the saucepan and bring to the boil, skim, then simmer for 15 minutes. Allow the peaches to cool in the liquid.

3. Beat the crème fraîche and Mascarpone together with the vanilla and icing sugar.

4. Remove the cold peaches from the cooking liquid. Halve and remove the stones. With a teaspoon, slightly enlarge the indentations where the stone was. Put the flesh you have removed into the cooking liquid.

5. Fill the cavities with the cream cheese mixture and push the two halves together again. Chill well.

6. Reduce the cooking liquid in volume to about $\frac{1}{2}$ pint (275 ml). Add the remaining demerara sugar and boil for a further 2 minutes until dissolved.

7. Purée the blackberries in a blender. Add enough of the sugar syrup to create the desired consistency and flavour.

8. Pass through a sieve and, if desired, add a little more Kirsch. Serve hot or cool.

To serve: Present the peaches in small glass bowls, covered in blackberry sauce, and garnished with toasted cob nuts and, if possible, bright blue fresh or candied borage flowers.

VARIATIONS

Substitute apricots or nectarines for the peaches. Substitute blueberries, raspberries or apricots for the blackberries.

DRINKS

With the starter, try a good chilled white wine like a Sancerre. The main course needs a basic red like a Chianti. The peaches are already flavoured with Kirsch and probably need no accompaniment.

ℳENU

WINTER

SERVES 6

*Butternut Pumpkin and Cider Soup
with Cheesy Garlic Croutons and Apple Purée*

—·—

*Steamed Winter Vegetable Pudding with Vegetarian
Gravy
Irish Mashed Potato
Food for friends' Cauliflower Cheese
Spicy Red Cabbage*

—·—

White Chocolate and Chestnut Pots

A dinner party in mid-winter is always a cheery occasion. Hosts become not only feeders of their guests but often warmers too. This second element gives both entertainer and entertainee a special rosy glow within, generated by mutual good cheer as much as the roaring log fire or thermostat on 80°. Having sorted out the temperature of the room to your own and your guests' mutual comfort there is nothing left but to decide on a suitably heartening menu. Once decided, I would strongly recommend that, if possible, the room in which you dine is several degrees cooler than the one in which you greet your guests, otherwise, after the second course, people will be removing articles of clothing, slipping shoes off and generally gasping for breath. One thing is for sure. After this dinner party no one will be going very far very quickly.

COUNTDOWN

2 days before
• Prepare the vegetarian gravy.

Day before
• Prepare the soup and the Apple Purée. Chill both, sep-arately. • Prepare the Spicy Red Cabbage and refrigerate. • Cook the cauliflower, *al dente*, refresh in cold water, drain and refriger-ate. • Prepare the cheese sauce for the cauliflower, cover with buttered paper and chill. • Prepare the White Chocolate and Chestnut Pots. • Prepare the filling for the steamed pudding. • Prepare the pastry for the steamed pudding.

On the day
• Prepare all garnishes and accompaniments and chill.

3 hours before • Prepare the steamed pudding and start steaming. Get the cheese out of the fridge (if serving) and the cork out of the red wine. Chill the white wine. • Make the Cheesy Garlic Croutons.

1 hour before • Put the cabbage in the oven, covered. Assemble the cauliflower and place in the oven. Cook and then mash the potatoes. Heat soup bowls.

30 minutes before • Put the gravy in a saucepan over a *bain-marie*. Start to heat the soup. • Put the Apple Purée in an attractive dish. Put the mash, covered, in the oven. • Serve and eat. Put main course plates into heat. • Transfer the Spicy Red Cabbage to an attractive serving dish. • Turn out the steamed pudding. Add a little hot gravy and chopped parsley. • Serve and eat. • Decorate the desserts and serve.

Butternut Pumpkin and Cider Soup

Pumpkins appear in England at the end of September and, depending on demand, sometimes last till after Christmas. Of course hundreds are sacrificed on Hallowe'en as crazed fathers and mothers, desperate to impress children with their handicraft, turn pumpkins into candle holders.

In this recipe we use butternut pumpkins. They are pear-shaped and have a pale yellow skin and probably more flavour than the average pumpkin. If you can't find butternut pumpkin, use ordinary pumpkin and serve the soup in the outer shell.

V G *Serves 6*

2 oz (50 g) butter or vegan
  margarine
1 tablespoon vegetable oil
4 shallots or 1 large onion, finely
  sliced
1¼ lb (550 g) butternut pumpkin,
  skinned, deseeded and roughly
  chopped
1 large carrot, chopped
1½ pints (900 ml) vegetable stock
1½ pints cider
fine sea salt and freshly ground black
  pepper
chopped fresh parsley to garnish

1. Heat the butter and oil in a large heavy saucepan. Cook the shallots until softening.

2. Add the pumpkin and carrot and cook for 5–10 minutes with the lid on. This should soften the vegetables slightly.

3. Add the stock and the cider and bring to the boil. Simmer for 20–30 minutes until all the vegetables are tender. Liquidise to a smooth consistency. Wash the saucepan.

4. Pour the soup back into the pan and reheat gently if you are serving immediately. Adjust seasoning.

5. Sprinkle generously with chopped parsley before serving.

To serve: Serve accompanied by Cheesy Garlic Croutons (below) and Apple Purée – perhaps too a dollop of sour cream or crème fraîche. For Apple Purée use the recipe for Apple and Pear Purée (see page 158) but omit the pears and substitute more apples.

Cheesy Garlic Croutons

Toast slices of wholewheat bread on one side. Spread the untoasted side with garlic butter. Top with grated Gruyère, Emmental or Cheddar. Sprinkle with chopped parsley. Grill under a hot flame until the cheese is bubbling and slightly browned. Allow to cool before cutting into shapes. When the croutons are immersed in hot soup, the cheese goes wonderfully gooey.

Steamed Winter Vegetable Pudding

V *Serves 6*

2 tablespoons olive oil or 2 oz (50 g) butter

8 oz (225 g) shallots, finely chopped

3 cloves garlic, crushed or chopped

3 medium leeks, cut into $\frac{1}{2}$ in (1 cm) slices

$\frac{1}{2}$ medium celeriac, cut into $\frac{1}{2}$ in (1 cm) dice

4 oz (100 g) carrots, cut into $\frac{1}{2}$ in (1 cm) dice

8 oz (225 g) button mushrooms, trimmed

6 oz (175 g) button onions

8 oz (225 g) Brussels sprouts, topped and tailed

6 fresh shiitake mushrooms or soaked dry ones

a sprig each of rosemary and thyme

1 bay leaf

2 tablespoons chopped fresh parsley

$\frac{1}{4}$ pint (150 ml) vegetarian gravy (see page 104)

12 oz (325 g) organic wholewheat pastry flour

salt

2 teaspoons baking powder

6 oz (175 g) vegetable suet

This has to be the ultimate vegetarian dream savoury dish and so we are going to spend a lot of time on flavour development. This is very important especially if the gravy is to be good. Follow the recipe on page 104 and don't take any shortcuts.

1. Heat the oil or butter and sauté the shallots, garlic and leeks until slightly browned.

2. Add the celeriac and carrots and cook for 5 minutes.

3. Add the button mushrooms, button onions, Brussels sprouts, shiitake mushrooms and herbs. Quickly pour in the vegetarian gravy and bring to the boil. Remove from the heat. It should not be necessary to adjust the consistency. You must, however, adjust the seasoning. The filling may be left like this overnight.

4. Next make the pudding pastry. Sift the flour, a pinch of salt and the baking powder together. Grate the suet and rub it in to form a crumbly texture. Stir in enough water to make a stiff dough.

5. Remove one quarter and reserve. Roll out the rest.

6. Grease a $2\frac{1}{2}$ pint (1.5 l) pudding basin and line it with the rolled-out dough.

7. Fill with the vegetable mixture (it's best if it's cold). Make sure there is not too much gravy and that the vegetables are well packed down.

8. Roll out the remaining piece of dough, lay it on top and seal the edges. Cover with silicone paper and foil and tie with string around the lip of the basin. Place the basin in a big saucepan. Half fill it with boiling water and cook, keeping the water at a rolling boil and topping up with water as necessary for 3 hours. Turn out the pudding and serve on an attractive plate with more vegetarian gravy. Garnish with fresh parsley.

VARIATION

Use cooked chestnuts or marinated tofu in the filling.

Vegetarian or Vegan Gravy

V *Makes 1 pint (600 ml)*

2 oz (50 g) butter or vegan margarine
1 tablespoon olive oil
4 oz (100 g) shallots, finely chopped
2 oz (50 g) carrots, finely chopped
2 oz (50 g) celery, finely chopped
2 oz (50 g) mushroom stalks, finely chopped
½ teaspoon dried thyme
½ teaspoon dried tarragon
1 teaspoon dried rosemary
1 bay leaf
pinch of salt
3 cloves garlic, finely chopped
½ pint (275 ml) red wine
2 tablespoons fresh tomato purée (see page 223)
3 tablespoons flour
2 pints (1.2 l) vegetable stock
1 tablespoon soya sauce
1 oz (30 g) butter, to serve

Here's a gravy to beat all gravies – it can be used as a base for other sauces too. Make at least 2 days in advance.

1. Heat the butter or margarine and olive oil in a deep heavy saucepan or casserole dish.

2. Add the shallots, carrots, celery, mushroom stalks, herbs, salt and garlic. Stir-fry for 5 minutes.

3. Add the red wine and reduce by half.

4. Stir in the tomato purée and flour and cook for 2 minutes.

5. Add the vegetable stock and soya sauce and bring to the boil.

6. Simmer until all the vegetables are tender, then pass through a fine sieve. You now have a pint (600 ml) of genuine Vegetarian Gravy. Best if kept for 1–2 days.

To serve: Simply reheat. Add 1 oz (30 g) butter if desired.

VARIATION

You can add lots of things to the gravy including: madeira, sherry, marsala, cream, redcurrant jelly, mustard, mint or horseradish.

Irish Mashed Potato

V **G** *Serves 4–6*

1 lb 2 oz (500 g) Maris Piper potatoes, peeled, eyed and cut into quarters
1 oz (30 g) butter or vegan margarine
1 large free-range egg (optional)
8 spring onions, finely chopped
1 tablespoon chopped fresh parsley
3 oz (75 g) vegetarian Cheddar, grated (optional)

Perfect for soaking up a delicious gravy or sauce and good in its own right too. Fry any leftovers for breakfast the next day.

1. Boil the potatoes in salted water until soft. Drain well and mash in a separate bowl.

2. Beat in the rest of the ingredients. Season at the end.

3. Serve immediately or, if you want to have it portioned out in advance, spoon into a piping bag with a large star tube.

4. Oil a baking tray and pipe the potato, 'Duchesse' style, onto it.

½ teaspoon freshly grated nutmeg

¼ pint (150 ml) milk or soya milk or
single cream

fine sea salt and freshly ground black
pepper

5. Brush with melted butter and reheat in the oven when desired. Serve when golden brown and piping hot.

'Food for friends' Cauliflower Cheese

Serves 4–6

1½ oz (40 g) butter

1½ oz (40 g) organic wholewheat
flour

½ pint (275 ml) milk

6 fl oz (180 ml) white wine

fine sea salt

freshly ground black pepper

½ teaspoon freshly grated nutmeg

4 oz (100 g) Gruyère or Cheddar
cheese, grated

2 teaspoons Dijon mustard

1 large head cauliflower

2 tablespoons grated Parmesan
cheese

¼ pint (150 ml) double cream
(optional)

toasted nuts for garnish (pine nuts,
walnuts or flaked almonds)

I don't know why, but I do feel slightly embarrassed using this dish in a book that is supposed to be the cutting edge of vegetarian cuisine. The thing is, I like it, and over the years have done some serious work on it. It's a great colour, texture, taste and smell to have on a plate! So here it is, food buffs, a truly original cauliflower cheese.

To turn Cauliflower Cheese into Cauliflower Cheese Sauce, see Variations on page 106.

1. Melt the butter in a non-aluminium saucepan.

2. Stir in the flour and cook gently for 1 minute.

3. Add the milk gradually, stirring all the time. As the mixture gets thick, add more milk until it is all used up. If the sauce is still obviously too thick add a little water.

4. In a separate saucepan, reduce the wine by half and add to the white sauce. Season with salt, pepper and nutmeg. Remove from the heat and add the Gruyère (or other cheese) and mustard.

5. Poach the cauliflower whole or broken into florets, for 10 minutes in boiling salted water. If poaching whole, place head down and cover with the saucepan lid.

6. Refresh the cauliflower in cold water to prevent further cooking. Place in an attractive dish.

7. If the sauce is cold and thick, reheat gently with extra cream or milk or even water. Whisk it briskly to avoid curdling. Then cover the cauliflower with the sauce.

8. Sprinkle with Parmesan and bake in the oven for at least 30 minutes at 180°C/350°F/Gas Mark 4 or until bubbling and brown. Garnish with toasted nuts.

VARIATIONS

- Cauliflower cheese can be turned into a wonderful Cauliflower Cheese Sauce by doubling the quantity of cheese sauce or halving the amount of cauliflower and cutting into florets.

- Add 2 cloves of garlic, crushed or chopped, with the mustard.

Spicy Red Cabbage

V G   *Serves 6*

1 large red cabbage, thinly sliced
1 oz (30 g) butter
2 tablespoons walnut or olive oil
2 medium onions, finely sliced
8 oz (225 g) Granny Smith apples, peeled, cored and sliced
2 cloves garlic, crushed
juice and zest of 1 orange
$\frac{1}{4}$ teaspoon each of powdered allspice, cloves, ginger and mace
$\frac{1}{4}$ pint (150 ml) red wine
1 tablespoon balsamic vinegar
1 tablespoon demerara sugar
fine sea salt and freshly ground black pepper
chopped parsley for garnish (optional)

Spicy Red Cabbage is one of my favourite vegetable dishes. It is especially good in a meal where the main dish has a fairly plain sauce to accompany it.

1. Heat the oven to 180°C/350°F/Gas Mark 4.

2. Prepare the red cabbage by removing the outer damaged leaves. Cut it into quarters and be careful to remove all the hard stalk. Shred it finely.

3. Melt the butter and oil together in a deep heavy casserole dish. Add the onions and cook gently for 5 minutes.

4. Add the cabbage, apples, garlic and orange zest and continue to cook for a further 5 minutes.

5. Add the rest of the ingredients, bring to the boil, cover and place in the oven. Cook for 30 minutes if you like your cabbage crisp or anything up to 3 hours if you prefer it really tender.

To serve: Place in an attractive serving dish and garnish with chopped parsley if you like.

VARIATION

Add 4 oz (100 g) sultanas with the apples.

White Chocolate and Chestnut Pudding

G   *Serves 4–6*

2 lb (900 g) fresh unpeeled
   chestnuts or 8 oz (225 g) dried
   chestnuts or 1 lb (450 g)
   unsweetened tinned chestnut
   purée
2 bay leaves
8 oz (225 g) demerara sugar
4 tablespoons rum or Kirsch
8 oz (225 g) white chocolate,
   broken into small pieces
8 oz (225 g) unsalted butter
½ pint (275 ml) double cream
6 marrons glacés
½ pint (275 ml) crème fraîche or sour
   cream

What a great dessert! It tastes good, looks good, is easy to prepare and can be frozen well in advance of the party. Not only that, but it doesn't necessarily require any strange, out-of-season ingredients that may be expensive or unavailable. Chocolate and chestnut are another of those strange 'right things' in life – they just do go together. I think white chocolate goes better than dark but both are very good. Always buy highest quality Belgian, French or Swiss white chocolate.

1. If using fresh chestnuts, score each chestnut through its skin. Place in a saucepan and cover with water. Add the bay leaves. Bring to the boil and simmer for about 1 hour or until the chestnuts are tender. Remove the chestnuts, one by one, from the hot water and peel. If using dried chestnuts, soak in water overnight, then boil for 1 hour or until very tender. Tinned purée can be used as it is.

2. Purée the chestnuts with the sugar and rum or Kirsch until smooth.

3. Place the purée in a saucepan and, over a low heat, add the chocolate and butter. Allow to mix thoroughly. Set aside to cool.

4. Whip the double cream and fold into the cooled chestnut mixture.

5. Spoon into individual ramekins and chill.

To serve: Serve decorated with marrons glacés or white chocolate shavings. Offer crème fraîche or sour cream as an accompaniment.

DRINKS

Bear in mind that the soup does have cider in it and most ordinary wines would not go well at all. So try a well chilled young Pineau de Charentes. The hearty steamed vegetable pudding demands a full flavoured red like Corbière or Barbera while the White Chocolate and Chestnut Pots would be best with a Californian Orange Muscat.

ℳENU

AN INDIAN DINNER PARTY

SERVES 8

*Poppadoms with Mustard and Cucumber Yoghurt
Sauce
Carrot, Cabbage and Onion Salad*

— . —

*Pakora with Lime and Peanut Relish
Spinach Bhaji
Fresh Pea Pilau
Blackeye Bean and Mushroom Korma*

— . —

Mango Flambé with Pistachio Cream

Quite early on in the restaurant's development we discovered that 'themed' days were fun things to do for customer and staff alike. Our Indian themed days became so popular that we ended up doing one a week. Apart from the wonderful flavours, textures and colours of Indian cuisine, the food appeals to vegan, vegetarian and non-vegetarian alike. People with wheat allergies, too, can find many dishes that are suitable for their own particular dietary needs.

Indian meals do not have the same rigid serving style as western ones. Ideally each dish would be brought separately to the table along with rice, poppadoms or breads where appropriate. At a dinner party this would be dreadful for the host, so here I've made the usual division of courses. For the first course the pakoras need to be quickly fried just before serving, so if you provide poppadoms, salad and some chutneys and raitas, people can be tucking into something while you disappear for three minutes.

COUNTDOWN

2 days before
• Cook and freeze the Spinach Bhaji.   • Soak the blackeye beans.

Day before
• Make the Mustard and Cucumber Yoghurt Sauce.   • Prepare and combine the carrots, cabbage and onion for the salad.   • Prepare the dressing for the salad but do not heat.   • Prepare the Lime and Peanut Relish.   • Make the korma. Store covered with buttered greaseproof paper in the fridge overnight.

On the day
• Prepare all garnishes and accompaniments. Take the bhajis out of the freezer and into the fridge.   • Parcook the pakoras. It is far less mess to do this earlier on in the day.   • Wash the rice and prepare all ingredients for the Fresh Pea Pilau.   • Prepare the mangoes.

1 hour before   • Turn the deep fryer on, and when it is ready fry the poppadoms.

30 minutes before   • Put the korma and aloo into the oven, covered. • Heat the Lime and Peanut Relish in a *bain-marie*.

10 minutes before   • Start to cook the pilau. Start to reheat the bhajis.

5 minutes before   • Serve poppadoms with salad and dip.   • Heat plates for the pakora.   • Cook the pakora while people are munching on poppadoms and salad.

0 minutes   • Serve and eat the pakora.   • Turn the pilau onto an attractive serving dish, garnish the main course and serve and, of course, eat.   • Serve the dessert according to recipe instructions.

Poppadoms

Poppadoms are thin wafers made out of dahl. We buy them dry and then just deep fry them for a few seconds. As they cook they bubble and blister, usually turning a lighter colour and expanding in size. Poppadoms can also be grilled, baked or pan-fried.

Once cooked they are best served hot or warm and are good with anything wet. For our dinner party you will have cooked them earlier and kept them warm near or in a low oven. There are several pickles and relishes described elsewhere in the book that are good with poppadoms (for example Zhooch (page 150), Sambal Olek (page 227), Mango, Apricot or Tomato Chutney (pages 226 and 173), and Rhubarb and Date Relish (page 78)).

Mustard and Cucumber Yoghurt Sauce

G *Serves 8*

1 cucumber, peeled and coarsely
  grated
fine sea salt
2 teaspoons black mustard seeds
1 bunch coriander, finely chopped.
  Retain a little for garnish
pinch of chilli powder
pinch of freshly ground black pepper
$\frac{1}{2}$ pint (275 ml) Greek yoghurt

Excellent before an Indian meal to get the taste buds going.

1. Prepare the cucumber and mix with the other ingredients except the yoghurt. Allow to marinate for 1 hour.

2. Stir in the yoghurt and adjust the seasoning. Serve in a small attractive bowl or two sprinkled with freshly chopped coriander.

Carrot, Cabbage and Onion Salad

V G *Serves 8*

6 oz (175 g) carrots, peeled and
  coarsely grated
6 oz (175 g) white cabbage, finely
  sliced
6 oz (175 g) red onion, or Spanish,
  if not available, finely sliced
1 fresh red chilli, finely chopped
8 mint leaves, chopped
juice and zest of $\frac{1}{2}$ lemon
2 tablespoons vegetable oil
2 teaspoons black mustard seeds
1 teaspoon sesame seeds
4 tablespoons finely chopped
  coriander leaves
fine sea salt and freshly ground black
  pepper

This is a simple salad that can be prepared well in advance. The combination of flavours and the crispness of the vegetables are irresistible.

1. Put the vegetables together with the chilli, mint and lemon juice in a bowl.

2. Heat the vegetable oil and add the seeds. Cook until they start popping. Add to the vegetables and finally stir in the fresh coriander. Stir well to ensure the oil and lemon juice are mixed. Season to taste.

To serve: This salad is excellent whether served immediately, with the dressing still warm, or cold after it has marinated for some time.

Pakora with Lime and Peanut Relish

V G *Serves 8*

The pakora
10 oz (275 g) gram flour
1 teaspoon bi-carbonate of soda
1 teaspoon garam masala
1 teaspoon ground cumin
3 teaspoons salt
1 teaspoon turmeric
$\frac{1}{2}$ teaspoon chilli powder
$\frac{3}{4}$ pint (450 ml) water
3 cloves garlic, crushed or chopped
2 avocados, cut into slices
1 medium aubergine, cut into
    smallish chunks
2 courgettes, cut into bite-sized
    pieces
1 cauliflower, cut into florets
2 red peppers, cut into strips
oil for deep frying

The Lime and Peanut Relish
juice of 2 limes
2 tablespoons peanut butter
6 cloves garlic
1 hot fresh chilli
1 tablespoon soya sauce
1 tablespoon demerara sugar
fine sea salt and freshly ground black
    pepper

Garnish
lime wedges

For the pakora, choose any vegetable you enjoy. Alternatives to the ones used here are carrots, broccoli, spinach, kohlrabi, artichoke hearts, fennel, celery, marrow, small onions, celeriac, potato, sweet potato, baby sweetcorn, green beans and mushrooms. You can even throw in a few succulent fruits like mango, pineapple or nectarine for contrasting flavour.

To make the pakora

1. Sieve all the dry ingredients into a bowl.

2. Gradually add the water, beating all the time. It should mix to a thick batter. Stir in the garlic and allow to stand for at least 30 minutes.

3. Beat again just before use and add the vegetables and/or fruit. Make sure they are well coated with batter.

4. Heat the oil in a deep saucepan or use a deep fryer.

5. Test the heat of the oil by dropping in a little of the batter. It should rise to the surface and start to bubble immediately.

6. Place tablespoonfuls of pakora mixture into the oil. Fry until lightly browned and remove with a slotted spoon. Drain on absorbent paper. This process will take some time but is worth the effort.

7. Just before eating refry the pakoras briefly. This will make them very crisp.
Drain on kitchen paper and serve immediately.

To make the lime and peanut relish

1. Put all the ingredients in a blender and whizz. Dilute with water to the required consistency and adjust the seasoning.

To serve: Serve the pakoras with wedges of lime. Put the relish in a separate dish and allow your guests to help themselves.

111

Spinach Bhaji

Serves 8

1 lb (450 g) fresh spinach leaves

2 tablespoons butter or vegan
   margarine

2 tablespoons vegetable oil

4 cloves garlic, crushed

1 large onion, finely chopped

4 oz (100 g) parsnip, cut into $\frac{1}{2}$ in
   (1 cm) cubes

4 oz (100 g) carrots, cut into $\frac{1}{2}$ in
   (1 cm) cubes

4 oz (100 g) courgettes, cut into $\frac{1}{2}$ in
   (1 cm) cubes

4 oz (100 g) aubergines, cut into
   $\frac{1}{2}$ in (1 cm) cubes

1 teaspoon finely grated fresh ginger

1 teaspoon ground cumin

1 teaspoon ground coriander seeds

1 teaspoon turmeric

1 fresh chilli, chopped

fine sea salt and freshly ground black
   pepper

Try to make sure the vegetables used in this dish do not clash with those already used in the pakora. Bhajis are often vegetables fried in a similar way to pakora, but here's one that isn't.

1. Prepare the spinach by washing it well and removing the stalks.

2. Heat the butter and oil in a deep heavy pan, add the garlic and onion and cook gently until becoming translucent.

3. Add the rest of the vegetables except the spinach and add the spices. Cover and continue to cook gently until all the vegetables are tender.

4. Fold in the spinach and cook with the rest of the vegetables, uncovered, until done. You must stir frequently. If necessary add a little water to prevent the spinach burning.

VARIATIONS

- You may wish to mash the end result with a potato masher.

- Add a tablespoon of fresh tomato purée (see page 223) to the vegetables before you add the spinach.

Tip: This dish freezes well. Make it in advance.

Fresh Pea Pilau

V G   *Serves 8*

10 oz (275 g) basmati rice
4 tablespoons ghee or vegetable oil,
    or mix of both
1 teaspoon ground cumin
3 bay leaves
5 cloves, whole
3 green cardamom pods
6 black peppercorns
$\frac{1}{2}$ teaspoon chilli powder
$\frac{1}{2}$ teaspoon turmeric
fine sea salt
1 pint (600 ml) boiling water
10 oz (275 g) fresh or frozen peas

An Indian meal isn't complete without a rice dish. This one features one of my favourite vegetables – heavily. Of course fresh peas are best but frozen ones have to do for most of the year.

1. Prepare the rice by washing it thoroughly three times. Allow it to soak for 30 minutes in water before use. Drain well.

2. In a heavy-bottomed saucepan or casserole dish heat the ghee or oil. Add the spices (except the turmeric) and sauté them gently for 2 minutes, being careful not to allow them to burn.

3. Add the turmeric and rice and cook together for a further 2 minutes, making sure the rice gets well coated with oil and spices.

4. Pour in the hot water and bring to the boil. Reduce the heat, cover tightly and cook for 20 minutes.

5. Quickly add the peas and mix into the rice. Cover and cook for a further 5 minutes.

6. Remove from the heat but allow to stand with the lid on for a further 10 minutes before serving.

To serve: Serve in an attractive bowl and warn your guests to look out for whole spices and bay leaves.

VARIATION

Add chunks of fried tofu or toasted cashews to make a simple meal.

Blackeye Bean and Mushroom Korma

G   *Serves 8*

4 oz (100 g) butter or 4 tablespoons
   vegetable oil
8 oz (225 g) onion, chopped
3 cloves garlic, crushed
1 teaspoon cumin
1 teaspoon garam masala
2 teaspoons fresh ginger, grated
$\frac{1}{2}$ teaspoon ground cardamom
$\frac{1}{4}$ teaspoon ground cloves
$\frac{1}{4}$ teaspoon ground nutmeg
1 fresh chilli, chopped
4 cardamom pods
$\frac{1}{2}$ teaspoon turmeric
1 tablespoon demerara sugar
1 lb (450 g) button mushrooms
juice of 1 lemon
1 pint (600 ml) double cream
4 oz (100 g) coconut cream
12 oz (325 g) blackeye beans,
   cooked
1 bunch fresh coriander
4 oz (100 g) toasted almond slivers

This might not be the classical korma but *Food for friends* korma does have a lot of fans. So many, indeed, that we started selling it frozen a couple of years ago.

1. Melt the butter or oil in a deep heavy pan.

2. Add the onions, garlic, spices and chilli and fry until the onion softens.

3. Stir in the cardamom pods, turmeric, sugar and button mushrooms. Cook for a further 1 minute.

4. Add the lemon juice and turn up the heat.

5. Add the double cream and the coconut cream and reduce the volume by half.

6. Stir in the blackeye beans and heat through. Keep warm in a *bain-marie*.

7. Before serving garnish with lots of fresh coriander and slivers of toasted almonds.

VARIATION

- If times are hard, substitute béchamel for cream and do not reduce.

- Omit blackeye beans and just use button mushrooms.

Mango Flambé with Pistachio Cream

V G *Serves 6*

3 oz (75 g) unsalted butter or vegan
  margarine
8 tablespoons light muscovado
  sugar
1 teaspoon curry powder
8 ripe mangoes, skinned, stoned and
  sliced
8 tablespoons rum or Kirsch

Pistachio cream
3 oz (75 g) pistachios
$\frac{1}{4}$ pint (150 ml) milk
$\frac{3}{4}$ pint (450 ml) double cream, well
  chilled
2 tablespoons icing sugar
dash of rum (optional)

At the end of a rich filling meal this is simplicity itself. If your mangoes aren't ripe, wrap them in newspaper and store in a warmish place. To chill mangoes simply drop into iced water.

1. Melt the butter in a large frying pan. Be careful not to burn it.

2. Add the sugar and curry powder and melt together for about 1 minute.

3. Add the slices of mango and stir to coat thoroughly. Cook for a maximum of 3 minutes.

4. Pour the rum or Kirsch over the mangoes. Ignite and serve hot with pistachio cream.

To make the Pistachio Cream

1. Cover the pistachios with boiling water. Leave for 2 minutes, then drain.

2. Remove the skins with your fingers, then finely grate or chop the nuts in a blender.

3. Add the ground pistachios to the milk and set aside in the fridge for at least 1 hour so that the flavours infuse.

4. Beat the milk mixture together with the cream, sugar and rum, if used, until it forms soft peaks. Chill and serve.

VARIATION

Use any exotic fruit. Serve with ice cream, sorbet or frozen yoghurt.

DRINKS

Indian food does present a slight problem when it comes to wine and many people just quaff beer all the way through. For a dinner party, though, I'd suggest drinking very cold Californian Chenin Blanc or a Barolo. For dessert treat your savaged tastebuds to a Muscat de Beaumes de Venise.

Chapter four

ENTERTAINING

CHILDREN

As a father of three young children I do feel particularly well qualified to talk about feeding children. Whilst all our children have been brought up on a vegetarian diet we have not indoctrinated them by saying 'Eating meat is wrong'.

Both Kate, my wife, and I believe people should decide for themselves and as time goes by I hope all three will reach their own decisions for eating whatever they eat.

Children have very conservative tastes when it comes to eating and generally speaking will not eat highly spiced or unusual-textured food. For instance, chilli and ginger or aubergine and mushrooms are generally taboo up to the age of twelve.

'Give 'em chips and burgers,' I hear you say. I say 'Don't.'

The reason children like burgers and chips is simply because of the millions of pounds spent on advertising them each year. Once children get to school, unfortunately, a large part of your influence over what they eat has gone.

No matter how you have brought them up, they will want to be the same as the other children and ideally eat the same too. This usually means burgers and chips and for a bit of variation the occasional pizza.

When your children entertain their friends at home, however, you have the ideal opportunity to break the mould – so don't blow it! I would advise against making them eat salad until they are well and truly addicted to your cooking. If you feel really nervous about it, start them on home-made veggie-burgers but don't tell them they're not meat. Large, home-cooked chips are a great improvement on frozen oven-ready or micro-chips – better still try them on sautéed potatoes. Only give them chips now and then, so that they're seen as a treat rather than the norm.

In this chapter on entertaining children the emphasis lies firmly on children who entertain their friends at home. I've only touched on birthday parties because the chapter on buffets and picnics should provide more than enough inspiration. The recipes in this chapter are well tried, tested and popular. Perhaps you could also adapt some of your own.

Children are generally more interested in sweets than desserts so make your second course simple, small and nutritious.

I've included two recipes for drinks, plus a list of recipes from the rest of the book which could be served at a children's party.

Friendly Burgers

V G *Serves 8–12 (depending on the size of burgers)*

1 oz (30 g) butter or oil
1 medium onion, finely chopped
4 cloves garlic, crushed or chopped
8 oz (225 g) mushrooms, finely diced
1 teaspoon each of thyme, marjoram and sage
4 oz (100 g) cooked rice
4 oz (100 g) cooked brown lentils
2 oz (50 g) walnuts, roasted and chopped
4 oz (100 g) wheatgerm or breadcrumbs
salt, pepper and soya sauce
vegetable oil for frying

Unfortunately Mr McDonald seems to have been successful in getting his message about burgers through to children. The silly thing is most children wouldn't mind if their burgers were vegetarian. So long as there's easy to eat and everyone else eats them there's no problem. A lot of vegetable burgers use textured soya protein, ours don't. We tend to sell them on a Saturday knowing that a lot of our clients will be young. We've tried all sorts of combinations over the years but this is a favourite.

1. Heat the butter or oil in a deep pan. Sauté the onion, garlic, mushroom and herbs until tender – about 10–15 minutes.

2. Partially blend together the rice and lentils. Fold the rice and lentils into the onion mix and stir in well. Add the chopped walnuts.

3. If the mixture is still a bit runny firm it up with wheatgerm or breadcrumbs.

4. Season with salt, pepper and soya sauce. Form into burgers and dust with wheatgerm. Chill for 1 hour before use. If you are not using them immediately simply wrap and freeze.

5. Either fry on each side for 8 minutes in a little vegetable oil and serve with vegetables or in a bun, or bake in a hot oven. Or grill for about 4 minutes on one side, turn, place a slice of cheese on the upper side and grill until the cheese is golden and bubbling.

VARIATIONS

For a novelty which children always enjoy, try shaping the burgers in other ways. Stars are good, but any shaped pastry-cutter will do. Then freeze before use so that the shape is clearly defined.

Remember most children up to the age of 12 enjoy small portions so they can finish their food and then ask for more. Don't try ramming huge half-pounders down their otherwise eager throats.

If you do want to serve them with potatoes why not wean them off oven fries and onto delicious home-made sautéed potatoes – children love them (see page 201).

Meatless Meat Sauce

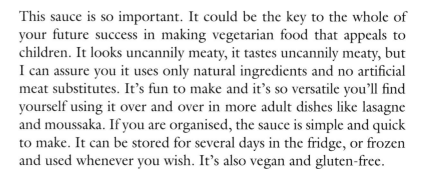

V G *Serves 6–8 depending on usage*

6 oz (175 g) brown lentils

3 tablespoons olive oil

1 medium onion, finely chopped

2 teaspoons chopped basil

1 teaspoon oregano

salt and pepper to taste

1 carrot, finely chopped

1 large red pepper, finely diced

6 oz (175 g) mushrooms, finely chopped

1 glass red wine or vegetable stock

1 tablespoon soya sauce

8 fl oz (250 ml) fresh tomato purée (see page 223)

3 cloves garlic, crushed or minced

This sauce is so important. It could be the key to the whole of your future success in making vegetarian food that appeals to children. It looks uncannily meaty, it tastes uncannily meaty, but I can assure you it uses only natural ingredients and no artificial meat substitutes. It's fun to make and it's so versatile you'll find yourself using it over and over in more adult dishes like lasagne and moussaka. If you are organised, the sauce is simple and quick to make. It can be stored for several days in the fridge, or frozen and used whenever you wish. It's also vegan and gluten-free.

1. Soak the lentils and cook them in boiling salted water so that they are well done. On no account undercook them. This can be done in advance of the rest of the recipe if you wish. Drain them and set them aside.

2. Heat the oil in a deep heavy pan, add the onion, herbs and a little pepper and sauté until the onions are softening.

3. Add the carrots and red pepper and continue to cook for another 5 minutes.

4. Stir in the mushrooms and cook for a further 5 minutes. When the whole mixture is very hot add the wine or vegetable stock and soya sauce. Reduce by half before adding the tomato purée and garlic. If the mix is a little thick at this stage, add some more wine or water. Bring to the boil and simmer for as long as you can with the lid on – at least half an hour.

5. When you are ready, remove at least half the mixture and roughly purée it in a blender, then return it to the pan. Stir the mix thoroughly, taste and adjust seasoning.

To serve: For children, serve this with attractive pasta shapes and cheese or with mashed or baked potatoes. It's even good with rice. The flavour will improve if kept in the fridge overnight.

Hamish's Turtle Pizzas

Makes 2 × 8 in (20 cm) pizzas

The base

1 teaspoon fresh yeast

1 teaspoon sugar

½ pint (275 ml) water, slightly warm

1 lb (450 g) unbleached plain white
    flour – white is best for children's
    pizzas

½ teaspoon salt

2 tablespoons olive oil

4 oz (100 g) Mozzarella cheese,
    grated

The pizza sauce

2 tablespoons olive oil

2 shallots, or 1 onion, chopped

2 teaspoons dried marjoram

2 teaspoons dried basil (or twice this
    quantity if fresh)

1 clove garlic, crushed or chopped

2 × 14 oz (400 g) tins Italian plum
    tomatoes, chopped roughly

1 tablespoon tomato purée (see page
    223)

1 bay leaf

3 teaspoons demerara sugar

salt and pepper

The topping

3 ripe avocados, halved, stoned,
    flesh scooped out and mashed
    with the juice of ½ lemon

½ pint (275 ml) sour cream

1 clove garlic, crushed or chopped

salt and freshly ground black pepper

4 oz (100 g) Mozzarella cheese,
    grated

strips of red or green peppers, olives,
    herbs etc. for decoration

Another dish that always goes down well when entertaining children. This one's probably healthier than most, containing, as it does, a good layer of puréed avocados.

Once again I can only rely on the evidence seen at home and in the restaurant but this pizza knocks the spots off almost any other pizza as far as children are concerned.

We use a deep base for this pizza. I don't think a thin base could support the topping. You'll need two deep sandwich tins.

Children do not like flavours that attract jaded adult palates, so the pizza sauce is distinctly less flavoured than it could be. It is best made the day before it is used to allow the flavour to develop.

To make the base

1. Dissolve the yeast with the sugar in the water.

2. Mix the flour and salt together. Add the dissolved yeast to the flour in a bowl and mix to form a soft dough.

3. Add the olive oil to the dough and knead for 10 minutes until the dough is smooth and elastic.

4. Oil two deep sandwich tins with a little olive oil. Divide the dough between them, pushing it thoroughly over the entire bottom of the tins. Cover and put in a warm place to rise for at least 1 hour. While the dough is rising make the pizza sauce and the pizza topping.

To make the sauce

1. Heat the oil in a deep heavy pan and cook the shallots until softening, with the marjoram and basil.

2. Add the garlic and tomatoes, bay leaf and sugar and bring to the boil. Simmer gently for as long as possible – at least an hour. The resulting sauce should be quite thick. Adjust the seasoning but remember it's for children, not you! It may be necessary to purée it to make the texture more suitable for kids.

3. Now you must prepare the topping, but first knock the dough back and push it so that it comes up the sides of the tins. Heat the oven to its highest setting.

OPPOSITE *Clockwise from top: Chimichangas (page 33) with Roasted Red Pepper and Chilli Sauce (page 227) and Guacamole (page 178), and Chickpea and Olive Tapenade (page 155) with Sesame Snaps (page 147) and crudités*

4. Sprinkle the base with the Mozzarella that you set aside earlier, then set the dough aside to rise again for half an hour.

To make the topping

Beat the avocados with the sour cream and garlic. Season with salt and pepper.

To assemble

1. Knock the dough back again, again pushing the dough up the sides of the tins.

2. Cover with the pizza sauce and on to this spread the pizza topping. Finally cover with the Mozzarella and decorate to your own taste. The topping will ultimately sell the pizza to your children so try to make it attractive. Faces are easy using strips of pepper, olives, herbs etc. Bake in the hot oven for 20 minutes or until the top is golden brown and the pizza crust cooked.

To serve: Well, really it's a meal in itself and most children would not want anything more apart from a drink.

Cheesy Croquettes

Serves 8–12 children

4 oz (100 g) rice, overcooked and sticky
1 tablespoon oil
1 medium onion, finely chopped
1 small red pepper, deseeded and finely diced
2 sticks celery, finely diced
1 clove garlic, or to taste
4 oz (100 g) sweetcorn
1 lb (450 g) cheese, grated
2 eggs, beaten
2 oz (50 g) breadcrumbs mixed with 2 oz (50 g) sesame seeds
salt and pepper

'Oh no!' I can hear the vegans saying, 'not another cheesy dish.' Well, the good news is that you can just replace the cheese with silken tofu (soft) and the egg glaze with soya milk to make a vegan version of this recipe.

Whether vegan or not, this dish is set to replace fish fingers for ever in the hearts of your children.

The grain/vegetable/cheese (or tofu) content is incredibly healthy and more than makes up for the seemingly rather unhealthy way of cooking it, but I've always said a successful deep fry is one where the oil is not noticeable. If you're dead against it simply shallow fry or bake. Brush with a little oil first, though, before you bake.

1. Heat the oil and sauté the onion, pepper, celery and garlic until just softening.

OPPOSITE: *Top to bottom: Rhubarb and Strawberry Cheesecake (page 42), Red Med Salad (page 31), Rosti (page 30) with Food for friends Cauliflower Cheese Sauce (page 106) and fresh Tomato and Garlic Sauce (page 80)*

2. Mix in the sweetcorn and grated cheese and stir well. Mould into rissole shapes about 3 inches (7.5 cm) long and 1½ inches (3 cm) wide.

3. Roll in the beaten egg and then in the seasoned breadcrumb/sesame seed mixture. Make sure the croquettes are all well coated.

4. Deep fry, fry or bake in a hot oven until crispy.

To serve: Serve garnished with parsley and lemon, with fresh vegetables and/or chips and Fresh Tomato and Garlic Sauce (page 80) or simply ketchup.

VARIATION

Vegans can use all sesame seeds in place of breadcrumbs.

Karen's Unbelievably Simple Tomato Soup

G   *Serves 8–12 children*

For the soup
8 oz (225 g) jar bottled tomato
   purée
½ pint (275 ml) milk
½ pint (275 ml) single cream
salt and pepper
sugar to taste

For the croutons
8 slices bread
butter (optional)
sesame seeds (optional)

It is well known that children only eat/drink one brand of tomato soup. Well, our Head Chef Karen has cracked how to make it, and when you realise how simple it is you'll never buy another can. What's more, you'll be in charge of the sugar content. Children love the soup – as I suspect do most adults.

1. Put the tomato purée in a deep heavy saucepan and start to heat.

2. Gradually add the milk, stirring all the time, until it is all absorbed.

3. Bring to the boil, then reduce the heat and stir in the cream. Season with salt and pepper and sugar to taste.

To serve: Serve with a dish of animal-shaped croutons. Butter 8 slices of bread on both sides. Cut out shapes with a suitable pastry cutter on a tray of sesame seeds. The seeds will stick on one side as you press the cutter through. Bake on a baking sheet for an hour at 150°C/300°F/Gas Mark 2 until crisp and golden. Serve hot or cold. Alternatively, if time is short, toast the bread under the grill or in the toaster then simply cut out shapes with a cutter.

Spanish Rice

[V] [G] *Serves 8–12*

2 tablespoons olive oil

1 large onion, sliced

2 cloves garlic, sliced and crushed

1 large green pepper, cut into small
$\frac{1}{2}$ in (1 cm) squares

1 large red pepper, cut into small
$\frac{1}{2}$ in (1 cm) squares

1 bay leaf

2 large tomatoes, skinned, deseeded
and chopped

2 oz (50 g) butter or vegan
margarine

14 oz (400 g) basmati or Arborio
rice

1$\frac{3}{4}$ pints (1 litre) wine mixed with
water (approx 1 part wine to 3
parts water)

saffron

salt and pepper

$\frac{1}{2}$ teaspoon paprika

4 oz (100 g) fresh or frozen peas

4 oz (100 g) fresh or frozen
sweetcorn

4 oz (100 g) tiny button mushrooms

juice of 1 lemon

lemon wedges and parsley for
garnish

Rice dishes follow pasta, pizza and burgers as firm favourites with children and when you are entertaining them it's important to select a dish that will be enjoyed by almost all the assembled tribe. You'll never please everyone but I think it's better to provide one decent dish that has a reasonable chance of success then just to cop out and serve junk you know everyone will eat a little of. This recipe for Spanish Rice can of course be adapted to suit any tastes. I've chosen ingredients that we've found appeal to most children.

1. Heat the oil in a large deep pan.

2. Add the onion, 1 clove of garlic, the peppers and bay leaf and sauté for a few minutes. Then add the tomatoes and fry them in the oil.

3. Now add the butter and melt it. When it has melted, stir in the rice. Stir until the rice is evenly coated, then allow to cook gently.

4. Bring the wine/water mixture to the boil separately. When the rice is turning opaque, add the liquid to it, bring to the boil and continue to simmer gently.

5. Mix the saffron, pepper and paprika together with the other clove of garlic (if you think your children can stand it) and salt. Mix with a little of the liquid before adding it to the pot. Stir in well, scraping the bottom of the pan as you do so to prevent sticking.

6. The rice will take 15–20 minutes to cook from this point, but it must be covered and you must resist the temptation to peek for at least 15 minutes. You then add the remaining ingredients and cover again.

If the rice is cooked, stir the ingredients in and cover the pan again. Leave for 10 minutes before serving.

To serve: Squeeze some lemon juice over the rice and serve garnished with lemon wedges and parsley.

Kate's Peanut and Raisin Flapjacks

V   *Makes about 24*

4 oz (100 g) demerara sugar
4 oz (100 g) butter or vegan
  margarine
1 tablespoon golden syrup
2 oz (50 g) organic wholewheat
  flour
6 oz (175 g) organic regular oats
1 oz (30 g) organic jumbo oats
1 oz (30 g) peanuts
2 oz (50 g) raisins

Before Kate and I had children she worked in the restaurant in the sweet department and produced the most more-ish flapjacks the restaurant has ever seen. The restaurant's loss has been our children's gain and now she produces flapjacks for them and their friends. They don't last long and are best eaten slightly hot. The important thing with flapjacks is to get the relative quantities correct.

1. Heat the oven to 180°C/350°F/Gas Mark 4.

2. Melt the sugar and butter together.

3. Add the rest of the ingredients and mix thoroughly.

4. Grease a baking tray of about 11 × 7 inches (27.5 × 17.5 cm) with at least 1 in (2.5 cm) high sides.

5. Pour the mixture in and spread evenly, resisting the temptation to push it down into the tin – this would result in hard, compacted flapjacks.

6. Cook until golden brown – approximately 20 minutes.

7. Allow to cool, then cut into small triangles or squares.

Banoffee Pie

I must admit to being quite ashamed that we have this recipe on the menu at the restaurant. The trouble is it's so good and everyone loves it – from the tiniest child to the most ardent wholefoodie, Banoffee Pie, it seems, just can't go wrong. Where did it come from? No one knows. We've taken the basic concept and tried to improve it, though the key to Banoffee Pie is of course the toffee-like substance made by boiling condensed milk in the tin. (Put it in a saucepan, covered with water. Cover the pan and cook for 2 hours. Top up the water now and again. Any less time and it tastes OK, but will be too runny.) When making this dish for children use much less cream than you would for adults. Making it is simplicity itself.

Serves 4–6

8 oz (225 g) sweet pastry (see page 222), chilled

1 tin sweetened condensed milk, boiled in its tin for 2 hours

3 large bananas, sliced and dipped in lemon juice

$\frac{1}{2}$ pint (275 ml) double cream

1 teaspoon coffee essence

cocoa powder for decoration

1. Roll out the pastry and line a well greased 9–10 in (22.5–25 cm) flan tin with pastry. Chill, covered in clingfilm, for 30 minutes. Cover the bottom with baking beans and bake blind in a preheated oven at 200°C/400°F/Gas Mark 6, until lightly coloured (about 20 minutes). Allow to cool in the tin.

2. Pour the condensed milk toffee onto the pastry case and top with banana slices.

3. Whip the cream with the coffee essence and spoon over the pie. Sprinkle with a little cocoa for decoration.

VARIATION

Use a biscuit base instead of pastry.

Lemon and Lime Meringue Pie

Serves 8–12 children

8 oz (225 g) sweet pastry (see page 222), chilled

2 large lemons, quartered

3 limes, quartered

$\frac{1}{2}$ pint (275 ml) water (for adults you can use water/wine mixture)

3 oz (75 g) demerara sugar

5 egg yolks

For the meringue

3 egg whites

6 oz (175 g) soft brown sugar

Children prefer the meringue to be soft and chewy in this slight variation of a classic sweet.

1. Heat the oven to 220°C/425°F/Gas Mark 7.

2. Roll out the pastry and line an 8 in (20 cm) flan tin with it, bake blind and allow to cool.

3. Boil the lemons and limes in the water and sugar for 15 minutes.

4. Remove any pips. Puree the lemons and limes in the cooking liquid, then add the egg yolks, one at a time, making sure they are blended thoroughly.

5. Pour this mixture through a fine muslin cloth into the pastry base.

6. Whisk the egg whites until stiff but not dry, then add the sugar a little at a time. Beat well between additions until the meringue is soft and shiny.

7. Put the meringue into a piping bag with a large star nozzle and pipe it onto the top of the lemon and lime custard.

8. Place the pie in the oven and cook for 8–10 minutes or until lightly browned. Allow to cool, then refrigerate.

Mollie's Home-made Lemonade

4 lemons
8 oz (225 g) white cane sugar
1 large bottle soda water
ice

My mother used to make this and as a result I was one child who never liked bottled fizzy lemonade. Impress your children's friends with fresh lemonade.

1. Wash the lemons and cut into pieces, keeping back enough to garnish the glasses.

2. In a blender or food processor blend the lemons together with the sugar, using a little water to get the process going.

3. Pass the blended lemons through a fine sieve, then dilute with the soda water. Serve with a slice of lemon and plenty of ice.

VARIATION

Replace lemons with limes, peaches, nectarines, oranges or strawberries.

Home-made Orange Barley Water

2 oz (50 g) pearl barley
2 oz (50 g) demerara sugar
juice of 1 lemon and 2 oranges

Here's another old-fashioned favourite the kids will love.

1. Place the barley in a saucepan. Cover with water and bring to the boil. Remove from the heat and empty into a sieve. Rinse with cold water.

2. Return the barley to the saucepan, add 1 pint (600 ml) of fresh water and bring back to the boil. Simmer for 1 hour.

3. Strain the liquid into a bowl. Stir in the sugar and leave to cool.

4. Add the juice and dilute to taste.

Party Nibbles

Of course, if you've got a lot of young children coming round, perhaps for a party, the success of the food will be judged by its snackability. Children hate having to sit down and eat properly when there are presents to open, games to play and lots of talking to do. Here are a few suggestions for some slightly healthier alternatives to crisps, nuts, and anything else out of a packet.

• Crudités with a dip. For crudités choose carrots, celery and baby sweetcorn with strips of red peppers, green peppers, and an innocuous cream cheese or avocado dip.

• Supply hot Garlic Bread (page 188) – not too garlicky.

• Tomari Roast Sunflower Seeds or nuts (page 160).

• Cheese Palmiers (page 159) or Tomato and Cheese Straws (page 160).

• Children do like small sandwiches so long as the fillings are chosen carefully and imaginatively. Try using different types of bread such as bagels, mini pittas, baps and granary rolls.

Try fillings like grated cheese and chives, hoummous and grated carrot, scrambled egg with a little mayonnaise and diced red pepper, cream cheese with pineapple and raisins, celery and grapes, or peanut butter and banana – all these are worth trying.

OTHER PARTY FOOD

And finally here are suggestions for a children's party:

Orange Juice (page 4)
Grapefruit Juice (page 11)
Banana Smoothies (page 17)
Honey Sultana Muffins (page 19)
Keith's Vegetable Basket (omit herbs)
   (page 148)
Herby Sweetcorn Fritters (page 97)
Sauté Potatoes (page 201)
Sesame and Potato Croquettes (page 14)
Spinach and Mozzarella Scramble (page 13)
Any fruit desserts
Ice cream, sorbet or iced soufflé (see Index)
Banoffee Pie (page 123)
Rhubarb and Strawberry Cheesecake (page 42)
Guinness Cake (page 44)
Vegan Date and Walnut Bread (page 45)
Mince Pies (page 216)

Shortbread (page 174)
Oaties (page 175)
Tartelettes Niçoise (page 131)
Rural Rolls (page 131)
Cheese Palmiers (page 159)
Tomato and Cheese Straws (page 160)
Garlic Croutons (page 161)
Arundel Tarts (page 172)
Sussex Pasties (page 173)
Poppadoms (page 109)
Filled Baked Potatoes (page 184)
Crespolini (page 49)
Ravioli (page 87)
New Season Salad (page 163)
Tuscan Rice Salad (page 164)
Karen's Unbelievably Simple Tomato Soup
   (page 121)

Chapter five

THE VEGETARIAN BUFFET

I'd never thought of completely vegetarian buffets until one occasion when Kate and I went to a wedding where every single savoury item on the buffet contained meat or fish. The whole thing had apparently cost a fortune yet was totally lacking in inspiration – chicken drumsticks, cocktail sausages, asparagus with ham wrapped round it – what a waste of good asparagus.

So I went away and immediately designed a buffet menu for *Food for friends*. Over the years this has grown and now contains both hot and cold, vegetarian and vegan dishes.

What immediately became apparent was that many dishes from around the world were already eaten with fingers and it is only in the western cultures that knives and forks are used. So many dishes, from the Middle East, India, China and Malaysia, can be readily amalgamated into a vegetarian buffet and, incidentally, many of these dishes are vegan too.

Once you are familiar with the concepts of the individual dishes it's not difficult to expand them into main courses in their own right.

Buffets can be one of the most spectacular ways of entertaining. Presentation is 80 per cent of the effort but at the same time the food has got to taste good. It's no good using the best table-linen, silver dishes and cut glass if the end result is bland, badly cooked or ill-conceived.

When planning your buffet bear in mind where you are having it. Will you be able to heat up the food? How will you keep things cold? Do you have enough fridge space? Should you hire more? What time of year is it? Will that affect your choice of menu?

A good buffet should always have hot and cold dishes in it, and the more contrasts the better. Colour is another aspect that is all too often forgotten. A good buffet should be pleasing to the eye as a whole, not just the individual dishes themselves. This can be achieved using fresh and dried flowers, mirrors, different levels of display on the table, and of course the attractive bowls and plates that the food is presented on.

Garnishes are a must and almost as much time will be spent on them as on the buffet itself! Quite often the display can be guided by a theme in the food – nationality and important festivals are two obvious examples.

All recipes in this chapter will be for ten or more individual items. Getting the quantity right for your buffet is vitally important and the best way to do it is to imagine what you yourself would eat – usually 5–6 main items – and multiply by the number of guests coming. Therefore if ten guests were coming, prepare ten each of five different main items. Always err on the generous side. There's nothing worse than running out early. Nibbles and dips would be extra.

Then there is the dessert to consider. Most sweet dishes in this book are suitable for a fork buffet, and I've included a few extra in this chapter that can be eaten in the fingers.

DRINKS FOR THE BUFFET

It is most important that you get the drink right and this will depend very much on the type of year. At Christmas you may serve some hot punch while in July it's probably wise to offer an ice-cold refreshing concoction. The thing about any buffet is there is so much variety of food that you will never match a single wine to it. Of course champagne or a good sparkling wine is the exception if you're feeling fairly wealthy. Try the fresh and creamy Carrington Brut from Orlando or the Sigura Vindas Brut, a good fresh Cava with fruit, or my favourite, a Crémant de Bourgogne. In winter try the mulled wine recipe I've given on page 206.

Any time of year Kir is another good alternative that is generally enjoyed by most people. Buy a good quality alcoholic Cassis (not a blackcurrant cordial) and have plenty of good inexpensive white wine to hand – a Czechoslavakian Pinot Blanc is an excellent candidate. Simply pour yourself a glass of wine – you deserve it, you've been working hard! Then replace the missing liquid in the bottle with cassis. Replace the cork and gently invert it a few times until it is mixed.

Alternatively make a nice ice-cold punch with freshly squeezed orange juice, strawberries and mint. Add ice-cubes and lots of sparkling wine.

When calculating drinks, allow half a bottle of wine per person. There is a distinct move away from red wine at parties, so divide it 60 per cent white to 40 per cent red. Always provide plenty of non-alcoholic drink – there are some lovely non-alcoholic sparkling fruit drinks about now that almost convince you that you're joining in the fun!

GARNISHES

Garnishes are very important for all food but especially a buffet. There are many ways of garnishing a dish. I prefer to keep them as simple and natural as possible.

Salad leaves make the perfect bed for dishes to sit on or nestle in, while fresh and dried fruit, vegetables, herbs, dried and fresh flowers, nuts and seeds are all good for decorating the top of dishes. Keep the garnish simple and wherever possible in line with the content of the dish itself.

Of course you may wish to have a theme for your buffet which is reflected in the garnishes, irrespective of the dish content. Garnishes will also be determined, to some extent, by the size and shape of your serving dishes. There are no fixed rules – if you think it'll make the dish look nice, use it.

Make sure the garnishes look fresh, dry and clean. There's nothing worse than limp parsley or soggy brown lettuce. Always leave the garnishing as late as you can, preferably within half an hour of eating. Some garnishes, like radish roses and spring onion brushes, can be made well in advance and kept in ice cold water in the fridge. Others are more delicate and must be made literally at the last minute. Remember that the first impression of your buffet will be the abiding one.

Four Useful Garnishes

V G *Radish Roses* These are perfect for garnishing cold dishes and salads, and make an attractive crudité in their own right.

1. Wash the radishes, trim off the root and remove the green stalk if you want the radish to sit up. If not, leave a small leaf or two on.

2. With the root side uppermost, now showing a circle of white, cut down to but not through the stalk end. Repeat this process on the other 3 sides of the radish.

3. Put the radish roses into iced water and leave until well opened out.

V G *Spring Onion Brushes* Good for decorating salads or barbecued foods.

1. Wash and trim the spring onions and cut into three equal sections.

2. Using a sharp knife, cut about halfway down the length of the onion. Continue with as many incisions as possible.

3. Put the brushes into iced water for at least 30 minutes until they have opened up.

VARIATION

Celery curls are made in exactly the same fashion.

V G *Cucumber Fans* Can be used for decorating nearly all savoury food. Try and buy young, under-sized cucumbers about 4 in (10 cm) long. If you can't get these, use pickling cucumbers or pickled gherkins.

1. Cut the cucumber in half lengthways, then slice in half widthways. Scoop out the seeds.

2. Place, cut face down, on your chopping board. Mark a series of cuts through the length of the piece, being careful not to cut all the way through.

3. Sprinkle the cucumber pieces with salt. After 20 minutes rinse thoroughly. Now lay the cucumber flat again and with the side of a knife flatten it, forcing it to fan out.

129

V G *Lemon Twists*   This is a very simple garnish and goes well with most food, especially fried food.

1. Cut a thin slice of lemon.

2. Make an incision into the centre of the lemon.

3. Hold each side of the incision with two fingers of each hand and twist in opposite directions.

VARIATION

Use orange or lime too.

Stilton Puffs

Makes about 20

6 oz (175 g) puff pastry (see page 221)
1 egg, beaten
1 oz (30 g) sesame seeds
4 oz (100 g) Stilton cheese
4 oz (100 g) cream cheese
2 cloves garlic, crushed or minced
fine sea salt and ground black pepper
a little milk (optional)
dill sprigs to garnish

Stilton Puffs are one of the oldest yet most popular items on the finger-buffet menu. They are simply a diamond-shaped sandwich of puff pastry and Stilton beaten with cream cheese. They look attractive and taste simply divine. The pastry can be cooked the day before, then split and filled just before serving.

1. Lightly flour the surface and roll out the puff pastry to $\frac{1}{8}$ in (3 mm) thickness. Trim the edges to form a neat rectangle.

2. Cut the rectangle lengthwise into 5 strips. Cut across each strip diagonally, making 4 cuts to produce 20 diamond shapes. Transfer to a baking sheet and brush with beaten egg and sprinkle with sesame seeds.

3. Allow to rest in the fridge for at least 20 minutes. Meanwhile, heat the oven to 220°C/425°F/Gas Mark 7.

4. Bake in the oven for about 15 minutes until risen and golden brown. Transfer the puffs to a wire rack to cool.

5. Beat the Stilton and cream cheese together with garlic and seasoning. If too stiff add a little milk.

6. When cool, split the pastry diamonds in half and sandwich them together with a little of the Stilton mixture. Serve at once, garnished with sprigs of dill.

Tartelettes Niçoise

Makes 20

8 oz (225 g) puff pastry (see page 221)

1 egg, beaten

1 tablespoon tomato purée (see page 223)

4 plum tomatoes, thinly sliced

1 tablespoon oregano

salt and freshly ground black pepper

8 oz (225 g) grated cheese (Cheddar, Emmental, Gruyère or Mozzarella)

grated Parmesan cheese (a little to taste if you like it)

10 black olives, halved and stoned

10 green olives, halved and stoned

Tartelettes Niçoise look like tiny pizzas. They have the advantage over their Italian cousins in being delicious both hot and cold – pizzas tend to toughen when served cold. Like pizzas, Tartelettes Niçoise are universally enjoyed by adults and children alike. You will need a 3 in (7.5 cm) round pastry cutter, plain or fluted. The tartelettes can be prepared on the morning of your party to the end of stage 6, and cooked at the last minute.

1. Preheat the oven to 220°C/425°F/Gas Mark 7.

2. On a floured surface roll out the puff pastry until it is $\frac{1}{8}$ in (3 mm) thick.

3. Cut out 20 × 3 in (7.5 cm) circles and place on a baking sheet. Glaze the edges of the circles with the beaten egg.

4. On each circle spread a little tomato purée, cover with sliced tomatoes and sprinkle with oregano, salt and pepper. Then cover with cheese and decorate with olives.

5. Bake for 15–20 minutes.

Rural Rolls

V *Makes 40*

2 oz (50 g) dried apricots

$\frac{1}{2}$ oz (15 g) unsalted butter or vegan margarine

1 small onion, finely chopped

$\frac{1}{4}$ recipe chestnut roast mixture (see page 210)

8 oz (225 g) puff pastry (see page 221)

beaten egg to glaze (optional)

soya milk (optional)

sesame seeds to sprinkle

I called these delicious little mouthfuls Rural Rolls because I wanted to get away from the idea that they had anything to do with sausages. For vegetarian cuisine to go forward, it must stop trying to emulate meat dishes.

Rural Rolls are the perfect party snack and will appeal to any age of guest. Obviously children will prefer plain ones while adults may enjoy a whole host of exotic additions. In this version I've used an apricot purée, but it could equally be prune, black cherry, a little peanut and chilli sauce or our own tomato purée recipe (page 223).

Rural Rolls can be prepared in advance and frozen at the end of step 11.

1. Soak the apricots in 1 pint (600 ml) water overnight. Bring to the boil and simmer until tender. Purée in a blender and adjust taste with a little sugar or honey and lemon juice. Allow to cool.

2. Preheat the oven to 220°C/425°F/Gas Mark 7.

3. Melt the butter in a saucepan and sweat the onion until translucent. Allow to cool.

4. Mix the cold chestnut roast with the onion.

5. Roll out the pastry on a lightly floured surface until it measures 12 × 10 in (30 × 25 cm). Divide it into 4 strips lengthways. Put a quarter of the chestnut mixture lengthways down one strip.

6. Using a piping bag with a small plain nozzle, pipe the apricot down the left-hand side of the chestnut mixture, where it meets the pastry (this will eventually be the top of the Rural Rolls).

7. Repeat the process with the other 3 strips.

8. Brush beaten egg or water along the edge of the pastry opposite to the apricot purée.

9. Fold the pastry over the apricot/chestnut mix and seal well. Prick with a fork.

10. Place all the rolls seam side down (apricot side up). Brush with beaten egg or a little soya milk and sprinkle with sesame seeds.

11. Cut into 1 in (2.5 cm) lengths using a sharp knife. The rolls can be frozen at this point.

12. Place on a lightly oiled baking sheet and bake in the oven for approximately 10 minutes or until the pastry is golden. If cooking from frozen, allow about 20 minutes. Serve warm – but they make an excellent addition to children's lunch-boxes too.

Vegetable Samosas

Vegetable Samosas are delightful – spicy, tangy and more-ish. They lend themselves to any buffet. In fact, it is easy to develop the theme around them and give the whole party a Middle Eastern flavour.

V   *Makes 40*

¾ oz (20 g) unsalted butter
2 tablespoons peanut oil
1 small onion, finely chopped
2 cloves garlic, crushed or chopped
1 fresh green chilli, deseeded and
    finely chopped
2 teaspoons curry paste (far superior
    to most curry powder)
8 oz (225 g) cooked potato, diced
3 oz (75 g) carrot, diced
4 oz (100 g) sweetcorn
3 oz (75 g) petit pois
fine sea salt
freshly ground black pepper
1 tablespoon chopped fresh
    coriander
5 large sheets filo pastry
oil for deep frying or for brushing

In India, samosas or samoosas are eaten at tea-time. This particular version would properly be known as a *singara* as it is filled with potatoes not meat. We think that you can eat them any time.

We use filo pastry rather than the traditional pastry (basically flour and water with a little oil and salt). This has the healthy benefit of allowing us to bake the samosas rather than deep fry. Personally, though, I prefer them deep fried.

1. Heat the butter and oil in a large frying pan or wok. Sweat the onion and garlic until the onion is soft.

2. Add the fresh chilli and curry paste and cook for a further minute, then stir in the rest of the vegetables and cook for 2–3 minutes.

3. Remove from the heat, season and stir in the chopped fresh coriander. Allow to cool.

4. Cut each sheet of filo with a sharp knife into 8 strips, width-ways.

5. Place a small amount of the filling at one end of each strip. Fold diagonally to cover the filling. Continue this process down the strip until you end up with a totally enclosed triangular parcel. Repeat the process to make 40 samosas.

6. If deep frying, fry in hot oil until crisp and golden. If baking, brush all over with oil, then place on a baking sheet and bake in a hot oven (220°C/400°F/Gas Mark 6) until crisp. The same all-over colour cannot be achieved by this method but it is much healthier.

To serve: Samosas will store, uncooked, in the fridge covered with clingfilm, so don't cook them until you are just about to eat them. Serve with a selection of dips. I particularly like Mango Chutney (page 226), Sambal Olek (page 227) and Banana Raita (page 158).

Two or three samosas and a salad make a lovely casual lunch too, and they're always popular as a starter at dinner parties.

Spring Rolls

[V] *Makes 40*

2 tablespoons sesame oil

2 tablespoons vegetable oil

1 medium red onion, thinly sliced

3 cloves garlic, crushed or finely
  chopped

2 green chillies, finely diced (remove
  seeds to make less spicy)

1 teaspoon finely grated fresh ginger

1 medium carrot, cut into fine
  julienne

1 stick celery, cut into fine julienne

4 spring onions, finely chopped

6 shittake mushrooms, sliced finely

12 water chestnuts, chopped

1 small red pepper, finely sliced

4 oz (100 g) thread vermicelli,
  cooked (see above)

3 oz (75 g) bean sprouts

soya sauce

salt and freshly ground black pepper

$\frac{1}{2}$–1 teaspoon cornflour (optional)

8 large sheets of filo pastry or 40
  spring roll skins

beaten egg white to glaze (optional)

sesame, poppy or aijun seeds
  (optional)

oil for deep frying or brushing

Just as samosas lend a Middle Eastern feel to any party, so do Spring Rolls bring an oriental flavour. You can be sure that no matter how many you make, there will never be enough. For an authentic touch you can buy spring roll wrappers from your local Chinese grocery – you'll be going there anyway to buy the bean noodles. These wonderful vegan noodles are made simply with green beans and are also known as thread vermicelli. They're gluten free too.

Buy two packs of frozen spring roll skins as there are usually 20 to a packet. Thaw before use, being careful when separating the skins. Cook thread vermicelli simply by pouring boiling water over to cover and leaving until soft but not overcooked, then rinse in cold water.

1. Heat the oils in a large frying pan or a wok. Add the onion, garlic, chillies and ginger. Fry for a couple of minutes.

2. Add the vegetables (except the bean sprouts) and continue to stir-fry for 1 minute.

3. Stir in the noodles and stir-fry once again for 1 minute.

4. Finally, add the bean sprouts and soya sauce. Adjust the seasoning and, if necessary, thicken by adding a little cornflour. Allow to cool.

5. Cut each sheet of filo pastry (if using) width-wise into 5. Put a small amount of the mixture at one end of the strip. Fold the long edges over the filling and roll up so that the filling is completely enclosed.

6. Brush the ends with water and press to seal.

7. Brush with egg white – unless you are vegan of course. If desired, sprinkle with sesame, poppy or aijun seeds.

8. Heat the oil and deep fry until golden brown. If using filo, you may also simply brush with oil and bake in a hot oven (200°C/400°F/Gas Mark 6) until crisp and brown on top. Drain on absorbent paper.

To serve: Serve on an attractive platter with as many dips as you can muster: plum sauce, soya sauce and Satay Sauce (pages 157 and 146) come readily to mind, and chilli sauce would be good too!

Curry Tarts

 Serves 30

12 oz (325 g) organic wholewheat
    shortcrust pastry (see page 218)
beaten egg white (optional)

The dahl
2 medium shallots, finely chopped
4 cloves garlic, crushed or finely
    chopped
1 tablespoon vegetable oil or ghee
2 oz (50 g) red lentils
1 teaspoon Thai curry paste

The curry sauce
$\frac{1}{2}$ pint (275 ml) garlic or vegan
    mayonnaise (pages 149 and 224)
1 tablespoon Thai curry paste
3 cloves garlic, crushed or chopped
fine sea salt and freshly ground black
    pepper

The onion salad
4 oz (100 g) red onion, finely
    chopped
6 oz (175 g) tomatoes, skinned,
    deseeded and chopped
2 sprigs mint leaves, finely chopped
coriander leaves and lemon wedges
    for garnish

The only way to describe these tarts would be 'an Indian meal in a mouthful'. They're a little bit fiddly but well worth the effort. They're also the ideal item for an Indian themed buffet or as appetisers before an Indian themed dinner party.

The filling and the pastry cases can be prepared in advance and assembled on the day.

1. Heat the ghee or oil in a large saucepan or wok. Add the shallots and garlic and sauté until they are slightly burnt. Add the lentils and continue to cook for 2 minutes.

2. Cover with hot water and bring to the boil, then simmer until the lentils are cooked and the mixture thick. Stir in the curry paste and allow to cool.

3. While the lentils are cooking prepare the mayonnaise and stir in the rest of the ingredients for the curry sauce. Adjust the seasoning and put to one side in the fridge.

4. Now prepare the pastry cases. Roll out the pastry on a lightly floured surface to about $\frac{1}{8}$ in (3 mm) thick. Using a round cutter cut out $2\frac{1}{2}$ in (6 cm) rounds. Place these in well oiled round-based tartlet tins and allow to rest in a cool place for 30 minutes. Meanwhile preheat the oven to 200°C/400°F/Gas Mark 6.

5. If desired, brush the edges of the pastry cases with a little egg white. Prick with a fork and bake for about 10 minutes. Allow to cool.

6. Mix together the onion salad ingredients.

7. Using a piping bag with a plain nozzle, pipe a little of the lentil mix into each tartlet. Spread evenly with a palette knife. With a teaspoon, put a little of the mayonnaise on top of the lentil mixture. Finally sprinkle with the onion salad and dot with coriander leaves.

To serve: Serve cold with plenty of coriander and lemon wedges to garnish.

Tiny Leek and Gruyère Croissants

Makes approx. 20 × 1 oz (30 g) croissants

½ quantity of Croissant Dough (see page 219)
1 oz (30 g) unsalted butter
3 oz (75 g) Gruyère, grated
3 oz (75 g) leeks, finely chopped
1 teaspoon chopped fresh basil
fine sea salt and freshly ground black pepper
1 egg, beaten, for glazing
seeds to sprinkle (optional)
extra Gruyère cheese, grated (optional)

We have experimented for years at the restaurant trying to get our croissant dough right. We started off using 100 per cent wholewheat flour but they would only work if we used French butter and this made them so expensive no one would buy them. Fortunately we've now secured an organic unbleached white flour which is suitable, and with which we can use ordinary unsalted butter. The flavour of this flour is delicious and it's well worth seeking out.

You can make the Croissant Dough well ahead and freeze it, or make it the day before and chill it overnight. The leek mixture, too, can be made ahead so that all you have to do on the day is shape and fill the croissants.

1. Melt the butter in a pan and sauté the leeks with the seasoning until soft. Increase the heat to reduce any liquid. Add the basil and season to taste.

2. Roll out the dough onto a lightly floured board until it measures 16 × 12 in (40 × 30 cm). Cut into 4 widthways, to make strips each 12 × 4 in (30 × 10 cm). Cut each strip into 5 triangles with a 4 in (10 cm) base.

3. Put some of the leek mixture on the base of each triangle, then sprinkle with Gruyère.

4. Roll up the triangle and twist the ends around to form a croissant.

5. Put the croissant on a lightly oiled baking tray. Allow to rest for 20 minutes in the fridge. Heat the oven to 200°C/400°F/Gas Mark 6.

6. Brush the croissants with egg and sprinkle with seeds or extra cheese, if desired. Bake for 20 minutes or until golden. Serve hot and bubbling.

Devonshire Blue Tartlets

Makes 30 × 2-in (5-cm) tartlets

1 quantity organic wholewheat
    shortcrust pastry (see page 218)
8 oz (225 g) Devonshire Blue
    cheese, rind removed
2 egg yolks
6 fl oz (180 ml) sour cream
pinch of mace or nutmeg
fine sea salt and freshly ground black
    pepper
fruit compote for garnish

Devonshire Blue cheese is a real treat for jaded tastebuds. These tartlets are really exotic quichelets. They're quite delicious.

1. Heat the oven to 200°C/400°F/Gas Mark 6.

2. Roll out the pastry and use it to line well greased tartlet tins. Weigh down with a few pastry beads and bake blind for 15 minutes. When cool, remove the pastry cases from the tins.

3. Put the rest of the ingredients in a food processor and blend to a smooth consistency.

4. Fill the tartlets with the cheese mixture, then place under a moderate grill until the tops are golden and the mixture has almost set. Eat them straight from the grill.

To serve: A nice idea is to garnish each tartlet with a sharp fruit compote. Gooseberry, blackcurrant or cranberry would all be wonderful.

Onion Tartlets

Makes 30 × 2-in (5-cm) tartlets

1 quantity organic wholewheat
    shortcrust pastry (see page 218)
4 medium onions, finely sliced
4 fl oz (120 ml) virgin olive oil
11 oz (300 g) fromage frais
5 egg yolks
16 fl oz (500 ml) double cream
pinch of nutmeg
fine sea salt and freshly ground black
    pepper
green olives, sun-dried tomatoes
    and parsley sprigs to garnish

More delicious tartlets, this time creamy onion ones.

1. Heat the oven to 200°C/400°F/Gas Mark 6.

2. Roll out the pastry and use it to line well greased tartlet tins. Weigh down with a few pastry beads and bake blind for 15 minutes. When cool, remove the pastry cases from the tins.

3. Cook the onions in the oil until soft.

4. Beat the fromage frais, egg yolks and cream together with the seasoning.

5. Fill the pastry cases with the mixture and bake for 25 minutes or until just set.

6. Garnish each tartlet with an olive, a sun-dried tomato and parsley. Serve hot or cold.

Mushrooms on Sticks

V G   *Makes 20*

80 small button mushrooms
(approx 1½ lb (675 g) depending
on size)
2 oz (50 g) unsalted butter or
4 tablespoons vegetable oil
4 oz (100 g) shallots, finely chopped
4 cloves garlic, finely minced
1 tablespoon soya sauce
1 tablespoon vegetarian
Worcestershire sauce
2 teaspoons demerara sugar or
honey
4 tablespoons fresh tomato purée
(see page 223)
3 carrots cut into fine julienne or
grated
1 bunch fresh coriander, leaves
picked from stems
lemon slices for garnish

The use of bamboo skewers for buffets has many advantages. Not only do the skewers look exciting, they're also easy to get hold of and great to eat from. Anything you can pierce can be served on a skewer whether it be sweet or savoury.

Food cooked on skewers is best barbecued over a charcoal grill, maybe with some hickory chips thrown in. If this is not possible, then grilling, baking, or even frying are options. In this recipe we cheated by cooking the mushrooms first, then putting them on skewers.

Choose the finest button mushrooms you can find. Small closed cup mushrooms will do though they're not quite so aesthetically pleasing. Bamboo skewers may be bought at most Chinese grocery stores. If they are too long, cut them in half.

1. Clean the mushrooms with a brush. Avoid immersing them in water unless they are particularly dirty.

2. Melt the butter or heat the oil in a large pan. Sauté the shallots with the garlic over a medium heat until softening, then add the mushrooms and continue to cook for 5 minutes with a lid on.

3. Stir in the sugar or honey, soya and Worcestershire sauces and cook for 2 minutes. It is important not to overcook the mushrooms.

4. Remove the mushrooms carefully with a slotted spoon and put to one side, preferably in a deep plastic container.

5. Bring the remaining cooking liquor to the boil and stir in the tomato purée. Adjust seasoning and allow to cook until the mixture thickens.

6. Remove from the heat and pour over the mushrooms. Allow to cool. Store overnight in the fridge, stirring occasionally as the sauce will tend to congregate at the bottom.

To serve: Cover a large oval dish with a mixture of grated carrot and fresh coriander. Skewer the mushrooms, four at a time, and place on the bed of carrot and coriander. Finally spoon the remaining marinade evenly over the mushrooms and sprinkle with more fresh coriander. Garnish with slices of fresh lemon.

Baby Sweetcorn on Sticks

V G   *Makes 20*

1 oz (30 g) unsalted butter or
    vegetable oil
2 spring onions, finely chopped
20 baby sweetcorn
½ teaspoon Dijon mustard
1 oz (30 g) demerara sugar or honey
2 tablespoons freshly squeezed lime
    juice

Baby sweetcorn are popular with most age groups. Children may find the sauce suggested here too strong – melted butter is all they need to enjoy these most innocent of vegetables.

1. Preheat the oven to 200°C/400°F/Gas Mark 6.

2. Melt the butter or heat the oil in a pan, then add the spring onion and cook for 2 minutes.

3. Add the baby sweetcorn and cook, with the lid on, for a further 3 minutes.

4. Add the rest of the ingredients and make sure that the baby sweetcorn are well coated.

5. Remove the sweetcorn from the pan with a slotted spoon and place in a baking dish. Taste the sauce and season if necessary, then pour over the sweetcorn, making sure they are well coated.

6. Cook in the oven for 6–7 minutes, agitating the tin occasionally. This will 'fix' a glaze on the corn.

Serving suggestion: Serve immediately. They are best eaten hot but are still delicious cold. Put onto halved bamboo skewers or cocktail sticks.

Stuffed Vine-leaves

What an obvious dish to have at a buffet and yet how rarely do you see it. Stuffed vine-leaves are simple to prepare and tasty and may be served cold or hot with a sauce or a series of dips. They originate from the Middle East and so may prove a little spicy for some more conservative British guests.

Vine-leaves themselves are readily available, in most good supermarkets or health food shops, preserved in brine. If you are lucky enough to have a vine in your garden just choose a few healthy-looking leaves from that.

The glutinous rice needed for the stuffing can be bought from Chinese groceries under the name *pulot*.

V G *Makes 30*

40–50 fresh or preserved vine-leaves
3 tablespoons virgin olive oil
1 medium onion, finely chopped
3 cloves garlic, finely diced
1 small chilli, deseeded and finely diced
1 small red pepper, finely diced
1 small green pepper, finely diced
2 tablespoons chopped parsley
2 teaspoons finely chopped mint
2 tablespoons finely chopped coriander
3 tablespoons pine nuts, lightly toasted
1 oz (30 g) currants
14 oz (400 g) cooked glutinous rice
juice of 3 lemons
salt and freshly ground black pepper
3 lemons, sliced
1 oz (30 g) butter or 1 tablespoon olive oil
lettuce, grapes and lemon wedges for garnish

1. Rinse the vine-leaves in cold water and blanch in boiling water for 2 minutes, no more than 10 at a time.

2. Transfer to cold water with a slotted spoon, then onto a colander to drain.

3. Heat the oil in a deep, heavy-bottomed pan. Gently fry the onion, garlic and chilli until the onion is beginning to soften.

4. Add the red and green peppers and the herbs and continue to cook for 5 minutes.

5. Stir in the toasted pine nuts, currants and rice. Add lemon juice until you are satisfied with the flavour. Adjust the seasoning.

6. Take 30 of the vine-leaves. Spread each vine-leaf, shiny side down, on a work surface. Trim its stem if necessary. Place a heaped teaspoon of rice filling near the stem end, roll over once, then fold in the sides and roll up completely to form a neat package. Repeat with the rest of the mixture until you have made 30.

7. Line the base of a heavy pan with the remaining vine-leaves, including damaged ones. Pack the stuffed vine-leaves in as tightly as possible. As each layer is completed cover with slices of lemon. Finish with a layer of lemon topped with any remaining vine-leaves.

8. Add the butter or olive oil, 6 fl oz (180 ml) of water and any remaining lemon juice.

9. Place a heavy metal saucepan lid or plate on the vine-leaves to weigh them down and make sure they keep their shape.

10. Bring slowly to the boil and reduce immediately to simmer. Cover and gently simmer for 50 minutes, then remove from the heat and allow to cool.

11. Carefully remove the rolls from the pan and place immediately on a serving dish.

To serve: Serve hot or cold on a bed of lettuce garnished with grapes and wedges of lemon. A yoghurt dip like Banana Raita (see page 158) would be ideal with this. Vegans may prefer a tangy vinaigrette.

Spicy New Potatoes

V G   *Makes 30*

3 tablespoons olive oil

3 medium red onions, chopped

2 teaspoons paprika

$\frac{1}{2}$ teaspoon chilli powder

2 teaspoons cumin seeds

5 cloves garlic, crushed

30 small potatoes (new if possible),
approx. $1\frac{1}{2}$ lb (675 g)

$\frac{3}{4}$ pint (450 ml) tomato purée (see
page 223)

$\frac{3}{4}$ pint (450 ml) water

fine sea salt and freshly ground black
pepper

1 bunch fresh coriander, chopped

salad leaves for garnish

For this dish I choose the smallest and, in summer, the newest potatoes I can find. Potatoes make a wonderful buffet dish – while they titillate the taste-buds, they're also soaking up the alcohol. For best results use a deep roasting-dish made of iron or copper.

1. Heat the olive oil in a roasting tray or deep-bottomed saucepan. Add the onions, spices and garlic and cook until the onions are softening.

2. Add the potatoes and make sure they are well coated in spice.

3. Add the tomato purée and water and a little salt and bring to the boil. Simmer gently for 30 minutes. If the liquid is loath to reduce turn up the heat for the last 5 minutes. The tomato sauce should be of a coating consistency.

4. Season and sprinkle with freshly chopped coriander.

To serve: Spear each potato with a cocktail stick and arrange in an attractive bowl or on a platter garnished with salad leaves.

Nori Sushi

Sushi make an unusual but delicious addition to buffets. They may also be served as a starter in their own right. There is no doubt that at first they're a bit time-consuming but once you've got all the unusual ingredients and have made them a couple of times you'll find making them easier and easier. To help you I've given here a brief description of each of the unusual ingredients. They can all be bought in Chinese supermarkets.

Nori seaweed is specifically cultivated in Japan from a red seaweed related to laver (as in Welsh laver bread). It is dried into black sheets in which form it is used for wrapping sushi. Alternatively, it may be crisped in the oven or under a grill and crumbled over a dish like a condiment. Nori crumbled into rice is delicious.

V G *Makes 36*

For the sushi rice
8 oz (225 g) short-grain rice
$\frac{1}{2}$ pint (275 ml) water
1 in (2.5 cm) piece kombu

For the dressing
2 tablespoons rice wine vinegar
1 tablespoon dry sherry
$1\frac{1}{2}$ teaspoons salt
1 tablespoon sugar

For the seaweed rolls
3 sheets of Nori seaweed
1 teaspoon wasabe powder,
    reconstituted with water
1 oz (30 g) Japanese pickled ginger
2 oz (50 g) daikon, cut into fine
    strips
1 cucumber, peeled and cut into fine
    strips

Sushi rice can be any short-grained, preferably glutinous rice flavoured with rice vinegar.

Wasabe powder is Japanese green horseradish powder, reconstituted with water like English mustard.

Kombu is a dried form of kelp.

Takuan or *daikon* is pickled yellow Japanese radish.

Rice vinegar is vinegar made from rice wine.

Japanese pickled ginger is pink and very pungent.

You will also need a bamboo sushi mat for rolling the sushi. If you cannot find one, a linen napkin will do.

Having got all the ingredients, first prepare the sushi rice. This can be done well in advance.

To prepare the rice

1. Wash the rice thoroughly until the water becomes crystal clear. Allow it to drain for 30 minutes. Also wash the kombu well.

2. Place the rice in a pan with $\frac{1}{2}$ pint (275 ml) fresh water. Add the kombu.

3. Bring to the boil quickly, then cover and simmer very gently without removing the lid for 15 minutes.

4. Remove from the heat and allow to stand for a further 10 minutes without removing the lid.

5. While the rice is cooking, prepare the dressing by mixing the ingredients so that the sugar completely dissolves.

6. Discard the kombu and turn the rice out into a large bowl.

7. Pour the dressing over the rice and mix in gently but thoroughly. Allow to cool.

To assemble the seaweed rolls

1. Divide the rice into 3 equal portions.

2. Gently toast the sheets of nori by passing them back and forth over a gas flame or electric hob.

3. Place a sheet of nori on the rolling-out mat.

4. Spread one portion of rice over two-thirds of the nori sheet, starting at the side nearest to you.

5. In a row down the middle of the rice arrange a combination of one-third of the other ingredients.

6. Roll up the sushi mat, keeping firm pressure on the rice to produce a neat cylinder.

7. Allow the rolls to rest for 10 minutes before cutting into 6 sections. Repeat with the other sheets of nori.

To serve: Arrange attractively on a tray (black is nice here), garnished with a few tiny leaves like flat parsley and some light Japanese soya sauce for dipping.

Stuffed Tomatoes

V *Makes 30*

15 small red tomatoes
15 small yellow tomatoes
1 small avocado
juice of $\frac{1}{2}$ lemon
1 tablespoon peeled, deseeded and
    finely diced cucumber
1 small green pepper, finely diced
1 small red pepper, finely diced
1 tablespoon chopped chives
1 tablespoon chopped fresh
    coriander
3 tablespoons vegan mayonnaise or
    crème fraîche or fromage frais
fine sea salt and freshly ground black
    pepper
chives to garnish

Stuffed Tomatoes are fiddly but they bring colour and freshness to your buffet. If you are vegan, use a vegan mayonnaise (see page 224).

Choose small ripe (not over-ripe) tomatoes. Cherry tomatoes are too small for most fillings except purées and creams.

1. With a sharp knife, slice the stalk end off the tomatoes, keeping the stalk intact.

2. Use the knife to loosen the pulp and seeds and scoop out with a small teaspoon. Retain any tomato fillets (pure flesh) but discard the seeds and pith. Avoid using excess pressure.

3. When the tomatoes are completely empty, sprinkle with a little salt and invert to drain on a cooling rack for 10 minutes.

4. Meanwhile, prepare the filling. Mix together the mashed avocado, reserved tomato flesh, peppers, chives, coriander and mayonnaise in a bowl and adjust seasoning.

5. Spoon a little of the filling into each tomato. There should be enough to slightly overfill each one.

6. Sprinkle with chopped chives and replace the lid at an angle, allowing a view of the contents.

To serve: Serve as a garnish for other dishes or as part of a selection, garnished with leaves or sprigs of basil.

143

VARIATIONS

Of course there are many other fresh vegetables that make ideal containers. Try:

- Artichoke hearts filled with hoummous, garnished with a little paprika and half a black olive. Use fresh artichokes if possible.

- Young celery stems with leaves intact filled with Cambozola cheese beaten with a little cream cheese. Decorate with a pecan.

Falafels

V G   *Makes 30 (cocktail size)*

1 lb (450 g) chickpeas
3 pints (1.8 l) water
1 large onion, finely chopped
2 sticks celery, finely chopped
4 cloves garlic, crushed or minced
1 bunch parsley, finely chopped
1 teaspoon chilli powder
$\frac{1}{2}$ teaspoon ground coriander seeds
1 teaspoon ground cumin
2 oz (50 g) sesame seeds
gram flour
olive oil
oil for deep frying
radicchio leaves, tiny lemon wedges
   and coriander leaves for garnish

Falafels are a delicious Middle Eastern treat. They are equally good as a starter with a dip or two, or as a main course, usually served in pitta bread with salad and a chilli or yoghurt sauce.

1. Cover the chickpeas with the water and leave to soak for 12–15 hours or overnight.

2. Put the chickpeas in a saucepan and cover with fresh water. Add a little salt. Bring to boil, cover and simmer until tender. This will take anything up to 2 hours, depending on their age and how long you've soaked them.

3. Drain in a colander, retaining some of the cooking liquid.

4. Blend the chickpeas in a food processor, using some of the liquid to get them going.

5. Mix with the onion, celery, garlic, parsley and spices.

6. Try to roll into 30 balls about 1 in (2.5 cm) in diameter. If they are too wet, add some gram flour to the mix. If they are too dry, add a little olive oil.

7. Mix the sesame seeds with more gram flour. Dip the balls in cold water, then roll in the sesame mixture.

8. Shallow or deep fry until golden brown. Remove from the oil and allow to drain on paper towels.

To serve: Serve hot, warm or cold in individual paper cases on a bed of radicchio with a tiny wedge of lemon and a coriander leaf.

Satay Sticks

3 oz (75 g) aduki beans

4 oz (100 g) couscous

$\frac{1}{2}$ pint (275 ml) vegetable stock (see page 225), heated

2 tablespoons peanut oil

1 small onion, finely chopped

4 oz (100 g) mushrooms, finely chopped

1 fresh green chilli, finely chopped

1 teaspoon ground coriander seeds

1 teaspoon ground cumin

$\frac{1}{2}$ teaspoon cayenne pepper

1 tablespoon chopped fresh mint

2 tablespoons chopped fresh coriander

4 tablespoons coconut milk (see page 146 – if not available soya milk will do)

4 oz (100 g) organic wholewheat flour

fine sea salt and freshly ground black pepper

oil for deep frying

strips of cucumber and spring onion frills for garnish

lemon wedges for garnish

Satay has become popular throughout the world in the last 10 years but up till now vegetarians have missed out on this delicacy. Of course seitan (wheat gluten) would be an ideal substitute for chicken, lamb, beef or pork as it soaks up the flavours of the marinade and emulates the texture of the meat. But if you don't have the time or patience to make seitan here's a good robust alternative – and it's vegan too!

You will need 25 small bamboo skewers, 6 in (15 cm) long.

1. Soak the aduki beans overnight and cook. Soak the couscous in hot stock.

2. Heat the peanut oil in a pan and sauté the onion, mushroom and chilli until the onion is softening.

3. Pour into a food processor with the coriander seed, cumin, cayenne, and cooked aduki beans. Blend until smooth.

4. Mix with the couscous and add the fresh mint and coriander. Bind together with coconut milk and a little of the flour. Season to taste.

5. Divide the mix into 25 portions. Mould each portion of the mixture around a bamboo skewer into a sausage shape, using your hands.

6. Roll in the remaining flour and chill for 30 minutes.

7. Deep fry in hot oil.

To serve: Serve on plates garnished with lemon, or for a more exotic presentation, put the leafy top of a pineapple in the centre of a serving dish and arrange the satay sticks around it. Have a large bowl of Satay Sauce (see page 146) to hand. Satay Sauce is spooned over the Satay Sticks before eating.

Satay Sauce

[V] *Enough for 25 satays*

6 tablespoons crunchy peanut butter
8 fl oz (250 ml) water
4 cloves garlic, minced
juice of 1 lemon
1 oz (30 g) sugar or honey to taste
2 tablespoons soya sauce
2 teaspoons Thai curry paste – (it's
   very hot – beware!)
$\frac{1}{4}$ pint (150 ml) coconut milk
salt and freshly ground black pepper

This is essentially a peanut sauce which can be as hot and spicy, crunchy or smooth as you like. Purists use freshly ground roasted peanuts. I use a mixture of good quality peanut butter (this thickens the sauce naturally) and freshly ground roasted nuts.

Coconut milk is made by combining 5 oz (150 g) of fine desiccated coconut with just under a pint (600 ml) of hot water in a blender for 30 seconds and then straining through muslin.

1. Mix the peanut butter and water together and bring to the boil.

2. Remove from the heat and add the garlic, lemon juice, sugar or honey, soya, and curry paste. Add the coconut milk to obtain a coating consistency. If the sauce is still too thick, add a little water. Adjust seasoning and stir in the peanuts.

Peppers on Toast

[V] *Serves 20*

1 stick of French bread (baguette)
4 tablespoons virgin olive oil
2 oz (50 g) shallots, finely chopped
1 clove garlic, finely chopped
3 oz (75 g) red pepper, finely diced
3 oz (75 g) green pepper, finely
   diced
4 oz (100 g) yellow pepper, finely
   diced
2 tablespoons fresh tomato purée
   (see page 223)
2 tablespoons chopped fresh basil
fine sea salt and black pepper
$1\frac{1}{2}$ oz (40 g) Pecorino cheese, finely
   grated

Find a good quality French stick for this simple recipe.

1. Cut 20 slices of French bread.

2. Heat the oil in a pan and cook the shallots and garlic until they are softening.

3. Add the diced peppers and cook for 3 minutes.

4. Stir in the tomato purée and continue to cook until most of the liquid has been absorbed. Remove from the heat and fold in the basil. Season.

5. Toast the French bread on both sides, then spread with the pepper mixture. Sprinkle with Pecorino and colour under a hot grill. Best served warm.

VARIATION

Replace peppers with mushrooms.

Black Olive Pâté on Sesame Snaps

V *Makes 20*

The pâté

6 oz (175 g) pitted black olives

2½ teaspoons lemon juice

3 cloves garlic

1 tablespoon chopped fresh basil

3 tablespoons pine nuts

4 tablespoons virgin olive oil

fine sea salt and freshly ground black
    pepper

small black olives to garnish

The Sesame Snaps

4 oz (100 g) organic wholewheat
    bread flour

½ teaspoon salt

½ teaspoon baking powder

1 oz (30 g) unsalted butter or vegan
    margarine

1 tablespoon sesame seeds (retain a
    few for sprinkling)

2 tablespoons sour cream

4 tablespoons water

beaten egg yolk to glaze (optional)

The pâté is best made a day or so before to allow flavours to mingle.

The Sesame Snaps are good on their own, with a variety of fillings, or simply with cheese.

To make the pâté

1. Put the olives, lemon juice, garlic, basil and pine nuts in a blender and purée.

2. Gently trickle the oil into the olive purée. Adjust the seasoning.

To make the Sesame Snaps

1. Mix the flour, salt and baking powder together.

2. Melt the unsalted butter or margarine in a pan and cook the sesame seeds in it until colouring.

3. Add the flour mixture, the sour cream and sufficient water to form a firm dough.

4. Roll out the dough thinly and cut 20 × 1½ in (3 cm) diameter biscuits.

5. Place the biscuits on an oiled baking tray and allow to rest in a cool place for 30 minutes. Meanwhile heat the oven to 170°C/325°F/Gas Mark 3.

6. Glaze the biscuits with egg yolk if you like, and bake for 12–18 minutes or until golden.

7. Transfer to a wire rack to cool. When cold store in an airtight tin.

To serve: Serve the biscuits spread with olive pâté and garnished with an olive half.

VARIATION

For a non-vegan alternative, top the pâté with a little Gorgonzola or Roquefort.

Herby Wholegrain Toast

V *Makes 20*

5 slices wholegrain bread
4 tablespoons garlic oil (see page 224)
$\frac{1}{2}$ quantity of Pesto (see page 225) made without oil or Parmesan

For a really deep garlic experience.

1. Heat the oven to 180°C/350°F/Gas Mark 4.

2. Brush the slices of wholegrain bread with the garlic oil and bake in the oven for 10 minutes.

3. Spread with Pesto, then trim off the crusts and cut each slice into 4, diagonally. Serve immediately.

Serving suggestion: Serve on a tray with plenty of parsley available for those who are worried about their breath. This form of canapé base lends itself to a myriad of toppings. Pipe pâtés and dips on garlic toasted wholegrain bread for a really sensational mouthful.

Keith's Vegetable Basket

A chap called Keith gave me this idea one summer in France. I immediately banned the ordinary way of serving crudités from our buffet menu, having always secretly thought them a bit outdated.

Keith's method is to choose celery, carrots, peppers, broccoli florets, cauliflower florets, cucumber and mushroom, where possible cut into chunky strips. Season them well with salt and pepper, then scrunch up plenty of fresh basil and mint leaves, mix them in with the vegetables and put them into a plastic container with a lid.

Leave, covered, in a cool place but not in the fridge, for a couple of hours and wait for the herbs to impart their magic. The vegetables don't need a dip. They are just beautifully perfumed with basil and mint. And what is more, they will not dry out and curl up at the edges like conventionally presented crudités.

Having said that, there are a number of dressings and dips that would go well with Keith's Vegetable Basket. The following section has plenty of ideas.

To serve: Find a suitably attractive wooden bowl or basket. Line it with a napkin and top with the fresh vegetables and herbs.

DRESSINGS AND DIPS

No buffet is complete without one or two dynamic dressings, apart from a standard vinaigrette. Dressings are amazing things and can transform salads, lubricate other dishes unintentionally and then be equally good with a simple biscuit or chunk of fresh bread.

I'm sure that many new ideas for combining different foods have originated at parties where a little bit of something has strayed onto a plate with a little bit of something it shouldn't have – end result: 'Wow, why did I never think of that before?'

Garlic Mayonnaise or Aïoli

G   *Makes nearly 2 pints (1.2 l)*

4 fl oz (120 ml) lemon juice, freshly squeezed
4 cloves garlic, crushed
4 egg yolks
½ teaspoon fine sea salt
1 teaspoon freshly ground black pepper
1 teaspoon dry English mustard
1 teaspoon soya sauce
1 pint (600 ml) olive oil (substitute vegetable oil if desired)

Real mayonnaise made with raw egg is the basis of many delicious and varied dressings. However, people who are pregnant, very old or very young should not eat raw egg mayonnaise because of the risk of salmonella infection.

Aïoli has garlic in it from the word Go, and makes a good substance to dip things into.

1. Blend together all the ingredients except the oil at high speed in a blender.

2. Turn the speed down and, ever so gently, start to trickle the oil in. The mixture should soon start to thicken. Continue to pour the oil until it has all been absorbed and the mixture is very thick. Turn the blender off immediately.

To serve: Serve as it is with precooked or raw vegetables.

VARIATIONS

- *Chilli Mayonnaise* Add chilli powder or a chilli paste like Sambal Olek (see page 227).

- *Curried Mayonnaise* Add curry paste.

- *Egg Mayonnaise* Hard-boil 6 eggs, mash and stir into the mayonnaise.

- *Herby Mayonnaise* Add freshly chopped herbs like basil, tarragon or chives. For a really green mayonnaise, try blanched puréed spinach and flavour with chopped herbs.

- *Cocktail Sauce* Add tomato purée (see page 223) or tomato ketchup, a little yoghurt, brandy and lemon juice.

- *Mustard Dip* Add 1 tablespoon Dijon mustard, chopped fresh herbs and, if enjoyed, chopped capers and gherkins.

Zhooch

V G *Enough for 4–6*
depending on usage

1 tablespoon olive oil
1 tablespoon lemon juice
6 cloves garlic
1 fresh chilli
1 bunch fresh coriander, washed and
    dried
fine sea salt and freshly ground black
    pepper

A simple vegan dressing that is powerful! Use sparingly.

Simply whizz to a thick purée in a blender.

Serving suggestions: • Dilute with Greek yoghurt to make a delicious non-vegan dip.

• Use as a condiment in salads or hot savoury dishes.

• Simply use to dip bread in, or mix with a little extra olive oil, spread on pitta bread and grill.

'Food for friends' Butterbean Mayonnaise

V **G** *Makes 2 pints (1.2l)*

1 quantity vinaigrette (see page 152) replacing basil with dill and reducing the mustard to 1 tablespoon
8 oz (225 g) butterbeans

This is a vegan mayonnaise that I invented on being told by the health authorities that we could no longer make fresh egg mayonnaise in the restaurants unless we used bulk homogenised eggs. These bulk eggs are not free-range, so I quickly came up with an egg-free alternative and certainly made a lot of vegan customers happy. If using canned butterbeans, double the weight.

There is another recipe for a vegan mayonnaise on page 224.

1. Soak the butterbeans overnight, then cook until soft.

2. Allow to cool, then blend with the vinaigrette in a blender until perfectly smooth and light. Adjust seasoning.

To serve: Use in any recipe where mayonnaise is used. Stored in a cool place it will actually improve, unlike real mayonnaise.

Kimizu – Japanese Salad Dressing

V **G** *Makes approx ½ pint (275 ml)*

2½ tablespoons sherry vinegar
3 teaspoons Dijon mustard
2 cloves garlic, crushed
3 tablespoons soft brown sugar
1 teaspoon vegetarian Worcestershire sauce
1 teaspoon tabasco sauce
2 oz (50 g) mixed leek and carrot, cut into fine dice and blanched
4 tablespoons sesame oil
2 tablespoons soya sauce
2 tablespoons tomato purée (see page 223)
fine sea salt and ground black pepper

This is more a Western interpretation than an actual Japanese dressing but it is excellent with raw or partly cooked vegetables.

1. Mix all the ingredients except the sesame oil, soya sauce and tomato purée.

2. Add the oil gradually. When starting to thicken, add the soy sauce and tomato purée. Adjust seasoning.

To serve: Serve in an attractive bowl or jug alongside freshly cut or lightly cooked vegetables and grains.

Vinaigrette

V G *Makes about 1 pint
(600 ml)*

1 shallot, finely chopped
3 or more cloves garlic, minced
1 tablespoon finely chopped basil
(or other herbs)
2 tablespoons Dijon mustard
fine sea salt and freshly ground black
pepper
1 tablespoon demerara sugar or
honey
8 fl oz (250 ml) virgin olive oil
6 tablespoons balsamic or sherry
vinegar

I love making vinaigrette. I always make it in large quantities because I love the thought of all those flavours marinating together. Eat my vinaigrette just after I've made it and it's very good. Eat it one week later and it's sublime. This basic vinaigrette can be embellished, extended, perverted and distorted in whichever way you like. It's best to make it in a wide-necked screw-top bottle.

1. Assemble the contents in a wide-necked screw-top jar and shake until all the ingredients have emulsified.

2. Taste and adjust seasoning if you have to.

VARIATIONS

- For a tomato flavour, substitute half or all the mustard with fresh tomato purée (see page 223).

- For a lighter vinaigrette, reduce the mustard and the sugar.

- For a spicy vinaigrette add 1 or more finely chopped fresh chillies.

- *Shallot Vinaigrette* Shake together 2 tablespoons chopped shallots, 5 tablespoons white wine vinegar, 5 tablespoons walnut oil, salt and pepper, finely chopped tarragon, chervil, parsley and chives.

- *Lime and Honey Vinaigrette* Shake together 3 tablespoons vegetable oil, 3 tablespoons olive oil, 1 teaspoon grated ginger, juice and zest of 1 lime, 1 tablespoon honey, 1 tablespoon chopped parsley, salt and pepper.

- *Stilton Vinaigrette* Shake together 2 tablespoons olive oil and 2 teaspoons lemon juice, then gently stir in 2 tablespoons double cream and 1 tablespoon finely chopped Stilton. Adjust seasoning to taste.

OPPOSITE: *Fresh Spinach and Goat's Cheese Ravioli with Coriander and Mint Sauce (page 87)*

Lemon and Tahini Dressing

V G   *Makes 1 pint (600 ml)*

4 cloves garlic
fine sea salt and freshly ground black
    pepper
4 fl oz (120 ml) tahini
8 fl oz (250 ml) olive oil
4 fl oz (120 ml) lemon juice
1 fresh chilli or 1 teaspoon Sambal
    Olek (see page 227)
1 tablespoon demerara sugar or
    honey
1 oz (30 g) grated fresh ginger
1 tablespoon fresh tomato purée
    (see page 223)

Sometimes a thought crosses my mind that our vinaigrette has got an awesome competitor. Lemon and tahini dressing has to run a close second, if not neck-and-neck. It's one of the most more-ish flavours known to humankind. Buy a good quality light tahini.

Put all the ingredients in a blender and whizz. The result should be thick and emulsified.

To serve: Serve with hot or cold vegetables or with a salad. Excellent also with hot rice and other grains.

Fresh Horseradish Dip

G   *Makes ½ pint (275 ml)*

2 tablespoons freshly grated
    horseradish
1 tablespoon chopped fresh chives
    or tarragon
fine sea salt and freshly ground black
    pepper
½ pint (275 ml) sour cream

Tangy horseradish is just what you need to liven up any dish that is potentially a bit heavy, or that has been fried. It would go well with Rösti (page 30) for instance.

Fold the horseradish, herbs and seasoning into the sour cream. If you do not have sour cream, add 1 tablespoon lemon juice to double cream. Retain a few fresh chives for decoration.

VARIATION

- For a sour cream and chive dip leave out the horseradish and add a few more chives.

OPPOSITE: *Top to bottom: Hamish's Turtle Pizzas (page 119), Garlic Bread (page 188), Karen's Unbelievably Simple Tomato Soup with animal-shaped croutons (page 121)*

Avocado and Fromage Frais Dip

G   *Serves 4–6 as a dip*

2 ripe avocados
juice and grated rind of $\frac{1}{2}$ lemon
$\frac{1}{2}$ teaspoon Sambal Olek (see page
    227)
4 oz (100 g) fromage frais
fine sea salt and freshly ground black
    pepper
pitted black olives, sundried
    tomatoes in oil and lemons, to
    garnish

Avocados are perfect candidates to be turned into dressings or dips. They have a high natural oil content and so need only a little lemon juice to form a good emulsion. They can be a bit heavy, so in this recipe we've added fromage frais to lighten the dish up. If you are vegan, omit the fromage frais and substitute soft tofu. Make sure the avocados you buy are ripe if you want to make this recipe immediately.

1. Combine the avocado flesh with the lemon rind and juice and Sambal Olek. Mix with a fork if you require a rough texture, otherwise use a food processor.

2. Fold in the fromage frais and adjust the seasoning.

To serve: Present in an attractive bowl garnished with olives, sun-dried tomatoes and lemon. Eat as a dip with nachos or slices of hot soft flour tortillas.

Aubergine Dip

V G   *Serves 4–6*

1 large aubergine, about 1 lb (450 g)
4 cloves garlic
$\frac{3}{4}$ teaspoon fine sea salt
1 tablespoon lemon juice
$\frac{1}{2}$ tablespoon ground cumin
1 tablespoon olive oil
1 tablespoon chopped fresh parsley
pinch of chilli powder
olives and lemons for garnish

Aubergines have long been used as the base of a dip in the Middle East. Some people call it poor man's caviar but personally, I'd prefer the aubergines any time.

1. Heat the oven to 190°C/375°F/Gas Mark 5. Meanwhile wash the aubergine and slit the skin deeply around its largest circumference.

2. Place on an oiled baking dish and bake for 30 minutes, or until soft and blackened. Leave to cool for 10 minutes.

3. Cut the aubergine in half and scoop out the flesh with a spoon.

4. Place the rest of the ingredients in a liquidiser. Add the aubergine flesh and blend to a smooth consistency. Adjust the seasoning.

To serve: Serve in an attractive bowl garnished with olives and lemons and surrounded by Sesame Snaps (page 147) or strips of hot pitta bread.

VARIATIONS

- Add 2 tablespoons of Greek yoghurt, mayonnaise or sour cream for a richer smoother dip.

- Add 1 tablespoon of tahini.

Chickpea and Olive Tapenade

V G   *Makes 1½ pints (900 ml)*

8 oz (225 g) dried chickpeas
1½ pints (900 ml) water
4 oz (100 g) black olives, pitted
2 tablespoons lemon juice
3 cloves garlic, crushed
fine sea salt and freshly ground black pepper
coriander leaves to garnish
1 tablespoon olive oil
paprika (optional)

Another versatile dip, easy to prepare well in advance if required as a starter – just double the quantities. You could use canned chickpeas to save time. If using canned, double the quantity of dried and omit stages 1 and 2.

1. Wash the chickpeas thoroughly in plenty of cold water. Cover with water and leave to soak for 12 hours or overnight.

2. Place the chickpeas in a saucepan with a little salt and, using the water they were soaked in, cook them for at least 3 hours or until very soft.

3. Place the chickpeas in the blender with the olives, lemon juice and garlic and a little of the cooking water. Blend to a smooth consistency. Adjust the seasoning.

To serve: Spread in a shallow serving dish, drizzle with olive oil, sprinkle with paprika, if liked, and decorate with coriander leaves.

Tomato and Basil Salsa

V G *Makes about 1 pint
(600 ml)*

1 small red onion, finely chopped
4 tablespoons chopped fresh basil
4 cloves garlic, crushed
1 lb (450 g) plump ripe fresh
    tomatoes, skinned, deseeded and
    chopped
fine sea salt and freshly ground black
    pepper
white wine vinegar, to taste

Salsas are the simplest of all sauces or dips as they are uncooked. There are many variations; in those where fresh tomatoes are used, choose only the best and ripest you can find.

1. Blend the onion, basil and garlic together with a little tomato for about 20 seconds.

2. Pour in the rest of the tomatoes and blend very briefly so as to retain the texture. Season and add a little vinegar if desired.

To serve: Salsas are excellent with any Mexican food or warm savoury pastries such as Cheese Palmiers (see page 159), mini croissants (page 136) or Tomato and Cheese Straws (see page 160). Serve in a small bowl garnished with basil leaves.

VARIATIONS

- *Salsa Verde* Blend shallots with fresh herbs, lemon peel, garlic, olive oil and lemon juice. Season to taste.

- *Salsa Picante* As for Tomato and Basil Salsa, but replace basil with fresh coriander and add a little Sambal Olek (see page 227).

- *Onion Salsa* As for Salsa Picante but use equal quantities of red onions and tomatoes. Add parsley too.

Kidney Bean Dip

V G *Serves 4–6 as a dip*

4 oz (100 g) dried kidney beans or
    an 8 oz (225 g) can
1 tablespoon vegetable oil
1 small onion, chopped
4 cloves garlic, crushed
2 chillies, sliced, or 2 teaspoons
    Sambal Olek (see page 227)
fine sea salt and freshly ground black
    pepper
4 tablespoons fresh tomato purée
    (see page 223)
lemon slices and paprika for garnish

Kidney beans made a good simple hearty dip, ideal for a quick lunch or as a pre-dinner snack.

1. Soak the kidney beans overnight. Drain and cook in boiling water for 45 minutes. Add the onion and garlic and chillies and continue to cook until soft.

2. Drain the cooking liquid and reserve.

3. Blend the beans in a processor, using some of the cooking liquor to get them going.

4. Fold in the tomato purée. Adjust the consistency with a little more cooking liquid if necessary. Season once more. Allow to cool.

To serve: Serve with nachos, garnished with sliced lemon and a little paprika.

OTHER USEFUL DIPS

Hoisin, Soya and Plum Sauces

V

Hoisin, soya and plum sauces are the only sauces I use that I don't make myself, and the same is true at the restaurant. Soya, it could be argued, is not a proper sauce or dip, more a condiment. But the fact is we cannot make it ourselves and we do use it as a dip, especially with sushi.

Hoisin is a sweet, spicy, dark reddish-brown sauce with a thick consistency. It is made from fermented soya beans, garlic and spices. Again it is a little too complex for us to start making and always seems to taste good when we buy it.

Plum sauce is made from special *umeboshi* plums, chillies, vinegar, spices and sugar. It is a great dip and a useful friend at any party and especially when there is an oriental theme.

All three sauces are available from Chinese supermarkets and specialist grocery stores.

Apple and Pear Purée

V G *Serves 4–6*

1 oz (30 g) unsalted butter or vegan margarine
1 lb (450 g) Granny Smith apples, peeled, cored and cut into small chunks
1 lb (450 g) William pears, peeled, cored and cut into small chunks
½ tablespoon soft brown demerara sugar
1 teaspoon freshly grated ginger
Calvados or Poire Williams liqueur (optional)

Fruit purées are underestimated as an accompaniment to buffet food. Yet their simplicity and clean palates are often just what is needed to counterbalance a rich dish or to brighten up a bland one.

1. Melt the butter in a saucepan. Add the apples, pears, sugar and ginger. Cover with a lid and simmer gently until all the fruit is soft. Be careful not to let it burn.

2. Add a dash of Calvados or Poire Williams if you are using it.

3. Purée or push through a sieve.

Serving suggestion: This purée is excellent with Rösti (page 30), which are ideal buffet food, as well as roasts, croquettes and even onion bhajis.

Banana Raita

G *Serves 4*

1½ oz (40 g) butter
2 teaspoons black or yellow mustard seeds (or a mixture)
1 oz (30 g) fine desiccated coconut
8 fl oz (250 ml) Greek yoghurt
1 large ripe banana, chopped
1 tablespoon chopped coriander

Another good accompaniment to spicy dishes such as biriyani, samosas or onion bhajis, the piquancy of mustard being offset by the cool, healing properties of bananas and yoghurt. Spoon it over Stuffed Vine-leaves (page 139) for a real sensation.

1. Melt the butter and skim off any milk solids. When the butter is hot, add the mustard seeds and cover with a lid (the mustard seeds explode). Agitate the pan to prevent the seeds burning.

2. When the popping eases, add the coconut. Stir continuously until it has become golden brown.

3. Allow to cool briefly, then stir into the yoghurt with the banana.

Chill. Serve cold garnished with coriander.

VARIATION

Add halved and deseeded Muscat or other grapes with the banana.

SNACKS AND NIBBLES

No buffet is complete without a selection of snacks and nibbles and what could be better than making your own? You can also serve a selection of these homemade items at a drinks party.

Cheese Palmiers

Makes 40

9 oz (250 g) puff pastry (see page 221)
egg white to glaze
2 oz (50 g) Parmesan cheese, grated
2 oz (50 g) unsalted butter

Cheese Palmiers are light savoury pastries that are good on their own or served with dips. They are best eaten on the day they are made.

1. Roll out the pastry on a lightly floured surface into a rectangle measuring 12×8 in (30×20 cm) and approximately $\frac{1}{8}$ in (5 mm) thick.

2. Brush the pastry with egg white, then sprinkle with half the Parmesan cheese.

3. Fold the short edges in to meet in the centre. Brush with egg white and sprinkle on the remaining cheese.

4. Fold in half along the joining place to enclose the surface you have just sprinkled with Parmesan. Cover the pastry and chill for 20 minutes in the fridge or 5 minutes in the freezer. Heat the oven to 220°C/425°F/Gas Mark 7.

5. Cut into 40 thin slices.

6. Use the butter to grease a baking tray well. Lay the Palmiers in the buttered tray about 2 in (5 cm) apart.

7. Bake for 7–10 minutes, then turn the Palmiers over and bake for a further 5 minutes.

8. Transfer to a wire rack to cool.

To serve: Serve on their own or with a firm dip or pâté piped onto them. Aubergine Dip (page 154) or Stilton and Walnut Pâté (page 197) would be good. Garnish as appropriate.

Tomato and Cheese Straws

Makes 40

13 oz (375 g) puff pastry (see page 221)

3 tablespoons fresh tomato purée (see page 223)

fine sea salt and freshly ground black pepper

3 teaspoons paprika

a little milk for brushing

3 tablespoons freshly grated Pecorino or Parmesan cheese

These are a delicious variation on an ever-popular theme. They may be frozen prior to baking and cooked on the day of the party.

1. Roll out the pastry on a lightly floured surface to a rectangle 14 × 16 in (35 × 40 cm). Trim the edges.

2. Spread the tomato purée over the pastry to form a thin coating. Season with pepper and salt and sprinkle with paprika.

3. Fold the pastry in half widthwise.

4. Brush with milk, then sprinkle with the Pecorino or Parmesan.

5. Fold in half again and roll out to its original size.

6. Cut into 20 × 1 in (2.5 cm) strips lengthwise. Twist gently, then cut in half. Place on lightly greased baking sheets and leave to rest in a cool place for 20 minutes. Heat the oven to 220°C/425°F/Gas Mark 7.

7. Bake for 10 to 12 minutes or until the pastry is crisp and golden.

Spicy Nuts, Seeds and Croutons

Little bowls of spicy, crunchy things are what everyone looks for when they arrive at a party.

⊻ Ǥ *Tamari Roast Sunflower Seeds* Choose how many seeds you want to roast. Choose a heavy-bottomed frying pan. Place over a medium heat, then add the sunflower seeds. Roast until all the sunflower seeds are very hot. Pour in the tamari and there should be an immediate 'Whoosh' as the thirsty sunflower seeds soak up the tamari very quickly. This will not work unless the sunflower seeds are very hot. Peanuts roasted like this are excellent too.

V G **Spicy Nuts** Choose your favourite nuts. Succulent macadamia, cashews, hazels and almonds are good. Cook them in oil with curry powder for Curried Nuts or chilli powder (or Sambal Olek, page 227) for Chilli Nuts. Make sure all the nuts are well coated in the seasoning. For Garlic Nuts use garlic powder as it will flavour the nuts more easily than fresh.

V **Garlic Croutons** Either cut up stale bread and fry in butter or vegan margarine with garlic until crisp, or coat slices of bread with garlic oil (page 224), cut into pieces and toast in the oven until crisp.

Home-made Crisps

V G

1 lb (450 g) potatoes, thinly sliced
  on a mandolin
oil for deep frying

Crisps can only be attempted by those of you with an electric deep fryer. It's too dangerous to do it the old-fashioned way, as the oil must be very hot. Don't limit yourself to ordinary potatoes, though – try sweet potatoes too. Always drain well on absorbent paper and sprinkle with salt before serving. Crisps are cut best with a fine mandolin.

All home-made crisps are best made at the last moment. Without the benefits of modern manufacturing techniques real ones tend to go a bit soggy if not eaten immediately. Choose waxy potatoes.

1. Heat the oil to 185°C/365°F.

2. Fry the potato slices, making sure they don't stick together.

3. Sprinkle with salt and drain on kitchen paper.

VARIATION

• Thin slices of courgette and aubergine are good cooked like this but must be coated in some sort of batter first. The simplest is just to dip them in milk and seasoned flour.

• Sprinkle with Parmesan cheese immediately.

BUFFET SALADS

If you are going to provide your guests with a fork then salads not only become feasible, but in fact will probably save you a lot of time and energy. A good salad is almost a meal in itself.

Salads are obviously affected more than most other dishes by the season. It's not that you can't buy the ingredients year round, it's that ingredients eaten raw must be of the highest quality. Quite often, out of season they're not!

I've chosen just five recipes to illustrate different aspects of salad-making.

Roasted Red Pepper and Pasta Salad

[V] *Serves 6*

2 red peppers, halved, deseeded, white ribs removed
1 yellow pepper, halved, deseeded, white ribs removed
6 tomatoes
2 cloves garlic, crushed or minced
6 tablespoons virgin olive oil
2 tablespoons white wine vinegar
fine sea salt and freshly ground black pepper
6 basil leaves, crushed
1 red onion, finely sliced
8 oz (225 g) fusilli pasta
4 oz (100 g) white bread, cut into cubes
2 tablespoons vegetable oil for frying
6 oz (175 g) soft goat's cheese

This is a great combination of flavours and textures – the sweet succulent red pepper contrasts with the tart dryness of the goat's cheese against a neutral backdrop of pasta.

1. Roast the peppers under a hot grill until the skin is blistering. Remove from the heat and allow to cool, then cut into diamonds.

2. Cut the tomatoes into strips and add to the peppers.

3. Blend the garlic, olive oil, vinegar, salt and pepper in a liquidiser until thick. Then add to the pepper mixture with the basil.

4. Cook the pasta in plenty of boiling salted water until just cooked (*al dente*).

5. While the pasta is cooking, fry the bread cubes in hot oil until golden.

6. Toss the drained pasta with the rest of the salad while still hot. Allow to cool.

7. Crumble in the goat's cheese and finally add the fried bread cubes. Adjust the seasoning.

New Season Salad

V G *Serves 4–6*

8 oz (225 g) Jersey Royal potatoes (or similar), washed

4 fl oz (120 ml) garlic oil (see page 224)

6 baby carrots, washed and trimmed but feathery green leaves left on

4 oz (100 g) french beans, topped, tailed and halved

4 oz (100 g) asparagus sprue, tips removed from stems, stems pared

1 small head cauliflower, cut into florets

1 yellow pepper, deseeded and cut into strips

2 oz (50 g) mangetout

1 tablespoon chopped coriander leaves

1 tablespoon chopped chives

1 tablespoon chopped basil

1 tablespoon chopped mint

4 fl oz (120 ml) lemon juice

Make this salad in May when new baby vegetables are available. Use only the youngest, freshest produce you can and if you can't get one ingredient, don't worry.

1. Cook the new potatoes until just tender then, while still hot, plunge them into the garlic oil.

2. Cook the carrots, beans, asparagus stems and cauliflower until just *al dente*. Cool with cold water, drain and add to potatoes.

3. Cook the asparagus tips, mangetout and pepper briefly in boiling salted water (or steam). Add to the other vegetables.

4. Stir in the herbs and some seasoning, cover and chill.

5. Just before serving add the lemon juice.

Minted Beetroot and Celeriac Salad

This one's bound to go down someone's dress or tie, but it'll be because they were trying to eat it too quickly. Beetroots, like most vegetables, are best in the summer. Choose small undamaged ones in the winter.

Celeriac is a very off-putting looking vegetable but has a quite unique nutty celery flavour. Both vegetables can be used raw in other salads though in this salad they must be cooked. Celeriac will not need as much cooking as beetroot. Once peeled, keep immersed in water with a little lemon juice.

163

V G *Serves 6*

6 small beetroots
2 medium celeriacs (peeled)
2 tablespoons walnut oil
1 tablespoon raspberry vinegar
4 cloves garlic, crushed or minced
4 oz (100 g) mint leaves, chopped
   (reserve 2 sprigs for garnish)
4 oz (100 g) Devonshire blue cheese
   (optional)

1. Cook the beets and celeriac separately by boiling them in salted water. The beets must be tender, the celeriac *al dente*. Drain the beets and remove their skins.

2. Slice the beetroots in half lengthways, then into thin slices. Cut the celeriac into similar sized slices. Place in a bowl.

3. Add the oil, vinegar, garlic and chopped mint. Cover and refrigerate overnight.

4. If liked, garnish with blue cheese and mint sprigs to serve.

Tuscan Rice Salad

V G *Serves 6*

12 oz (325 g) basmati rice or
   basmati wild rice mixture
6 tablespoons olive oil
4 fl oz (120 ml) freshly squeezed
   lemon or lime juice
2 cloves garlic, crushed or chopped
1 tablespoon runny honey or maple
   syrup
fine sea salt and freshly ground black
   pepper
1 medium red onion, finely chopped
2 oranges, peeled and sectioned,
   then cut again into quarters
4 oz (100 g) fresh peas
2 oz (50 g) currants
1 small yellow pepper, diced
1 small red pepper, diced
1 tablespoon chopped parsley
1 tablespoon chopped chives
1 tablespoon chopped mint
few small seedless grapes and toasted
   cashew nuts for garnish

Rice salads are almost unanimously enjoyed and so are a good bet at a large party where there are bound to be many different tastes. The secret with any rice salad is to dress it while it is still warm.

1. Cover the rice with $2\frac{1}{4}$ pints (1.3 l) of cold salted water. Bring to the boil and simmer, covered, for 30 minutes. Remove the lid and continue to cook until all the water is absorbed and the rice is tender. If you wish, add the squeezed lemon skins to the water in which you cook the rice. Discard the lemon skins when the rice is cooked.

2. Mix the oil, lemon or lime juice, garlic and honey or maple syrup together to make a dressing.

3. Add the rice to the dressing. Allow to cool.

4. Add the rest of the ingredients and chill well.

5. Garnish with grapes and cashew nuts before serving.

To serve: Serve in an attractive salad bowl or on a platter decorated with leaves and the garnish.

Chapter six

PICNICS AND BARBECUES

Most of the dishes described in the chapter on buffets are eminently suitable for picnics and barbecues. The deciding factor is transportability, as far as picnics go, and grillability, as far as the barbecue is concerned. Picnics and barbecues are, of course, quite different events, common only in the fact that they are usually held outside in the summer.

I have had a few wonderful barbecue parties myself in mid-winter, surrounded by snow and temperatures well below zero. These are perfect conditions for the cook who would otherwise sweat buckets over the grill – but what of the guests? Well, they were all sitting snug and warm inside watching me perform through the patio window.

Food for friends is beside the sea, and over the years we have often been asked to provide picnics for the beach, picnics for the opera interval at Glyndebourne, as well as food for *alfresco* lunches in the wonderful Sussex countryside.

SAVOURY PICNIC FOOD

Picnic sandwiches and rolls

There are endless sandwich and roll fillings. I think it's nice to let the filling suit the bread.

Fillings for organic wholewheat bread

1. Fill with cream cheese mixed with a little chopped spring onion.

2. Cream cheese mixed with mashed banana, lemon juice, a few raisins and some chopped roasted nuts.

3. Cream cheese with fresh herbs like parsley, chives, tarragon, dill and oregano.

4. Peppers, cucumbers, tomatoes, salad leaves, watercress and radish all make exciting vegetable additions to cream cheese.

5. Try boiled or scrambled eggs mashed with home-made mayonnaise. Liven it up with a little dry mustard, curry paste, chilli powder or Sambal Olek (page 227). Again add chopped spring onions, chives, cress, cucumber or any other vegetable that catches your fancy.

6. Nut and seed butters make good fillings for wholewheat sandwiches. Easily available are peanut, cashew, sesame and sunflower butters. They do tend to be a little dry, so add salad or fruit (grapes are good) to liven things up.

Fillings for organic unbleached white bread
This lovely soft bread is ideal for pâté and cheese. Try Stilton and Walnut (page 197) or Hazelnut (page 168) for a change.

Fillings for walnut bread

Cheese is also excellent in this bread. Use a good mature vegetarian cheese with a home-made pickle or chutney such as the recipe on page 226.

Blue cheese is also an excellent filling for walnut bread. Vegetarian Stilton is still a bit difficult to find but good old Devonshire Blue is a wonderful alternative, probably having more in common with Dolcelatte than crumbly Blue Stilton. On its own it is too harsh and dry in a sandwich, so either add a salad vegetable or two or blend it with mayonnaise and yoghurt. Cold roasted red and green peppers make excellent additions to blue cheese sandwiches.

Tip: Wrap potentially soggy sandwiches in outer lettuce leaves then clingfilm.

Fillings for pitta or pocket breads

Pitta, of course, are dying to be filled with something. On a picnic they would be filled with salad and then wrapped with clingfilm. Alternatively add a pâté like Chickpea and Olive Tapenade (page 155) or Aubergine Dip (page 154).

Olive breads

Breads like *focaccia* or *ciabatta* are great on their own but do try filling them. Ripe tomatoes, Mozzarella, a good thick vinaigrette made with olive oil and a little fresh oregano or basil are good. If you are vegan, why not try alternating slices of ripe avocado with sweet William pears and perhaps a little orange, all topped off with a racy lemon vinaigrette? Another favourite at the restaurant is Pan Bagna. For this we make large rolls with olive bread dough, slice off the top and hollow out the insides. Into the cavity stuff a well-dressed salad of onion, lettuce, fresh tomato, sun-dried tomatoes, cucumber, olives and toasted pine nuts. Chunks of Mozzarella, or fried cubes of marinated tofu, would be good too. Then replace the lid, wrap in clingfilm and enjoy later on. Unlike many sandwiches, Pan Bagna will actually improve with age so long as it's not stored in a warm place.

V G Edible bowls

While salads are good warm-weather food, sometimes it's not practical to take them on picnics. But what if they were stored in edible bowls? A neat and hassle-free way to take salads with you is simply to store them inside other vegetables.

Peppers are the obvious choice, but equally good would be tomatoes or crisp lettuce leaves. They must be wrapped for transportation so bear that in mind when choosing your receptacle – you wouldn't want it to wilt on you. Grain or pasta salads suit this mode of transportation best but do try any salad that you feel is appropriate.

Tomatoes and peppers should be washed and dried. Slice off the stalk end and remove the seeds and any unnecessary flesh. You now have a receptacle for your salad. Spoon it in, replace the stalk end and wrap in clingfilm.

Choose large crisp leaves of lettuce (Webbs are best), fill with salad, fold over and wrap firmly with clingfilm. These delicate parcels are not suited to long periods of incarceration in a picnic box.

Red and Green Pepper Terrine

G   *Serves 8*

2 red peppers, halved and deseeded
2 green peppers, halved and
   deseeded
1 tablespoon olive oil
4 cloves garlic, crushed
1 large onion, finely sliced
fine sea salt and freshly ground black
   pepper
$\frac{1}{2}$ pint (275 ml) milk
5 free-range egg yolks
$\frac{1}{2}$ pint (275 ml) double cream
1 teaspoon Sambal Olek (page 227)
3 teaspoons agar-agar

Pâtés and terrines are of course ideal to take on a picnic and serve with fresh bread or good biscuits. This and the following recipe not only look good but taste good too.

1. Roast the peppers in a hot oven or under a grill until they are blistered and blackened all over. Place in cold water, remove the skin and cut into strips.

2. Heat half the oil in a saucepan and cook the green peppers with half the garlic and onion until softening. Allow to cool. While it is cooling repeat the process with the red peppers and the remaining oil, garlic and onion. Purée each colour of pepper separately in the food processor and push through a sieve. Season with salt and pepper.

3. Put the milk into a saucepan and bring to the boil. While you're waiting, beat the egg yolks together. When the milk is very hot, pour it onto the egg yolks, whisking continuously. When the eggs are completely absorbed return the mixture to the saucepan and continue to heat gently until the custard has a coating consistency. Do NOT allow it to boil. Divide it equally between the two purées. Allow them to cool a little.

4. Beat the cream a little and mix it with the Sambal Olek. Fold half the cream into each custard.

5. Put $\frac{1}{4}$ pint (150 ml) of water into a saucepan, then add the agar-agar and set aside for 5 minutes. Lightly oil a 2-pint (1.1 l) terrine mould.

6. Heat the water and agar-agar mix gently until it is totally dissolved (up to 20 minutes). Now boil it for 3 minutes before adding to the two custards. Pour the red pepper custard in first and then the green. Refrigerate until set.

7. To turn the terrine out, dip the mould into hot water. For carrying to a picnic it is wise to then return it to the mould and seal it with clingfilm for transportation.

Chickpea and Coriander Pâté

V G *Serves 8*

6 oz (175 g) dried chickpeas or a
    12 oz (325 g) can
1 teaspoon salt
4 tablespoons lemon juice
2 tablespoons virgin olive oil
1 large Spanish onion, chopped
2 oz (50 g) fresh coriander, chopped
2 cloves garlic, chopped or crushed

This is an ideal pâté to take on a picnic. You can spread it on bread or dip into it with raw or marinated vegetables. It'll keep well in transportation too.

1. Cover the chickpeas in plenty of salted water and bring to the boil. Turn off the heat and allow to soak overnight.

2. If necessary, add more water, then bring back to the boil and simmer until tender – up to 2 hours.

3. Drain and while still hot add the lemon juice and olive oil.

4. Purée in a food processor until thick and creamy – if too dry add more olive oil. Turn into a bowl and stir in the chopped onion, coriander and garlic.

Hazelnut Pâté

V G *Serves 8*

1 bunch spring onions, chopped and
    cooked in a little butter
2 oz (50 g) roasted hazelnuts
2 hard-boiled eggs (vegans can use
    tofu)
1 tablespoon white wine
10 oz (275 g) french beans, cooked
fine sea salt and freshly ground black
    pepper
1 pinch nutmeg
2 tablespoons mayonnaise (vegans
    can use Butterbean Mayonnaise –
    see page 151)

This is very quick to make and it's a great sandwich filling.

1. Combine all the ingredients except the mayonnaise in a blender. Add more wine if too stiff.

2. Transfer to a bowl and fold in the mayonnaise. Adjust the seasoning, then chill.

Spinach and Carrot Roulade

G *Serves 6*

4 oz (100 g) spinach
4 oz (100 g) carrots
4 eggs, separated
pinch nutmeg
fine sea salt and finely ground black
    pepper

For the filling
4 oz (100 g) cream cheese
2 tablespoons sour cream
6 spring onions, finely sliced
$\frac{1}{2}$ tablespoon chopped fresh parsley
$\frac{1}{2}$ tablespoon fresh thyme
grated rind of $\frac{1}{2}$ lemon
pinch nutmeg
fine sea salt and finely ground black
    pepper

The nice thing about roulades is that they not only taste good, but look good too, and are lighter than many other vegetarian snacks. They are ideal for picnics or buffets, being easy to eat. For a picnic, transport the roulade whole and slice it up when you get there.

1. Heat oven to 190°C/375°F/Gas Mark 5. Line a roasting tin with greaseproof paper and lightly oil it.

2. Cook the spinach in a tiny amount of boiling water until tender. Drain and cool, then whizz in a food processor with 2 egg yolks. Season with salt, pepper and nutmeg.

3. Cook the carrots in water until nearly tender. Drain and place in a mixing bowl with the rest of the egg yolks and the spinach mixture.

4. Whisk the egg whites until they form peaks and gently fold into the carrot and spinach mixture.

5. Pour this mixture into the lined tin and spread it flat. Bake for 10–12 minutes or until dry to touch.

6. While it's in the oven, make the filling by combining the ingredients.

7. Turn the roulade out onto greaseproof paper, trim the edges and spread with the filling. Roll it up.

Raw and Marinated Vegetables

[V] [G] *Enough for 6*

1 lb (450 g) small globe artichokes
1 large aubergine
3 or 4 small courgettes
1 large pepper
olive oil

The marinade
1 large onion, chopped
1 carrot, finely diced
juice of 1 lemon
1 large glass white wine vinegar
   (8 fl oz/250 ml)
$\frac{1}{2}$ glass white wine
10 whole peppercorns
6 cloves garlic, peeled and halved
1 tablespoon fresh or freeze-dried
   tarragon leaves
1 bay leaf
3 sprigs parsley
1 pint (600 ml) water

No picnic would be complete without a selection of crisp raw vegetables – but why not take along some marinated ones for a change? After all, pickled onions and gherkins are always popular, so why not try a few of their marinated cousins? You can transport them still in their marinade in large screw-top jars.

I've chosen a combination of baby artichokes – so small they're nearly all heart and very little choke – red peppers, courgettes and aubergines. But any of your favourite vegetables can be treated in the same way. Remember always to just cook the vegetables and add them to a hot marinade so they can soak up the juices.

1. First of all prepare the vegetables. Trim the artichokes with a pair of scissors. Trim the ends of the courgettes and aubergines and cut into quarters lengthways. The aubergine may need to be cut into eighths, depending on its size. Try to get the aubergine pieces roughly matching in size. Spread the aubergine pieces out on a baking tray and sprinkle with salt. Leave them for 30 minutes to release any bitter juices. Cut the pepper into sixths and deseed. Now prepare the marinade.

2. Combine all the ingredients for the marinade in a saucepan. Add the artichokes and boil rapidly for 40 minutes, then remove the artichokes and reduce the liquid by half.

3. While the marinade is reducing and the artichokes are cooking, wash and dry the aubergine and courgettes. Pop the peppers into a hot oven until they are black and blistering. Remove, cool and peel. Sauté the aubergine and courgettes in a little olive oil, bearing in mind that the aubergine will take longer to cook.

4. When all the vegetables are ready put them in a plastic container and cover them with the hot marinade and artichoke. Allow to cool, then store in the fridge for at least 2 days. Make sure the marinade is at room temperature before you eat the vegetables.

Rellenos

V Makes 6

The filling

1 tablespoon vegetable oil

1 large onion, chopped

2 tablespoons chopped fresh
coriander

3 cloves garlic, crushed

1 teaspoon ground coriander

1 teaspoon ground cumin

$\frac{1}{2}$ teaspoon chilli powder or 1 fresh
chilli, chopped

14 oz (400 g) red kidney beans, well
cooked

3 tablespoons fresh tomato purée
(see page 223)

1 tablespoon soya sauce

grated cheese or mashed avocado
(optional)

The wrapping

6 sheets filo pastry

2 oz (50 g) butter or vegan
margarine, melted

I called these Rellenos simply because they were rolled, and later discovered the Mexicans had a different version. Still the name has stuck and I must apologise in advance to all those lovers of South American food. I'm sure you'll find this version equally delicious. Make sure the beans are really well cooked.

1. Heat the oil in a frying pan or wok and sauté the onion with the garlic, coriander, cumin and chilli until the onion is soft.

2. Put the kidney beans into a blender with the onion mixture, tomato purée and soya sauce. Zap to a rough purée. Alternatively mash with a potato masher. Put to one side and allow to cool.

3. Heat the oven to 200°C/400°F/Gas Mark 6.

4. Lay a sheet of filo pastry on the work surface and brush with melted butter or margarine. Fold in half lengthwise so that now you have a double thickness. Brush again with melted butter.

5. Spoon one-sixth of the bean mixture onto one end of the pastry. Sprinkle with grated cheese or spread on a little avocado. Fold the sides in and then roll up.

6. Brush with more butter.

7. Repeat this process with the other five sheets of filo pastry.

8. Lay the six Rellenos on a baking sheet with the join underneath. Bake for 20–25 minutes or until golden brown. Serve hot or cold.

Note: If making Rellenos for children, reduce the spices in the bean mix.

Arundel Tarts

Makes 12

1 lb (450 g) organic wholewheat
   shortcrust pastry (see page 218)

For the mushroom pâté

1 oz (30 g) butter or 1 tablespoon
   vegetable oil
1 large onion or shallot, chopped
1 teaspoon dried sage
8 oz (225 g) flat mushrooms,
   chopped
1 glass white wine
3 oz (75 g) breadcrumbs
salt and pepper to taste
soya sauce

For the topping

8 oz (225 g) grated cheese
4 fl oz (120 ml) mayonnaise or
   cream
12 oz (325 g) potatoes, cooked and
   sliced
paprika

Alongside your carefully prepared sandwich you'll probably want to take some savoury pastry on your picnic. Here's one with real mouth-feel.

1. Heat the oven to 180°C/350°F/Gas Mark 4.

2. Roll out the pastry and using a fluted cutter line 12 well greased 4 in (10 cm) tartlet tins.

3. Leave the pastry in the fridge while you prepare the mushroom pâté.

4. Melt the butter or heat the oil in a saucepan, add the onions or shallots and sage and sauté until the onions are softening.

5. Add the mushrooms and continue to cook until they are soft.

6. Pour in the white wine and briefly reduce before adding the breadcrumbs.

7. Purée in a blender and adjust the seasoning with salt, pepper and soya sauce.

8. Beat the grated cheese and mayonnaise or cream together and season.

9. Put a spoon of mushroom pâté into each tartlet. Cover neatly with overlapping slices of cooked potato. Finally top with the grated cheese mixture and sprinkle with a little paprika.

10. Bake in the oven for 15 minutes or until the pastry is cooked and the cheese is golden brown.

Sussex Pasties

V *Makes 6 large or 12 small*

1 tablespoon vegetable oil
2 leeks, finely sliced
1 medium carrot, finely diced
pinch cayenne (optional)
pinch curry powder (optional)
1 teaspoon thyme
8 oz (225 g) potato, cooked and
    finely diced
2 oz (50 g) frozen peas (optional)
1 quantity mushroom pâté (see
    Arundel Tart Recipe, page 172)
salt and freshly ground black pepper
1 lb (450 g) puff pastry (see page
    221) made with hard vegan
    margarine

These are an excellent vegan alternative to Arundel Tarts (page 172). They're good hot too.

1. Heat the oven to 220°C/425°F/Gas Mark 7.

2. Heat the oil in a pan. Add the leeks, carrot, spices and thyme. Stir-fry until the carrot is starting to soften. Throw in the potato and peas and cook for a further 4 minutes.

3. Stir in the mushroom pâté. Mix well and adjust the seasoning. Put to one side and allow to cool, then refrigerate.

4. When the filling is cold, roll out the pastry then cut out 6 × 5 in (12.5 cm) circles or 12 × 3 in (7.5 cm) circles, using a plain cutter.

5. Spoon enough of the filling onto the centre of each pastry circle. Brush a little soya milk around the edges of the pastry before bringing them together to form a traditional pasty shape. Seal the edges with a pastry crimp or with your fingers. Brush the outside of the pasties with soya milk, then bake in the oven for 10–15 minutes or until the pastry has cooked.

Tomato Chutney

V **G** *Makes 2½ pints (1.5l)*

8 oz (225 g) shallots, chopped
6 oz (175 g) soft dark sugar
5 large cloves garlic, crushed
¼ teaspoon ground cloves
¼ teaspoon grated nutmeg
1 teaspoon chilli powder
1 tablespoon coriander seeds
1 tablespoon black mustard seeds
3 tablespoons grated fresh ginger
6 tablespoons white wine vinegar
2¼ lb (1 kg) tomatoes, cut into
    chunks
fine sea salt and pepper

Here's a recipe for chutney that you can make in early autumn when tomatoes are fresh, ripe and cheap. Use plum tomatoes if you can.

1. Put all the ingredients, except 1 tablespoon of vinegar and the tomatoes, into a large preserving pan.

2. Bring to the boil and simmer for 45 minutes. If the mixture becomes a bit dry add a little water.

3. Add the tomatoes. Bring back to the boil and continue to cook gently until the mixture has cooked down to a dry soft mushy texture – about another 40 minutes.

4. Season and add the rest of the vinegar before bottling.

PICNIC DESSERTS

For dessert, my obvious choice would be whole fresh fruit: grapes, nectarines, apples, oranges, peaches, pears, plums, strawberries, raspberries, melons and bananas all come to mind. They're easy to transport, refreshing and universally popular. You could even take a fresh fruit salad packed in a large sculpted watermelon, wrapped in clingfilm and transported in an ice bag.

For an adult picnic, marinate chunks of Charentais melon in Pineau de Charente, watermelon in Tequila or fresh berries in Pernod.

Inevitably, however, many guests will want something more substantial to get their teeth into. Anything with cream and chocolate is obviously out of the question. The best sweets are easy to eat with your fingers, ready sliced and wrapped in a serviette or clingfilm. Here are a few from our repertoire.

Cinnamon Shortbread

Makes 12 fingers

8 oz (225 g) unbleached plain white flour

4 oz (100 g) rice flour

1 teaspoon ground cinnamon

4 oz (100 g) vanilla sugar (sugar in which a vanilla pod has been kept)

8 oz (225 g) soft salted butter

Cinnamon Shortbread is great in its own right, especially with a nice cup of tea. But you can also use it to make an impromptu dessert with the addition of some fresh berries marinated in Pernod or Kirsch.

1. Preheat the oven to 150°C/300°F/Gas Mark 2.

2. Sift the flours and cinnamon into a bowl and add the sugar. Work in the butter with your fingertips until it forms a dough. Knead it gently but thoroughly.

3. Grease and flour a 8 × 10 in (20 × 25 cm) tin, then pack with the shortbread dough.

4. Bake in the preheated oven for about 1 hour. When cooked, leave to cool and sprinkle with more of the vanilla sugar. Cut it into fingers before it is completely cool.

VARIATION

Add 2 oz (50 g) of your favourite ground nuts to this mixture for a nutty shortbread, and flavour with lemon, lime or orange zest.

Spicy Apple Cake

V *Makes 1 × 9½ in (24 cm) cake, enough for 16 slices*

The apple purée

1½ lb (675 g) cooking apples, peeled, cored and chopped
4 fl oz (120 ml) maple syrup
¼ pint (150 ml) water

The cake mixture

4 oz (100 g) lexia raisins
10 oz (275 g) wholewheat pastry flour
½ teaspoon ground cinnamon
½ teaspoon ground ginger
½ teaspoon ground cloves
1 teaspoon baking powder
pinch of salt
4 fl oz (120 ml) soya oil
juice and zest of 1 lemon

This is an extremely nice, moist and fruity cake that has the bonus of containing no eggs or refined sugar.

1. Cook the apples with the syrup and water until soft. Mash with a potato masher to form a thick purée.

2. Heat the oven to 170°C/325°F/Gas Mark 3. Grease a 9½ in (24 cm) springform cake tin.

3. Combine the raisins and all the dry ingredients.

4. Add the soya oil and lemon juice to the apple purée and blend in a food processor.

5. Fold the purée into the dry ingredients. Tip into the prepared cake tin.

6. Bake for 1 hour 15 minutes or until a skewer inserted in the centre comes out clean.

7. Allow to cool before removing from the tin.

Peach Oaties

V *Makes 18*

5 oz (150 g) wholemeal flour
5 oz (150 g) regular oats
5 oz (150 g) demerara sugar
1 teaspoon baking powder
6 oz (175 g) butter or vegan margarine
6 oz (175 g) no-soak dried peaches, chopped

These and their variations have always been a great favourite at the restaurant. If you can't buy no-soak peaches use dried peaches reconstituted by poaching in water, then puréeing.

1. Heat the oven to 180°C/350°F/Gas Mark 4. Prepare a baking tin about 14 × 10 × 1½ in (35 × 25 × 3 cm) by lightly greasing it.

2. Mix the flour, oats, sugar and baking powder together. Then rub in the butter until it resembles breadcrumbs.

3. Spread half the mixture over the base of the prepared tin. Spread the peaches over this layer. Top with the remaining crumb mixture and press down well.

4. Bake for 25–30 minutes until golden brown. Allow to cool in the tin for about 1 hour.

VARIATION

Substitute dates, apricots, figs or nectarines for the peaches.

DRINKS FOR THE PICNIC

The best thing about taking drinks on a picnic is that invariably you don't have to bring them back – at least not externally. Obviously the type of drinks you take will be determined by the time of year, the occasion and who exactly you are taking. Coffee or tea can be taken hot or iced in vacuum flasks (remember never to add milk to tea in the flask), while the rest of the drinks must reside in the cool bag – except the red wine of course.

Alcoholic and non-alcoholic fizzes

The most famous of these is Bucks Fizz (fresh orange juice and champagne) but the same principle can apply to almost any soft succulent fruit. Use sweet ripe fruits like peaches, nectarines, strawberries, raspberries and mangoes. Purée them with a little sugar or honey to adjust their sweetness, pass through a fine sieve and then store in a screw-top jar in your cool bag. On the picnic simply dilute with cold sparkling wine or soda water to make a lovely refreshing drink for adults and children alike. Some children may prefer the addition of apple juice to soda.

Wine

On chilly days take mulled wine in a vacuum flask as an alternative to tea, coffee or chocolate, but on perfect picnic days take chilled whites and rosés, still or sparkling. Red wine has a terrifically somnolent effect which does not always ensure the picnic goes with a swing.

Children may like to feel grown up and drink a non-alcoholic sparkling grape drink. These are eminently suitable for the driver too. It is my experience that children will greatly appreciate drinks which are a little bit special, as opposed to run of the mill drinks like Coke or bought lemonade.

Barbecues

For a lot of vegetarians this is the one chance they get to experience a different form of cooking. All too often vegetarian food is baked, fried, boiled or steamed. Grilling rarely seems to get a look in, let alone grilling over charcoal.

Cooking over wood is probably the oldest way of cooking in the world, very satisfying to do and even more satisfying to eat the end results. You can flavour the food by adding hickory chips or branches of rosemary to your fire. So, vegetarians, here it is at last – the complete vegetarian barbecue, with tips about how to run it too.

Barbecue Tips

1. Ensure you have plenty of charcoal and an odourless firing liquid. There's nothing worse than the smell and taste of meths or paraffin in the end result.

2. Keep the charcoal dry. It easily absorbs moisture.

3. To light the barbecue, spread the charcoal, one layer deep, over the entire base of the barbecue. Then heap more coals up in a pyramid in the centre. Light this and when it has a light coating of ash (30–40 minutes), spread it into one layer again and begin to cook.

4. Allow up to 50 minutes for the barbecue to light and achieve the right temperature.

5. Oil the grill well before placing anything on it, otherwise you will leave the best bits stuck to the grill.

6. When turning the food on the grill take the opportunity to baste it in oil or marinade.

7. The cooking time will depend on the thickness of the food, the quantity on the grill, the amount of charcoal burning, the proximity of the grill to the coals and even the weather.

8. Cook the larger items first, moving them to the edges of the grill when almost done to leave space for faster-cooking items.

While guests are arriving and the cooking is commencing, provide some tasty nibbles and dips, such as guacamole (page 178), for people to snack on with their drinks.

All the recipes in the following section are for 8 people.

Guacamole with Corn Chips

Serves 8

flesh of 4 ripe avocados, mashed
juice of 2 lemons
6 cloves garlic, chopped or crushed
1 red pepper, diced finely
1 bunch spring onions, finely
   chopped
$\frac{1}{2}$ cucumber, finely diced
2 tomatoes, skinned, deseeded and
   diced
$\frac{1}{2}$ teaspoon chilli powder
fine sea salt and ground black pepper
$\frac{1}{2}$ pint (275 ml) sour cream, yoghurt,
   mayonnaise or crème fraîche

For the corn chips
24 × 6 in (15 cm) corn tortillas, cut
   into quarters
corn oil for frying

Let your guests tuck into this while they wait for their barbecued food.

1. Mix the dip ingredients together, adjust the seasoning and refrigerate.

2. For the corn chips, heat $\frac{1}{2}$ in (1 cm) of corn oil in a frying pan and fry the corn tortillas in relays until crisp and golden. Drain on kitchen paper and season. If possible serve warm with the guacamole.

| V | G | *Serves 8*

1 large onion, roasted in tinfoil until
   soft
1 large red pepper, roasted in the
   oven until black and soft
$\frac{1}{2}$ teaspoon ground ginger
$\frac{1}{2}$ tablespoon Sambal Olek (page
   227)
1 tablespoon vegetarian
   Worcestershire sauce
2 tablespoons demerara sugar
1 tablespoon molasses
2 tablespoons white wine vinegar
3 tablespoons fresh tomato purée
   (see page 223)
1 teaspoon soya sauce
4 cloves garlic, crushed

Barbecue Sauce for Vegeburgers

The vegeburgers can be prepared well in advance and frozen. Use the recipe for Friendly Burgers on page 117.

You will probably want to double the quantities at least. Find some good quality burger baps or bagels to serve the burgers in. And you must, simply must, make this Barbecue Sauce recipe. It's simply delicious.

1. Whizz everything together.

2. Keep at room temperature overnight before use.

Flavoured Butters

[V] [G] These are invaluable at barbecues, adding a brief taste sensation to whatever they are put on. All these butters are made using 8 oz (225 g) of unsalted butter or vegan margarine. Soften the butter, add the flavourings, then wrap it up in some greaseproof paper to form a sausage and freeze. Simply slice the butter from the end of the sausage when you want to use it.

Garlic Butter – 4 cloves of garlic (chopped), a little salt and a dash of lemon.

Herb Butter – 2 tablespoons chopped chives, 2 tablespoons fresh chopped parsley, 2 tablespoons chopped tarragon and 2 tablespoons fresh dill.

Lemon Butter – Juice and zest of $\frac{1}{2}$ lemon (equally good with limes and oranges).

Tomato Butter – Add 1 tablespoon of fresh tomato purée (see page 223).

Curry Butter – Add 1 tablespoon of curry paste.

Spicy Butter – Add $1\frac{1}{2}$ teaspoons paprika, $\frac{1}{2}$ teaspoon cayenne pepper, $\frac{1}{4}$ teaspoon black pepper and 2 teaspoons oregano.

Mustard Butter – Add 1 tablespoon dry English mustard and a little fresh tomato purée (see page 223).

Basil Butter – Add 4 tablespoons chopped fresh basil and a squeeze of lemon juice.

Flavoured Oils

[V] [G] Almost equally important are flavoured oils, of which the most important are garlic, chilli and herb. To produce these simple oils, heat 8 fl oz (250 ml) of virgin olive oil with 8 cloves of minced garlic for 4 minutes, or 4 fresh chillies or about 4 oz (100 g) of assorted fresh herbs. It's best to use these oils warm.

179

Marinades

In the earlier part of this chapter we looked at taking marinated vegetables on picnics. We cooked most of them first, then marinated them. For barbecues it is simply the other way round; we marinate them first before cooking them, the reason being that most vegetables contain very little fat or sugar and in order to be grilled successfully they must be encouraged to absorb some, otherwise they will simply shrivel up.

So the key to successful vegetarian or vegan barbecueing is to marinate what is going on the grill for as long as you can before cooking – 12 hours should be the minimum, 24–36 is ideal.

Let them marinate for 4 hours at room temperature before storing them in the fridge. If the marinade does not cover all the ingredients you will have to turn them every 2 hours to make sure they are evenly coated.

Marinades in general are extremely close relations to salad dressings. When your vegetables have finished their spell of duty in the marinade you can simply turn it into a vinaigrette. Here are some marinades to experiment with. The method in all cases but one is simply to whizz up before coating the vegetables. All except one are vegan, and all are gluten-free.

Each marinade makes enough to marinate sufficient vegetables to serve 8 people.

V G *Marinade 1* (very basic)

½ pint (275 ml) virgin olive oil
8 fl oz (250 ml) cider vinegar
6 cloves garlic, crushed
1 tablespoon oregano or
   2 teaspoons thyme, basil
   or marjoram
fine sea salt, to taste
freshly ground black pepper, to taste

V G *Marinade 2* (a slightly more oriental version)

8 fl oz (250 ml) olive oil
8 fl oz (250 ml) cider vinegar
6 tablespoons soya sauce
4 cloves garlic, crushed
1 tablespoon demerara sugar or
   honey
fine sea salt, to taste
freshly ground black pepper to taste
pinch of chilli powder

V G *Marinade 3* (a little more Caribbean)

4 fl oz (120 ml) olive oil
4 fl oz (120 ml) soya sauce
4 oz (100 g) demerara sugar
6 cloves garlic, crushed
5 tablespoons Dijon mustard
freshly ground black pepper, to taste
fine sea salt, to taste

V G *Marinade 4* (definitely for adults only)

4 tablespoons olive oil
1 tablespoon white wine vinegar
1 tablespoon vegetarian
  Worcestershire sauce
4 tablespoons tomato ketchup
1 medium onion, roughly chopped
3 cloves garlic, crushed
1 tablespoon molasses
freshly ground black pepper, to taste
fine sea salt, to taste

V G *Marinade 5* (very spicy)

4 tablespoons olive oil
½ pint (275 ml) red wine
grated zest and juice of 3 lemons
3 tablespoons demerara sugar
3 cloves garlic, crushed
1 medium onion, chopped
2 teaspoons each ground ginger, salt
  and ground coriander seeds
1 teaspoon each chilli powder,
  turmeric and mustard seeds
½ teaspoon each ground black pepper
  and ground cardamom

G *Yoghurt Marinade* – This is the one marinade which should not be whizzed but stirred. Marinate in the fridge only.

1 pint (600 ml) plain yoghurt
2 cloves garlic, minced or crushed
4 tablespoons finely chopped fresh
  mint
2 teaspoons finely chopped fresh
  coriander
2 tablespoons olive oil
1 fresh chilli, chopped
juice and zest of 1 lemon
1 tablespoon honey or sugar
1 bunch spring onions, chopped
1 teaspoon black mustard seeds,
  crushed
salt and pepper

Grilled Marinated Vegetables

V G *Serves 8*

1 large aubergine cut into 8 × ¾ in
  (1.5 cm) thick slices
4 courgettes, cut into halves
  lengthwise
2 red peppers, deseeded and cut into
  quarters lengthwise
8 baby artichokes, trimmed and
  pared (parboil if not tiny)
16 button mushrooms
1 recipe of your chosen marinade

Having chosen a suitable marinade, now it's just a question of what you choose to marinate in it. Here's a selection of vegetables for about 8 people.

1. Wash and prepare the vegetables. The aubergine slices are better if sprinkled with salt and left for 30 minutes to discharge any bitterness.

2. Make sure all the vegetables are dry before they go in your chosen marinade. Allow to marinate at room temperature for 4 hours before transferring to the fridge for a further 8 or more hours (see page 180).

3. When they are all suitably marinated, barbecue them on a hot barbecue but away from any extreme direct heat. Baste them with a little marinade as you cook, being careful to avoid flare-ups. Cook the aubergines first (they will take up to 6 minutes) followed by the courgettes, peppers, artichokes and mushrooms. Cook the courgettes and peppers cut side down for 2 minutes, then finish their cooking skin side down.

Marinated Vegetable Kebabs

Using the same ingredients as above, cut the vegetables into bite-sized pieces before marinating, then thread onto wooden or metal skewers. You could add a fresh cherry tomato or two for colour. Cherry tomatoes need no marinating.

To serve: Serve with hot rice or rice salad or in a pitta pocket with a little salad and a good thick dressing.

Barbecued Marinated Tofu

V G Tofu can be barbecued in a variety of ways but must always be marinated first. Bought tofu comes in rectangular 1 lb (450 g) blocks about 5 × 3 × 2 in (12.5 × 7.5 × 5 cm). If you are cooking on its own, slice the block in half lengthways, then through the centre three times to give 8 pieces about $2\frac{1}{2}$ in (6 cm) long, 3 in (7.5 cm) wide and $\frac{1}{2}$ in (1 cm) thick. Marinate the slices when cut. If you are cooking the tofu as part of a vegetable brochette, then cut it into cubes to match the vegetable sizes.

Tofu will take up to 8 minutes to cook; the thicker the slice the longer it will take.

I've taken a tip from my partner Jerry's Chinese wife Tammy. Before removing the tofu from the barbecue, she likes to brush it with a little mixture of lemon or lime juice, honey, oil and garlic. The contrasting flavours and added moistness of this last-minute addition make any brochette extra nice.

Corn on the Cob with Spicy Butter

[V]   *Serves 8*

4 large or 8 small corn on the cob
chilli oil (see page 179)
lemon wedges
spicy butter (see page 179)

I recommend only half a large corn on the cob or 1 small one per person, to leave room for other dishes on the menu. Make sure the cobs you buy have their husks intact and in place.

1. Carefully peel back the corn husks and remove all the threadlike strands.

2. If possible, brush the exposed corn with some chilli oil before carefully replacing the husks.

3. Cook the corn over the hottest place on the barbecue, turning frequently until the outer husk is blackening – usually 15–20 minutes.

4. Remove from the heat and as soon as possible strip the husks off and cut in half.

5. Present to your guests with a wedge of lemon and a chunk of spicy butter. Encourage them to squeeze the lemon over the corn cob first, then to smear it in the butter.

Filled Baked Potatoes

G *Serves 8*

4 large baking potatoes
$\frac{1}{2}$ pint (275 ml) sour cream
2 bunches spring onions, chopped
1 bunch fresh chives
1 teaspoon cayenne pepper
2 tablespoons chopped parsley
fine sea salt and ground black pepper

Everyone's favourite – so prepare plenty.

1. Bake the potatoes in the oven in the normal way.

2. When cooked, remove from the oven. Halve and scoop out the flesh, being careful not to damage the skins.

3. Mix the potato pulp with the other ingredients. Mix well and spoon back into the skins. Wrap in tin foil and, when the time comes, reheat on the barbecue for up to 1 hour.

Sweet Potatoes with Garlic Butter

V G *Serves 8*

2 lb (900 g) sweet potatoes (approx.
   2 average sweet potatoes),
   washed
a little chilli oil (see page 179)
8 oz (250 g) garlic butter (see page
   179)

These make a delicious alternative to the usual baked spud.

1. Bake the potatoes in the oven until tender (do not overcook).

2. Slice into $\frac{1}{2}$ in (1 cm) slices and brush with a little chilli oil.

3. Barbecue or grill for 5 minutes each side, away from intense heat.

4. Serve with garlic butter on each slice.

OPPOSITE: *A selection from the Vegetarian Buffet, clockwise from top: Stuffed Vine Leaves (page 139), Peppers on Toast (page 146), Stuffed Tomato (Page 143), Spicy New Potatoes (page 141), Tiny Leek and Gruyère Croissant (page 136), Mushrooms on Sticks (page 138), Nori Sushi (page 141) and Tartelette Niçoise (page 131)*

Grilled Onions with Herb Butter

V G *Serves 8*

8 medium-sized onions
4 oz (100 g) herb butter or
    margarine (see page 179), melted
salt and pepper

These take a little while to cook on the barbecue, but they are worth the wait.

1. Peel the onions and remove a thin slice from top and bottom of each.

2. Cut the onions into quarters, but NOT all the way through.

3. Brush some of the herb butter into the incisions. Season with salt and pepper and wrap in foil. Cook on the barbecue for 40–50 minutes.

Grilled Tomatoes with Herby Garlic Ciabatta

V *Serves 8*

4 large beef tomatoes
$\frac{1}{4}$ pint (150 ml) olive oil heated with
    8 cloves garlic
1 loaf *ciabatta* bread, cut into 8
2 tablespoons chopped fresh
    marjoram

This will bring a taste of the Mediterranean to your barbecue.

1. Cut the tomatoes in half, brush with oil and cook, cut side down, for 1 minute on the barbecue. Turn them over, brush again with oil and continue to cook until extremely mushy.

2. Slice the *ciabatta* and brush with the oil. Cook on both sides until warmed through. Brush with oil again.

To serve: Pile the tomatoes onto the *ciabatta* and push down firmly. Sprinkle with marjoram. ENJOY!

OPPOSITE: *Vegetarian Christmas Lunch (pages 195–206) comprising Festive Feast with Tangy Tomato and Sour Cream Sauce; Honey Roast Parsnips; Nutty Brussels Sprouts; Red, Green and Yellow Pepper Marmalade; Sauté Potatoes; followed by Christmas Pudding and Real Rum Custard*

VARIATIONS

- Substitute red, yellow or both peppers for tomatoes. Cook them, skin side up, for 3 minutes, then skin side down until the skin is burnt and blistered. Eat on warm garlicky *ciabatta*.

- Eat tomatoes cooked like this mashed onto the top of a hunk of grilled polenta (see page 186).

Grilled Polenta

V G *Serves 8*

1¾ pint (1 litre) water
salt
11 oz (300 g) cornmeal
¼ pint (150 ml) garlic oil (see page 224)

It is possible to buy an instant variety of cornmeal specially designed for making polenta. It certainly makes light work of something that otherwise involves 30–40 minutes of vigorous stirring. There is no noticeable reduction in the quality, so I must encourage you to use it.

Traditionally, polenta was cooked in a huge copper cauldron hanging above an open fire, so the risk of it burning was far less than it is today when cooked on a stove.

1. Bring the water to the boil with plenty of salt.

2. Gradually sprinkle in the cornmeal, stirring all the time with a wooden spoon.

3. Continue to stir until the mixture starts to come away from the sides of the pan (5 minutes with instant polenta or 30–40 minutes with natural cornmeal).

4. Remove from the heat and shout 'God my wrist aches!'

5. Brush a deep rectangular dish generously with some garlic oil. Pour in the cooked polenta and smooth it down. Put aside to cool and set. When it is cool, let it stand in the fridge for a further 2 hours until solid. Cut into wedges.

6. Heat the garlic oil and brush over all sides of the polenta wedges.

7. Grill on the barbecue for up to 10 minutes each side. It will form a golden brown crust and, with luck, acquire the rather attractive markings of the grill. While barbecuing, brush as much garlic oil onto it as possible to avoid sticking and to enhance the flavour.

Serving suggestions: Serve spread with Pesto (see page 225), Black Olive Pâté (see page 147), Preserved Peppers (see page 89), sun-dried tomatoes, cheeses or flavoured butters (page 179).

Grilled Buckwheat Stuffed Mushrooms

V G *Serves 8*

7 oz (200 g) roasted buckwheat
1 pint (600 ml) water
1 tablespoon soya sauce
1 medium onion, finely chopped
1 small green pepper, finely chopped
½ teaspoon chilli powder
½ oz (15 g) butter or vegan
    margarine
4 oz (100 g) mushrooms, finely
    chopped
1 tablespoon peanut butter
1 tablespoon fresh tomato purée
    (see page 223)
a handful of grated Mozzarella or
    Cheddar cheese (optional)
fine sea salt and freshly ground black
    pepper
4 oz (100 g) lemony garlic butter
    (see page 179) or some garlic oil
    (see page 224) with lemon juice
    (optional)
8 large field mushrooms
herb butter (page 179) to serve

If they haven't been marinated, mushrooms tend to curl up and die on a barbecue – unless they're wrapped in foil. This technique brings with it the added advantage of being able to slip in something tasty like a knob of flavoured butter, a bit of cheese like Brie, or even a complete and genuine stuffing as shown below. Cooking here will depend on the size of your mushrooms; 5–10 minutes on high heat is usually enough.

1. First cook the buckwheat by covering with the water and soya in a saucepan. Bring to the boil and simmer for 15–20 minutes, being careful it doesn't burn.

2. While it is cooking, sauté the onions, peppers and chilli powder in the butter or margarine for 5 minutes before stirring in the chopped mushrooms. Put the lid on and cook for a further 5–8 minutes. Now stir in the peanut butter and tomato purée.

3. When the buckwheat is cooked, fold it into the rest of the mixture. It should form quite a stiff stuffing. Those of you who enjoy cheese may like to add a little to the mix at this stage. Adjust the seasoning with salt, pepper and soya sauce.

4. Brush the field mushrooms clean. Remove the stalks and trim any untidy bits. If you like extra flavours, put a knob of lemony garlic butter or squeeze some lemon juice over the gills of the mushrooms and brush with garlic oil. Don't forget to season them at this stage.

5. Next put in the filling – top with a little cheese and herbs, if desired, and wrap in foil. They are now ready for the barbecue. Put them on the barbecue for 10–15 minutes, then serve, to gasps of delight, accompanied with a slice of herb butter.

Garlic Bread

Enough for 8

1 baguette made from unbleached, untreated flour, about 18 in (45 cm) long
4 oz (100 g) butter or 4 tablespoons extra virgin olive oil
8 cloves garlic, crushed (more if you like garlic)
fine sea salt and freshly ground black pepper
squeeze of lemon

No barbecue is complete without moist hot garlic bread. In fact just about any party is bolstered by its presence. Funny thing is, I've never heard anyone complain that there is too much garlic or butter in their garlic bread; once it is hot and melted it would seem it is beyond even the most fervent food faddist's sphere of demarcation.

Choose good organic bread to make your garlic bread. It could be long baguette style, round *focaccia* or even tin loaves if you're desperate. White or brown, it doesn't matter so long as there is plenty of garlic and butter or olive oil and other goodies if you like them, and it's wrapped tightly in foil to prevent the flavours and juices escaping.

If you have bread left over from the day before, it too can be transformed by the judicious use of garlic and butter or olive oil.

1. Heat the oven to 200°C/400°F/Gas Mark 6.

2. Beat the butter, garlic, seasoning and lemon juice together well, or simply whizz up the olive oil with the other ingredients.

3. Cut the baguette across at suitable intervals, taking care not to cut right through the loaf. Butter the interior of the slices generously. If using olive oil, simply brush it into the crevices.

4. Wrap the loaf well in tin foil, making sure no juices can escape.

5. Pop it into the hot oven or on top of the barbecue for about 10 minutes. If on the barbecue, turn it as you would a sausage.

6. Serve immediately.

VARIATIONS

- Add handfuls of herbs to the mix, whether butter or oil. Parsley, chives, coriander and basil are all excellent.

- Spice the mix with chilli powder or even curry paste.

- For a very trendy and completely different sensation make *fettunda* on your barbecue. Brush slices of baguette with lots of garlic and olive oil and toast it on the barbecue. When ready eat it as it is or with squashed ripe tomatoes and basil on top.

BARBECUE DESSERTS

What could be more natural after all that barbecued savoury food than to cook a few fruits for dessert? With the prudent provision of various creams, ice creams and sorbets it will be all you need on a hot summer day.

I've included recipes for a simple vegan ice cream and a vegan sorbet. It helps if you have an ice cream machine but it is by no means essential.

Barbecued Fruit

Many fruits actually barbecue very successfully. The trick is to use them before they get so ripe they just disintegrate, and yet when they are ripe enough to contain sugar that will caramelise in the barbecueing process. Some fruits lend themselves quite naturally to marinating. The liqueur is normally either neat brandy, rum, Kirsch, Grand Marnier, Cointreau or white wine, or a syrup made using one of these as a base. Here are some suggestions for your barbecue.

BBQ Bananas   Choose firm bananas or even plantain (the large green variety) or else they will dissolve into a mush. Place them, skins on, on the barbecue over a moderate heat. When they are completely black they are done.

To serve: Remove from the barbecue, quickly remove a strip of skin about an inch (2.5 cm) wide. Ease the skin either side of the banana away from the flesh. Then, if it's for an adult, drizzle in some brandy, rum or even green Chartreuse with perhaps a little melted butter. For children, use honey or maple syrup. Serve accompanied by ice cream, cream, sour cream or cashew cream.

BBQ Pineapple   Peel and cut a pineapple into slices $\frac{1}{2}$ in (1 cm) thick or into wedges. If desired, marinate in white wine and rum for not less than 2 hours. Cook over a hot heat for 5 to 10 minutes each side or until starting to brown.

BBQ Peaches and Nectarines Choose large firm fruit (ripe but not soft). Halve and remove the stone. Cook, cut side down, on tin foil for 5 minutes, then turn and remove the tin foil to cook the other side for 5 minutes. Good eaten with crème fraîche or fromage frais.

BBQ Figs Figs must be cooked whole over a medium heat on squares of tin foil for about 5 minutes. Excellent with acacia honey and Greek yoghurt.

BBQ Pears Pears are excellent when barbecued but must be bought in the right condition. Pears have a life of about 1 day when ripe so don't leave them hanging around. Use firm ripe William pears. Cut them into quarters or halves, depending on their size. Remove what little core there is with a fruit knife. Cook over a moderate heat for about 5 minutes each side. Serve with a little kirsch and Ginger and Vanilla Ice Cream (see below).

BBQ Fruit Kebabs You can of course barbecue any of these fruits threaded onto a 6 in (15 cm) wooden stick. You can also grill smaller or more delicate fruits like cherries, apricots, greengages, wedges of orange, lime and melon. Marshmallows can be popped on to the ends of the sticks too. Serve the kebabs coated with a thick fruit purée sauce like apricot or rhubarb.

Ginger and Vanilla Ice Cream

G   *Serves 6*

½ pint (275 ml) milk
½ pint (275 ml) double cream
2 vanilla pods
6 egg yolks (size 2)
2 oz (50 g) caster sugar
2 tablespoons ginger syrup
7 oz (200 g) chopped stem ginger

When making ice cream, use the freshest eggs possible. Use the lowest setting on the freezer.

1. Bring the milk and the cream just to the boil. Remove from the heat.

2. Expose the seeds in the vanilla pods with a sharp knife and throw into the hot milk and cream. Set to one side for at least 30 minutes to infuse.

3. Beat the egg yolks, sugar and syrup together until roughly doubled in volume and quite thick.

4. Stir into the cooled cream mixture with the chopped ginger.

5. Pour into a shallow freezable container. Cool completely, then freeze. If you have an ice cream machine allow the mixture to cool, then pour it into the machine.

6. Remove the ice cream every 20 minutes from the freezer, stir and occasionally beat with a fork or whisk to give a smooth ice cream.

VARIATIONS

Many ice creams can be made by infusing a flavour into the milk and cream. For instance, substitute 6 heads of elderflowers for the vanilla, and omit the ginger, for Elderflower Ice Cream.

Pecan and Maple Tofu Ice Cream

V G   *Serves 6*

4 oz (100 g) chopped pecans
4 oz (100 g) soft tofu
$\frac{1}{2}$ pint (275 ml) soya milk
2 oz (50 g) vegan margarine
$\frac{1}{2}$ pint (275 ml) maple syrup
1 teaspoon vanilla essence

Vegan ice creams are even easier to make. Simply put most of the ingredients in a blender, whizz and freeze, stirring occasionally.

As this ice cream is very low in fat the texture is less creamy than recipes using cream and eggs.

1. Lightly toast the pecans and allow to cool.

2. Blend all the ingredients except the nuts.

3. Stir in the pecans, pour into a freezable container and freeze. Stir every 20 minutes until completely frozen.

To serve: Remove from the freezer about 20 minutes before serving to allow to soften.

Raspberry Sorbet

V G *Serves 8*

1½ lb (675 g) fresh ripe raspberries
    (defrosted frozen will do)
8 oz (225 g) granulated sugar
1 pint (600 ml) water
juice of ½ lemon

Raspberries are available fresh or frozen, all year round. This is one recipe where you can use either successfully. You could substitute any fresh berry. Adjust the amount of lemon juice accordingly.

1. Purée the raspberries and sieve. Chill for 2 hours.

2. Bring the sugar and water to the boil. Boil rapidly for 5 minutes without stirring. Remove from the heat, cool and chill.

3. Mix the purée and the syrup together and pour into a shallow freezable container.

4. Freeze, stirring occasionally. When you judge it to be half-frozen, add the lemon juice and, if you're lucky enough to possess an ice cream machine, pop it into that. Otherwise, continue to beat the sorbet occasionally as it freezes.

DRINKS AT THE BARBECUE

There are no set rules when it comes to drinks for a barbecue. Unpredictable summer weather usually means barbecues are planned literally the day before they happen if not actually on the day. So drinks must be simple and effective, cooling thirsts while complementing often spicy food.

Wine is probably the best all-round option. For a barbecue where meat is the main thing on the menu, young reds like Shiraz, Chianti or Zinfandel would be chosen. However our barbecue is based solely around vegetables and so I would choose dry to medium dry white – a Sauvignon Blanc or a Riesling. Bearing in mind the amount of oil used in basting and marinating, a sparkling white Cava would be a good choice too.

As an alternative to wine, Pimms is always a good option and gives you plenty of scope for attractive decoration with fresh flowers and fruit. But if you want to break the mould, here are a couple of ideas for drinks you may not have tried – both alcoholic and non-alcoholic.

Fruit Cup

Serves 16–18

16 fl oz (500 ml) orange juice
1¾ pints (1 l) pineapple juice
4 pints (2.5 l) white grape juice
1¾ pints (1 l) pure sparkling water
strawberries, raspberries, black-
    currants, redcurrants, slices of
    lemon, lime, oranges and kiwi
    fruit, any edible garden flowers
    that are available, plus sprigs of
    mint for garnish

This is such a delicious and refreshing fruity drink that no one will miss the alcohol. Include as much fruit as you like, in any combination.

1. Ensure all the ingredients are well chilled.

2. Combine all the liquids in a bowl. Add the fruit.

3. Ladle into large glasses over ice and decorate with a sprig of mint and a petal or two.

Blackcurrant Wine Cup

Serves 16–18

4 pints (2.5 l) white wine (use a
    Sauvignon Blanc)
1¾ pints (1 l) white grape juice
1¾ pints (1 l) sparkling mineral water
8 fl oz (250 ml) Crème de Cassis
pairs of cherries, small bunches of
    blackcurrants and any suitable
    flowers for decoration

Here's a variation of the classic aperitif, Kir. It is diluted with white grape juice and sparkling mineral water and so is not as alcoholic.

Mix well chilled ingredients and pour over a cube or two of ice. Decorate with fruit and flowers.

Chapter seven

A VEGETARIAN
CHRISTMAS

Christmas has always been the greatest feast of all. Even before Christ lent his name to the mid-winter solstice, earlier cultures were celebrating the coming of lighter days at this time of year.

Entertaining at Christmas can be vast and it is no new thing to start preparations way back in September or October. Planning, forethought and prudent use of your freezer will take the burden of entertaining off your shoulders and allow you to enjoy not only Christmas Day but equally the rest of the holiday and all its multitudinous meals and snacks.

If you're going to entertain at any time then it's not worth approaching it half-heartedly. Christmas is the perfect excuse to make an effort, a wonderful chance to enjoy families and friends, children and elderly relatives. If you're short of money make Christmas your focus of entertaining for the year; presents can be kept small but thoughtful. What people remember about Christmas is not the socks or the gloves but the party.

Also it's quite possible to spread the cost by advance planning and preparation.

In our house the children get excited about Christmas as soon as they start opening their Advent calendars. We don't put the tree up until Christmas Eve as this special ritual seems to encapsulate the Christmas spirit and capture the children's imagination.

If possible, lay the table for Christmas lunch on Christmas Eve as it will be one less job to do on the day. By now Christmas presents will have been wrapped and stowed enticingly beneath the tree. The restaurant will have been put to bed for two whole days – what luxury! We usually have a few friends round so we light the fires, turn on the Bing Crosby and open a few bottles of wine! Christmas Eve entertaining has to be simple – perhaps just mince pies and booze or a stroganoff with rice. If you value your marriage, don't go over the top!

Christmas is all about birth and renewal – the kindling of a new and good light. I think a vegetarian Christmas is particularly appropriate, expressing, as it does, the feeling of care and compassion we have for all living things. At the end of the day what could be better than enjoying yourself in the knowledge that you have not hurt anything – and that the food is doing you and the world some good.

Christmas entertaining is a vast subject on which whole books can be written. I think that you will find within the pages of this book enough tips on entertaining to cover almost every aspect of Christmas except the Christmas meal itself.

So I have limited the recipes in this section to two Christmas meals – one vegetarian and one vegan – but both equally delicious to all.

It is no coincidence that both main dishes involve chestnuts. The flavour and texture of these seasonal nuts are unique and a special treat at this time of year.

MENU

VEGETARIAN CHRISTMAS

SERVES 4–6

Stilton and Walnut Pâté

—·—

*Festive Feast with Tangy Tomato and Sour Cream
Sauce
Red, Green and Yellow Pepper Marmalade
Nutty Brussels Sprouts
Sauté Potatoes
Honey Roast Parsnips*

—·—

*Christmas Pudding with Real Rum Custard or
Gingered Brandy Butter
Danish Apple Cake
Exotic Fruit Salad or Hot Fruit Salad
Suggested drinks: Piesporter, Valpolicella, Muscat,
madeira or port*

COUNTDOWN

Several months, if not years before
Make the Christmas pudding and store in a cool dry place. If you like, add a dash of brandy or rum every now and then and rewrap it securely.

Two weeks before
Make individual Stilton and Walnut Pâtés and the Festive Feast and freeze them. Festive Feast should be frozen with the pastry uncooked.

Christmas Eve
• Make the Red, Green and Yellow Pepper Marmalade. Cook until still fairly crunchy. • Prepare the Brussels sprouts ready for cooking.

• Prepare and parcook the potatoes ready for sautéing. • Prepare the parsnips and store, covered in water. • Make the Brandy Butter. • Put the white wines in the fridge. • Lay the table for Christmas Day if you have the space. • Just before bed, remove the pâté and Festive Feast from the freezer and put them in the fridge.

Christmas Day

3 hours ahead • Put the Christmas Pudding on to cook. The longer it cooks the better it is. • Decant the port. • Make the Danish Apple Cake. • Make the Exotic Fruit Salad. • Make the Rum Custard. • Make the tomato sauce and keep warm in a *bain-marie* on the stove.

2 hours ahead • Uncork the red wine and allow to breathe.

1 hour ahead • Heat oven to 200°C/400°F/Gas Mark 6. • Prepare the Hot Fruit Salad and put in the oven. • Put the parsnips on to cook. • Decorate the plates with salad leaves for the pâté. • Slice wholewheat bread for toast.

30 minutes before • Start recooking the Pepper Marmalade. • Sauté the potatoes, drain on a kitchen towel and store in serving dish in oven. • Glaze Festive Feast and put into the oven.

5 minutes before • Remove parsnips from the oven, decant into serving dish and replace in oven. • Put salted water on to boil for Brussels sprouts. • Put toast in the toaster.

0 minutes • Remove Festive Feast from the oven and set aside to cool slightly. (It will carve better if allowed to cool a little.) Serve the toast with the pâté.

5 minutes later • Steam or boil the Brussels sprouts. • Drizzle honey over the parsnips. • Decant the tomato sauce into a sauce jug. • Decant the peppers into a serving dish. • Sprinkle the potatoes with chopped parsley or basil. • By now the Brussels sprouts will be cooked and should be finished off by adding a few tablespoons of peanut butter. Allow to melt, shake to coat, and serve.

10 minutes later • Put everything on the table and carve the Festive Feast. • Enjoy yourself. • When serving the Christmas Pudding, gently ease it away from the sides of the basin with a spatula before you invert it onto your serving dish. • If flambéing the pudding, always heat the alcohol before igniting it. This will avoid disappointment and an over-use of matches and brandy.

Stilton and Walnut Pâte

To serve 4–6 persons (makes 1 lb (450 g) of pâté)

4 oz (100 g) butter
1 small onion, finely chopped
1 small green pepper, finely chopped
salt and pepper to taste
2 oz (50 g) mushrooms, finely chopped
2 cloves garlic, minced
2 oz (50 g) walnuts, toasted and ground
2 tablespoons port
1 oz (30 g) breadcrumbs
3 oz (75 g) Stilton, crumbled
2 oz (50 g) cottage cheese
soya sauce, to taste
4–6 bay leaves
about 10 juniper berries

Stilton and Walnut Pâté is something we invented in 1989. I wanted to create a really special pâté, that would stand out at a Christmas feast. Properly made, this pâté has an uncanny meatiness which may prove unnerving to the devoted vegetarian at first. It's rich and powerful so don't overdo the portions. It can be frozen for up to 2 months.

1. Melt just over 2 oz (50 g) of the butter in a deep pan until gently bubbling. Then add the onion, green pepper, salt, and pepper. Cook until the onions are starting to soften.

2. Add the mushrooms and garlic. Continue to cook until the mushrooms have softened.

3. Stir in the walnuts and increase the heat. Continue to cook until the whole mixture is very hot.

4. Add the port and cook until reduced by half. Stir in the breadcrumbs and continue to cook for 1 minute. Remove from the heat and allow to cool.

5. Beat the Stilton and cottage cheese together thoroughly, using a hand whisk or a blender. Fold into the rest of the mixture thoroughly. Taste and adjust seasoning (add soya if necessary).

6. Transfer three-quarters of the mixture to a blender and blend. Add back to the original mixture and stir in thoroughly. This is important for the final texture.

7. Pour the mixture into individual ramekins and decorate with juniper berries and bay leaves. Melt the remaining butter and pour over the top. Chill well before eating.

To serve: Eat with hot buttered organic wholewheat toast or fingers of hot pitta bread, and salad leaves.

Festive Feast

Serves 4–6 persons

For the chestnut purée

4 oz (100 g) Italian organic dried
   chestnuts
6 oz (175 g) shallots, finely chopped
4 tablespoons vegetable oil
1 teaspoon chopped sage
1 teaspoon chopped thyme
1 teaspoon chopped parsley
salt and pepper
2 tablespoons soya sauce
2 tablespoons brandy
1 oz (30 g) breadcrumbs
2 oz (50 g) hazelnuts, roasted and
   ground
2 eggs
2 teaspoons cream

For the mushroom ragout

2 teaspoons brandy
4 oz (100 g) onion, finely chopped
2 cloves garlic, minced
1 lb (450 g) field mushrooms, finely
   chopped
$\frac{1}{2}$ pint (275 ml) red wine
1 lb (450 g) puff pastry (see page
   221)
beaten egg yolk
sesame seeds (optional)

The Festive Feast is really a rich chestnut roast in a lovely home-made puff pastry case topped with an incredibly alcoholic mush-room ragout. It's very special and quite time-consuming to make – but the good news is that it can be frozen uncooked. Just get it out of the freezer on Christmas Eve and pop it into the fridge. It should be ready to cook by the next morning. Festive Feasts are equally nice served cold with salad and pickles on Boxing Day.

If you wish to use fresh chestnuts you will need about 10 oz (275 g) good sized chestnuts. Make an incision through the skin with a sharp knife, then boil in salted water for 20 minutes. Drain, and remove the skin when cool enough to handle. Discard the water and use a little stock in place of the chestnut juice.

To make the chestnut purée

1. The day before cooking, soak the dried chestnuts in plenty of salted water (they swell up a lot). Leave overnight, then bring to the boil until tender – about $1\frac{1}{2}$ hours.

2. Drain the cooking liquor but retain. Allow to cool.

3. Keep 12 chestnuts whole and grate the rest. This is best done by hand.

4. Sauté the shallots in the vegetable oil until softening. Add the herbs and seasoning. Pour in the soya sauce, brandy and 4 tablespoons of the chestnut cooking liquor. Bring to the boil and fold in the breadcrumbs, hazelnuts and grated chestnuts. Cook for a further 5 minutes before beating in the eggs and cream. The mixture should be fairly stiff. Allow to cool.

To make the mushroom ragout

1. Place all the ragout ingredients in a pan.

2. Bring to the boil and allow to simmer until all the liquid has evaporated.

3. Purée roughly in a liquidiser or food processor. Adjust the seasoning.

To assemble the Festive Feast

1. Roll out the pastry on a lightly floured surface until it resembles the size of a piece of A4 paper – perhaps slightly wider.

2. Put the mushroom mixture down the centre of the pastry.

3. Spoon the chestnut mixture exactly on top of the mushroom mixture.

4. Bring up the two narrower ends of the rectangle and wrap one slightly over the other. Seal by brushing the overlapped end with egg yolk, then pressing to seal.

5. Quickly turn the whole roll over so that the seam is directly underneath. Now seal each end of the roll by tucking the pastry underneath the roll.

6. Decorate the top by scoring diagonally with a sharp knife. Brush with egg yolk and, if desired, sprinkle with sesame seeds or decorate with Christmas pastry shapes.

7. Keep in the fridge until ready to cook.

8. Heat the oven to 230°C/450°F/Gas Mark 8. Place the Festive Feast on a baking sheet and bake for 10 minutes before reducing the temperature to 200°C/400°F/Gas Mark 6. Continue to cook for another 25–30 minutes.

Serving suggestions: Festive Feasts are incredibly versatile whether you serve them with all the trimmings (as we have for Christmas), hot with a salad, cold with a salad or indeed just on its own with a delicious sauce. It's very rich so don't overdo the portions.

I recommend varying the mushroom ragout. It could be replaced with a tangy pipérade or a sharp but sweet fruit purée. Why not experiment and see?

One thing is for sure, Festive Feasts are a great dish at any time of the year. For picnics or buffets, make individual Festive Feasts in little parcels.

Tangy Tomato and Sour Cream Sauce

G *Serves 4–6*

½ pint (275 ml) sour cream
½ pint (275 ml) double cream
salt
1 tablespoon Dijon mustard
2 tablespoons fresh tomato purée
    (see page 223)
1 tablespoon chopped chives

This sauce is a little on the fattening side but it's simple to make and goes well with our Festive Feasts. It needs to be made just before serving. It's also extremely versatile. Instead of tomato purée and Dijon mustard, try marsala, madeira or white wine (reduce them by half before adding them to the cream). Chopped fresh herbs, like dill, parsley, tarragon or chervil, may also be stirred into the sauce just before serving.

1. Put the sour cream and cream in a saucepan with a little salt and bring to the boil over a gentle heat.

2. Simmer for about 45 minutes or until reduced by half.

3. Mix together the mustard and the tomato purée, then gradually add to the cream.

4. Finally, add the chives and serve immediately.

Red, Green and Yellow Pepper Marmalade

V G *Serves 4–6*

1 tablespoon olive oil
1 medium red onion or large shallot,
    chopped
2 large red peppers, cut into strips
2 large green peppers, cut into strips
1 large yellow pepper, cut into strips
2 teaspoons light brown muscovado
    sugar (optional)
salt and pepper
soya sauce to taste
fresh tomato purée (optional; see
    page 223)

This dish never fails to get compliments and it's so simple. If you are short of time, prepare the peppers the night before. If you're really desperate you could cook them the day before and then reheat, either conventionally or in the microwave – but the recipe is so simple it's hardly worth it.

1. Heat the oil in a deep, heavy-bottomed pan.

2. Add the onion and sauté until it softens.

3. Add all the peppers and the sugar if liked.

4. Cover and simmer until the peppers are soft. Adjust the seasoning with salt, pepper and soya and serve. You may wish to add just a little tomato purée at the end to bring all the flavours together, but once again it is not absolutely necessary.

Serving suggestions: This 'marmalade' is great with just about anything, but especially nice to counter-balance rich food. More adventurous cooks may wish to flavour it with garlic, ginger or chilli or even all three. Once again, it is the quality of the peppers that will determine what you add to them.

Sauté Potatoes

Serves 4–6

2¼ lb (1 kg) waxy potatoes
3 oz (75 g) butter, or 2 oz (50 g)
    butter plus 2 tablespoons oil
fine sea salt
parsley or basil for garnish

This is one of the simplest potato dishes, but how often do you see it these days?

1. Boil the potatotes – unpeeled – until almost cooked. Allow to cool.

2. Peel and cut into slices or cubes.

3. Heat the butter or the butter and oil mix in a large frying pan over a high heat.

4. Sauté the potatoes vigorously at first, then turn down the heat and cook gently for 10–12 minutes, turning frequently. Season with salt and pepper.

5. If necessary, drain on kitchen towels and store covered in the oven until needed.

To serve: Serve garnished with fresh chopped parsley or basil.

VARIATIONS

- Hash Browns – Instead of cutting the cooked potatoes into slices, chop them roughly, then sauté. As you sauté, squash the potato down to form a sort of cake. Allow to brown.

- Add onion and garlic and roast in the oven instead of sautéing.

- Cut cooked potato into larger pieces, sauté for 10 minutes, then roast in the oven for the rest of the time. (Oven should be at 200°C/400°F/Gas Mark 6.)

Honey Roast Sesame Parsnips

G *Serves 4–6*

1½ lb (675 g) parsnips, cut into
   sections according to size
sesame oil or vegetable oil to coat
   the roasting dish
2 teaspoons sesame seeds
2 teaspoons honey, warmed

Roast parsnips are quick and easy to prepare and are an excellent addition to many meals. Parsnips are rather nice overcooked: they go all sweet and gooey. In this recipe we just cook the parsnips and baste them with honey before serving. Parsnips are rarely favourites with the children, so make less than potatoes.

1. Preheat the oven to 200°C/400°F/Gas Mark 6.

2. Heat the sesame or vegetable oil in a roasting dish on top of the stove. When it is hot, add the parsnips and stir them round to ensure they are coated in hot oil. Sprinkle with sesame seeds and place in the oven. Depending on the size when you cut them they will take 15–30 minutes.

3. When ready, baste them with honey, using a pastry brush, and place in their serving bowl. They will keep hot quite happily whilst you get on and do other things!

'Food for friends' Christmas Pudding

The *Food for friends* Christmas Pudding was introduced by Phil Taylor, one of our best chefs ever. He was kindly lent the recipe by his grandmother and the rumour is that she was taught how to make it by her grandmother. However many grandmothers were involved, it is certain that its origins were in the misty depths of time.

You will need to buy two 2-pint (1.2 l) Christmas pudding bowls. There's no point in just cooking one. If you can't eat the other one, keep it for next year, sealed in a plastic container or tin in a cool dark place.

Don't rush out and buy a steamer for cooking the pudding; simply choose the deepest saucepan or casserole pot you have and rig up a platform for the pudding to sit on. Make sure you can still keep the lid on the pot. Pour water into the pan so that the bottom of the pudding only is immersed. You will have to

V *Makes 2 (each serves 6)*

8 oz (225 g) vegetable suet
4 oz (100 g) demerara sugar
8 oz (225 g) raisins
8 oz (225 g) sultanas
8 oz (225 g) currants
4 oz (100 g) mixed peel
8 oz (225 g) breadcrumbs
3 oz (75 g) organic wholewheat
  flour
3 teaspoons mixed spice
2 teaspoons cinnamon
1 teaspoon salt
2 eggs (vegans may omit the eggs)
juice and zest of 2 lemons
juice and zest of 2 oranges
1 small cooking apple, grated
1 small carrot, grated
¼ pint (150 ml) Guinness

top it up from time to time. Remember to top it up with boiling water otherwise you will crack the pudding bowl.

The uncooked pudding mixture will keep quite happily in the fridge for up to a week. Some people say this actually improves its flavour. It's best to attend to the preparation of Christmas puddings and mincemeat back in October; this will not only save work nearer to Christmas but also give them a chance to mature in flavour.

1. Beat the suet and sugar together in a large bowl until creamy.

2. Add all the remaining ingredients and stir (don't forget to invite the children in to make a wish – or just have one yourself).

3. Leave covered overnight.

4. Grease two 2-pint (1.2 l) bowls. Pour the mixture into these bowls.

5. Cover with a greased circle of greaseproof paper.

6. Secure in a muslin cloth or wrap in tin foil – basically you want to avoid water getting into the pudding.

7. Steam for at least 5 hours. The longer you steam it, the better the flavour develops. Leave to cool, then store in a cool place.

8. Steam for a further 2 hours on Christmas Day or before eating.

Serving suggestion: When the pudding is cooked you may wish to insert 20p pieces wrapped in greaseproof paper. Decorate with a well berried sprig of holly or simply flame it. To flame a Christmas pudding heat about 2 tablespoons of the favoured alcohol, whether it be rum, brandy, or whisky, in a ladle over a hot flame. After a few minutes it should ignite. When it does this, pour it carefully over the pudding and serve immediately.

Real Rum Custard

G *Serves 4–6*

10 egg yolks
9 oz (275 g) fine demerara sugar
1¾ pints (1 l) pints milk
1 vanilla pod, split
2 or 3 teaspoons rum

If you don't like rum, any well flavoured spirit will do – brandy or whisky or Cointreau. This custard is very rich but delicious.

Make this sauce two to three days before Christmas and keep it in the fridge, covered with buttered greaseproof paper to prevent a skin forming. You may wish to pass the sauce through a sieve before serving.

1. Combine the egg yolks with one-third of the sugar. Beat with a whisk until it is thick enough to trail a ribbon of mixture on the surface.

2. Put the milk, vanilla pod and rest of the sugar together in a saucepan and bring carefully to the boil.

3. Add the boiling milk to the egg mixture gradually, whisking continuously.

4. Pour back into the saucepan and, using a wooden spoon, stir the mixture over gentle heat until it is thick enough to coat the back of the spoon. Do not allow to boil. Add the rum.

Gingered Brandy Butter

G *Serves 4–6*

4 oz (100 g) unsalted butter, softened
4 oz (100 g) fine soft brown sugar
1 tablespoon brandy
2 oz (50 g) preserved ginger, drained

Here's an old favourite that is given an even more festive edge with the introduction of finely chopped preserved ginger.

Brandy butter can be prepared in advance and frozen. When you want to use it, defrost and cut into circular sections.

1. Place the butter in a basin. Add the sugar and beat to a creamy consistency (best done in a processor).

2. Add the brandy gradually.

3. Fold in the finely chopped preserved ginger.

4. Fashion into a log shape, wrap in greaseproof paper and keep in the fridge until needed.

Danish Apple Cake

Serves 4–6

$2\frac{1}{4}$ lb (1 kg) eating apples (Granny Smiths), peeled, cored and roughly chopped

$\frac{1}{4}$ teaspoon ground cloves

2 oz (50 g) brown sugar

juice and rind of 1 lemon

4 oz (100 g) unsalted butter

12 oz (350 g) fresh brown breadcrumbs

4 oz (100 g) light muscovado sugar

$\frac{1}{4}$ teaspoon ground cinnamon

$\frac{1}{2}$ pint (275 ml) Greek yoghurt, fromage frais or whipped cream

It is quite often the case that one of your family or a guest at Christmas can't eat Christmas pudding. So it is wise to have an alternative or two available, preferably with a festive aspect to them, such as this traditional spicy dessert. It is not a cake as such, but comes from the trifle school of gooey cookery.

If vegans are present, keep the topping separate.

1. Put the apples, cloves, brown sugar and lemon juice into a pan with enough water to prevent sticking. Cook until soft, with the lid on. Purée roughly.

2. Melt the butter in a pan and fry the breadcrumbs until crunchy. Remove from heat and stir in the muscovado sugar, cinnamon and lemon peel.

3. Take a rectangular glass dish and coat the bottom with a third of the apple mixture. Top with a third of the breadcrumb mix and so on until all the mixture has been used up.

4. Finally top with Greek yoghurt, fromage frais or whipped cream. Sprinkle with a little ground cinnamon. This dish can be prepared the day before. Keep well chilled.

Serving suggestions: You could serve in individual glass bowls. Also, a glass of sweet sherry or Calvados makes an excellent addition to the apple purée.

Exotic Fruit Salad

V G A simple fruit salad is definitely a must at Christmas. It will revive jaded tastebuds and balance the other more weighty dishes of the meal. Choose your favourite exotic or out-of-season fruit, such as strawberries, raspberries, muscat grapes, lychees, mango, figs, cape gooseberries and star fruit. Arrange attractively on your favourite fruit salad dish. Serve with a sorbet or good quality ice cream or alternatively Greek yoghurt, fromage frais or cream.

Hot Fruit Salad

G *Serves 4–6*

2 large apples
2 pears
2 large oranges
2 bananas
4 oz (100 g) seedless grapes
6 oz (175 g) demerara sugar
½ teaspoon allspice
½ teaspoon grated nutmeg
Greek yoghurt to serve

If the weather is extremely bitter, try this warming fruit salad.

1. Heat the oven to 200°C/400°F/Gas Mark 6.

2. Prepare the apples and pears. Do not peel but cut each into 12.

3. Cut the oranges in half (remove pips); slice each half into 6.

4. Peel the bananas and cut into ½–¾ in (1–1.5 cm) pieces. Mix together and add the seedless grapes. Place everything in a large shallow dish and sprinkle with the demerara sugar and spices.

5. Place in the oven and bake for 1 hour, turning the fruit once. Allow to cool for 5 minutes before serving with Greek yoghurt.

Mulled Wine

V G *Serves 4–6*

1 apple
8 cloves
1 lemon
3 cinnamon sticks
8 oz (225 g) light brown sugar
3 pints (1.75 l) red wine
¼ pint (150 ml) brandy
lemon slices to serve

Mulled wine should never be simmered for long as this drives off the alcohol.

1. Cut the apple into 4 and stud with cloves.

2. Remove the zest from the lemon.

3. Combine all the ingredients in a saucepan and gently bring to the boil. Simmer for 2 minutes – no longer.

4. Strain and serve hot with slices of lemon.

DRINKS

When guests arrive offer them mulled wine.

With the Stilton and Walnut Pâté you need a young red like a Dolcetto from the Piedmont region of Italy. There are several worth trying.

The Festive Feast is rich, delicious and quite sophisticated so try a substantial white like Chablis Grand Cru or even champagne.

Christmas Pudding requires a deviation from wine to tawny port or madeira or a sweetish sparkling wine.

A VEGAN CHRISTMAS MENU

Vegans tend to have a hard time when other people are catering for them, but there is absolutely no reason why this should be so at Christmas. Entertain a vegan well and you will have a friend for life. A vegan Christmas menu tends to be slightly lighter, leaving you feeling great on Christmas Day evening, when all your neighbours are passing out.

In this small section I've included the basics of the vegan meal without the trimmings, as it were. Vegetable accompaniments are very much a matter of personal choice; most of them are already vegan or, if not, may be made so by the judicious use of soya milk and other dairy substitutes.

*M*ENU

VEGAN CHRISTMAS

SERVES 4–6

Fassoulatha with Olive Bread

—·—

Chestnut Roast with Black Cherry and Red Wine Sauce
Candied Yams
Sloshed Leeks and Carrots
Garlic Potatoes
Hot Courgette and Tomato Salad

—·—

Christmas Pudding
Mince Pies with Vegan Ice Cream

COUNTDOWN

At least 3 months ahead
Make the Christmas Pudding and store.

1 month ahead
Make the Mince Pies, Vegan Ice Cream, Black cherry and Red Wine Sauce and the Chestnut Roast. Freeze them.

Christmas Eve
• Make the soup. Cool and refrigerate. • Make the Black Olive Bread.
• Prepare the potatoes and cook to the middle stage. • Prepare the Candied Yams and the salad ingredients. • Lay the table. • Take frozen food out of the freezer and put it into the fridge. • Put white wine into the fridge.

Christmas Day
3 hours ahead • Put the Christmas Pudding on to cook.
• Prepare any garnishes. • Decant the port. • Open the red wine.

1 hour ahead • Heat the oven to 200°C/400°F/Gas Mark 6.
• Put the Chestnut Roast and the yams in to cook.

30 minutes ahead • Put the potatoes into the oven along with the Black Olive Bread. • Finish preparing the salad. • Reheat the soup.
• Start reheating the Black Cherry and Red Wine Sauce in a *bain-marie*. • Put plates in to warm.

0 minutes Serve lunch. When you remove the last of the savoury food from the oven put the Mince Pies in to warm, sprinkled with a little icing sugar if you like it.

Fassoulatha

V G *Serves 4–6*

4 oz (100 g) baby green lima beans, washed well
water to cover
1 medium onion, finely chopped

This delicious bean soup is common throughout the Middle East; this particular variation is Greek. If you can, serve it with olive bread; home-made is obviously the best but it would be perfectly understandable if, at Christmas, you bought some.

8 oz (225 g) tomatoes, peeled,
    deseeded and chopped
2 tablespoons fresh tomato purée
    (see page 223)
4 oz (100 g) celery, chopped,
    including leaves
4 oz (100 g) carrots, diced
2 bunches parsley, chopped (retain
    half for garnish)
1 tablespoon extra virgin olive oil
freshly ground black pepper
$\frac{1}{2}$ teaspoon sugar
fine sea salt

1. Boil the beans vigorously for 2 minutes in unsalted water, then allow to stand until the beans plump up. Time will vary on this – anything from 1 to 2 hours.

2. Add all the remaining ingredients except the salt and bring to the boil. Simmer gently for $1\frac{1}{2}$ hours. Add salt to taste, then cook until the beans are tender.

Serving suggestion: Serve sprinkled with parsley, accompanied by wedges of hot Black Olive Bread.

Black Olive Bread

[V] *Serves 4–6*

$\frac{1}{2}$ oz (15 g) fresh yeast
6 fl oz (175 ml) hand-hot water
1 teaspoon sugar
10 oz (300 g) strong flour
1 teaspoon fine sea salt
3 tablespoons extra virgin olive oil
10 dried black olives (stones
    removed)
1 teaspoon coarse sea salt

Olive bread is always a success at any celebration. Once you've mastered the dough, you can flavour it with green olives, onion, sun-dried tomatoes or indeed garlic. I always think that day-old olive bread heated up is superior to fresh olive bread because the flavour of the olive oil seems to have had time to develop. So, if you're making it for Christmas lunch, make it the day before or well in advance and freeze it. It freezes excellently.

We use a mixture of organic wholewheat and unbleached white flour.

1. Crumble the yeast into a little of the hand-hot water. Add the sugar. Allow it to stand until it starts frothing.

2. Warm a large mixing bowl and place in it the flour and the fine sea salt. Mix thoroughly.

3. Make a well in the flour and add the yeast mixture together with a generous tablespoon of extra virgin olive oil.

4. Mix the dough, adding the rest of the water when needed. The resulting dough should be on the soft sticky side.

5. When the dough has formed a ball, knead it on a lightly floured board with your fingers. Only add extra flour to very sticky patches. Form the dough into a ball, cut the top with a sharp knife and place in a lightly floured bowl. Cover and leave in a warm place to rise for about an hour.

6. While the dough is rising, lightly oil a 12 in (30 cm) round tin or a baking sheet and have a drink!

7. When the dough has doubled in size knead it again, this time gently, and add the black olives. Push it down into a circular shape, handling gently all the time. Place in the tin or on the baking sheet and push out to its 12 in (30 cm) diameter. The dough will have a rough surface and be about $\frac{1}{2}$ in (1 cm) thick. Puncture the surface with a fork, wooden if possible, and leave to rise a second time for about 45 minutes, covered, in a warm place. It should grow in volume again to about 1 in (2.5 cm) thick.

8. When satisfied the rising is complete, trickle a generous tablespoon of the extra virgin olive oil over the surface and sprinkle on some of the coarse sea salt.

9. Bake in the middle of the oven for 15 minutes, then reduce the temperature to 200°C/400°F/Gas Mark 6 and bake for another 10 minutes.

10. Remove from the oven and allow to cool on a wire rack. Paint with the remaining olive oil and sprinkle with the remaining coarse sea salt.

Serving suggestion: Black Olive Bread is fabulous served hot or cold and is a perfect accompaniment to soups, salads and dips.

Chestnut Roast

Dare I say it – the ultimate nut roast. If it wasn't so good it'd be a cliché. Chestnuts have a unique texture and flavour which combine to make Chestnut Roast one of the very best vegan mixes. Chestnuts have a binding capability usually found only in eggs, consequently chestnut roast is close textured and easy to serve in slices.

The basic unroasted mixture can be altered and extended *ad infinitum*. You can fill mushrooms with it, wrap it in pastry, or

V   *Serves 6–8*

8 oz (250 g) dried Italian organic
    chestnuts
8 oz (250 g) peanuts, skinned and
    roasted
2 tablespoons vegetable oil
6 oz (175 g) onion, finely chopped
8 oz (250 g) field mushrooms, finely
    chopped
2 tablespoons finely chopped fresh
    parsley
3 teaspoons herbes provençales
$\frac{1}{4}$ pint (150 ml) red wine
freshly ground black pepper
fine sea salt
4 oz (100 g) organic wholewheat
    breadcrumbs
1 tablespoon soya sauce
parsley and orange slices for garnish

fry it as burgers. It's so simple and it freezes well too. This is definitely one dish that you will have cooked well in advance.

1. Soak the chestnuts in water overnight.

2. When the chestnuts are plump, place in a heavy pan and cover with salted water. Bring to the boil and simmer for about $1\frac{1}{2}$ hours or until the chestnuts are tender. This will vary according to the length of time soaked and the age of the chestnuts. When they are ready, drain and cool. Retain the chestnut water.

3. Keep a handful of chestnuts whole to one side and finely grate the rest.

4. Roast the peanuts in a hot oven or under a grill, being careful not to burn them. Grate these too.

5. Heat the oil in a deep pan and add the onions. Cook until softening, then throw in the mushrooms with herbs, wine and seasoning.

6. Fold in the chestnuts and peanuts and continue to cook for a further 2 minutes.

7. Fold in some of the breadcrumbs. The texture of the mixture now needs adjusting. If it's too wet, add more breadcrumbs. If too dry, add chestnut water. Stir continuously to avoid burning.

8. When you are happy with the texture, mix in the remaining chestnuts, remove from the heat and adjust the seasoning with soya sauce, salt and pepper. Set the oven at 180°C/350°F/Gas Mark 4.

9. Oil a 2 lb (900 g) loaf tin and spoon the mixture into it. Place the tin in the oven and cook for about 40 minutes or until it has set. Serve hot.

To serve: Gently ease the sides of the roast from the sides of the tin with a spatula. Choose a favourite serving plate and place on top of the tin. Invert it and 'hey presto!' there's Christmas lunch. Decorate with parsley and a few slices of orange with peel removed.

Serve with Black Cherry and Red Wine Sauce (see page 212).

If frozen, allow to thaw and then heat for 40 minutes at 180°C/350°F/Gas Mark 4.

VARIATIONS

• For a more refined Chestnut Roast you can remove half to two-thirds of the mixture at stage 8 and blend it till smooth in a blender, then add it back to the rest.

• For a more vegetably roast, substitute carrot, celeriac, celery, capsicums or leeks wholly or partly for the peanuts.

• Use other nuts instead of peanuts. Walnuts and cashews are best.

• Add a couple of handfuls of grated cheese.

Black Cherry and Red Wine Sauce

V G *Serves 4–6*

1 tablespoon extra virgin olive oil
1 large shallot, finely chopped
$\frac{1}{2}$ pint (275 ml) red wine
2 teaspoons cornflour
2 tablespoons madeira (optional)
1×10 oz (350 g) tin pitted black cherries (or, if available, fresh cherries)
fine sea salt
freshly ground black pepper
lemon juice and soya sauce (optional)
brown sugar (optional)
chopped parsley and coriander for garnish

This rather decadent sauce is the perfect accompaniment to a rich roast. It is essentially sweet and sour and so cuts across the tastebuds like a razor. This sauce can be made well in advance and frozen, or it can be made the day before and left for the flavours to develop.

1. Heat the oil in a saucepan. Add the shallot and cook till softening (about 10 minutes).

2. Pour in the red wine and bring to the boil. Cook until reduced to $\frac{1}{4}$ pint (150 ml).

3. Mix the cornflour to a paste with the madeira (if not using madeira, just water). Pour into the wine and stir until it has thickened slightly.

4. Add the cherries and bring to the boil.

5. Adjust the seasoning. If too sweet add a little lemon juice and soya sauce; if too sour, add a little sugar.

To serve: When the sauce is hot, transfer it to a sauce boat and sprinkle with chopped parsley and coriander.

Candied Yams

Serves 4–6

1½ lb (675 g) yams
juice of 1 lemon or lime
1 tablespoon olive oil
1 tablespoon demerara sugar
fine sea salt and freshly ground black
    pepper

Yams have a mild flavour and are larger and creamier than the more common sweet potatoes. Choose unblemished yams with firm undamaged skins.

1. Heat the oven to 170°C/375°F/Gas Mark 3.

2. Cut the yam(s) in half lengthwise. Score the top of each one, trellis style, about ¼ in (5 mm) deep. Don't mark the skins.

3. Brush the top of each half with first lemon or lime juice then olive oil. Sprinkle each half with an equal amount of brown sugar. Season with salt and pepper.

4. Bake the potato for 1 hour or until a knife slides easily into the middle of the flesh.

Sloshed Leeks and Carrots

Serves 4–6

4–6 good sized leeks, trimmed and
    thoroughly washed. Large ones
    may be cut in half.
1 or 2 large carrots, peeled, grooved
    and sliced quite thinly
1 large glass Riesling – enough to
    semi-immerse the leeks
1 teaspoon thyme
fine sea salt and freshly ground black
    pepper
chopped parsley for garnish

This was my invention one Sunday, using up what I had left in the fridge. Sunday lunches (or Christmas come to that) are notorious for filling all the space in the oven and more. Well, a few years ago Kate and I were given a Le Creuset dish shaped like a long loaf tin with a lid and I never did find out what it should be used for. So it sat in a cupboard without meaning to its life until that Sunday when I put whole trimmed leeks in it decorated with prettily shaped carrots and moistened with the remnants of a bottle of Riesling. It just squeezed in by the side of the potatoes and, as it happened, took exactly the same time to cook. Fellow cooks will know the satisfaction this brought me.

1. Cram the leeks, carrots, wine and thyme in a lidded casserole dish. Cover and place in the oven alongside the roast potatoes.

2. Remove from the oven when the roast potatoes are done. Sprinkle with parsley and serve in the casserole dish.

More precisely, bake in the oven heated to 190°C/375°F/Gas Mark 5 for 40 minutes–1 hour depending on how well cooked you like your leeks. They're delicious when they melt in the mouth.

Hot Courgette and Tomato Salad

V *Serves 4–6*

2 tablespoons virgin olive oil
3 shallots, finely chopped
1 bunch basil, finely chopped (retain
   a little for garnish)
1 teaspoon lemon juice
1 teaspoon balsamic vinegar
1 teaspoon Sambal Olek (see page
   227) or $\frac{1}{2}$ teaspoon chilli powder
1 tablespoon demerara sugar
   (optional)
1 tablespoon Dijon mustard
fine sea salt and freshly ground black
   pepper
1 lb (450 g) courgettes, topped,
   tailed and sliced, about $\frac{1}{8}$ in
   (2 mm) thick
4 fresh ripe tomatoes, chopped
chopped fresh parsley for garnish

Courgettes are a nice treat at Christmas – a welcome taste of summer months gone by. Surprisingly they are often of excellent quality at this time of year, originating in Spain or the Canaries. This hot salad makes best use of them, adding in the process two lovely colours and textures to your plate. Don't be tempted to turn it into a stew.

1. Heat the oil in a pan and cook the shallots for 2 minutes.

2. Add the basil, lemon juice, balsamic vinegar and Sambal Olek and bring to the boil.

3. Stir in the sugar (if used) and mustard. Adjust the seasoning.

4. Add the courgettes and cook for 1 minute only in the liquor. Stir in the chopped tomatoes and serve in an attractive salad dish garnished with fresh parsley.

Garlic Potatoes

V *Serves 4–6*

$1\frac{1}{2}$ lb (675 g) Maris Piper potatoes,
   peeled and finely sliced
3 cloves garlic, crushed or chopped
4 tablespoons extra virgin olive oil
fine sea salt and freshly ground black
   pepper
chives for garnish

Here's a potato dish that can be parcooked the day before your Christmas lunch. Parcooking and covering reduces the likelihood of discoloration, which can be further prevented by choosing a potato like Maris Piper that is known for keeping a good colour.

1. Heat the oven to 200°C/400°F/Gas Mark 6.

2. Prepare the potatoes and pat dry with a tea towel.

3. Heat the garlic in the oil for 5 minutes very gently. Do not allow the oil to bubble violently or burn the garlic.

4. Using a brush, coat the bottom of a baking dish with the garlic oil. Cover it with a layer of potato, then generously brush these

214

with garlic oil and season with salt and pepper. Continue this process, being careful to keep the potato slices overlapping, until they have all been used up.

5. Bake for 15 minutes, remove and allow to cool, then cover with clingfilm. Store in the fridge until needed. When finishing the cooking, the oven can be slightly cooler – 180°C/350°F/Gas Mark 4 – and the potatoes must be cooked for a further 20 minutes or until done. Garnish with chopped chives.

Tofu Ice Cream

V G *Serves 4–6*

8 oz (225 g) tofu (use soft or medium)
2 teaspoons natural vanilla essence
2 tablespoons vegetable oil
3 oz (75 g) raw cane sugar
6 fl oz (150 ml) organic soya milk

Tofu Ice Cream is a really unexpected treat to whisk out of your freezer at Christmas. It is really easy to make, especially if you have an ice cream machine.

1. Blend all the ingredients to a smooth consistency.

2. Put into an ice cream machine or alternatively place in a bowl in the freezer and stir thoroughly every 10 minutes until completely frozen.

Mince Pies

Our mince pies are rather more-ish. I often wondered why so many people liked them. The reason I discovered is simple – real mincemeat should be fruit, alcohol and spice but what many people do is add sugar and lots of apple to bulk it out, and in some cases fat. These are all ways of making a little go a long way but the result is patently inferior and terribly sweet.

The mincemeat recipe I've provided will make enough for about 50 mince pies, not an untidy sum for the whole of the festivities. Store what you don't use first time in an airtight plastic container or glass jar for up to a month.

V   *Makes 48*

1 quantity organic wholewheat
    short pastry (see page 218) made
    with vegan margarine
icing sugar for dusting

For the mincemeat
1 lb (450 g) chopped dates
10 oz (300 g) currants
10 oz (300 g) sultanas
10 oz (300 g) raisins
5 oz (150 g) mixed peel
zest and juice of 2 lemons
zest and juice of 2 oranges
$2\frac{1}{2}$ oz (60 g) blanched nibbed
    almonds
1 lb 2 oz (500 g) cooking apples
3 teaspoons mixed spice
2 teaspoons cinnamon
2 oz (50 g) brown sugar (optional)
4 tablespoons brandy

1. To make the mincemeat, stir all the ingredients together well.

2. Heat the oven to 200°C/400°F/Gas Mark 6.

3. Lightly grease two 12-hole mince-pie tins with approximately $2\frac{1}{2}$ in (6 cm) diameter bases.

4. Select a 3 in (7.5 cm) cutter and $2\frac{1}{2}$ in (6 cm) cutter. On a lightly floured board, roll the pastry out quite thinly. Cut out 24 large cases and 24 smaller ones.

5. Push the large circles of pastry into the mince-pie tin moulds, add a spoonful of mincemeat and top with a smaller circle. Press together at the edges and make a small hole in the centre. Bake for 15–20 minutes, until the pastry is browned slightly.

6. Dust with icing sugar and allow to cool in the tin.

To serve: Serve with Tofu Ice Cream or Vegan Brandy 'Butter' made by substituting good quality soft vegan margarine, such as Granose or Tomor, for butter in the recipe on page 204.

DRINKS

The soup has a definite Greek feel to it so why not try a fresh white Greek wine like a Mantinia from the Peloponnese?

The Chestnut Roast would be best with a Cava or even a good St Emilion.

Fruity Mince Pies will suit tawny port, madeira or perhaps a sweet German wine like a Beerenauslese.

Chapter eight

BASIC RECIPES

There are certain recipes that I use all the time. Rather than keep repeating them, I've herded them together and given them their own little corner of the book. Vegetarian, vegan or carnivore, you'll find these recipes invaluable.

Wholewheat shortcrust pastry

There is a lot of nonsense talked about cooks having 'pastry fingers'. Anyone can make good pastry if the ingredients are good and used correctly. The key to making successful short pastry is to do the mixing quickly and then to chill the dough well before use. To mix pastry quickly the butter must be soft (room temperature). If you use water it should be ice cold; eggs may be used wholly or partially instead of water as a binding agent that also enriches the pastry, and they too should be cold.

Sugar can be added, up to a maximum of half the weight of the flour. Pastry with this amount of sugar is more commonly known as shortbread and is so crumbly it is impossible to roll out. Subtle flavourings can be introduced to short pastry – vanilla is often used either directly by adding extract or indirectly by flavouring the sugar. Nuts, too, may be added – almonds, walnuts and hazelnuts are best. They should be lightly toasted, finely ground and added in addition to or as part of the flour quantity. Spices like cinnamon are often used too.

If you do not wish to use butter, substitute a hard vegan margarine like Tomor. Flour should be as fine as possible – organic wholewheat pastry

flours, milled extra fine, are commonly available now. Try and find a good source of freshly milled flour. When adding water to your pastry mix do so gradually. The amount you need will vary from day to day according to the humidity of your kitchen, and short pastry needs very little water; the more you add, the tougher the pastry will be. Wholewheat pastry does tend to need a little more water than white short pastry.

Finally, try to make sure everything used in the making of the pastry is cool. If your hands are naturally hot, dip them in iced water before you mix the pastry. If possible, chill the equipment, make sure the room is cool. Marble work surfaces are excellent for making pastry.

When rolling pastry use as little extra flour as possible. Roll away from your body using only light strokes. Avoid over-rolling and frequently turn the pastry to keep a good shape. When you have lined a tin ready for baking, chill it for 30 minutes (or as instructed in the recipe) before you cook it.

Short pastry is frequently wholly or partially baked blind, depending on how much cooking, if any, the filling is going to need. Simply line your chosen tin with pastry, prick it with a fork, cover the interior with greaseproof paper and onto this paper pour a suitable quantity of baking beans. Set the oven to 200°C/400°F/Gas Mark 6 and bake for 15–20 minutes, when the pastry will have coloured slightly. To parbake the pastry, remove it from the oven 5 minutes earlier.

Uncooked short pastry can be frozen, wrapped tightly in clingfilm, and must be defrosted at room temperature when you want to use it.

Organic Wholewheat Shortcrust Pastry

(also known as Lining Pastry)

V *Makes approx 1 lb (450 g) (enough for 1 × 10 in (25 cm) flan tin/ring)*

8 oz (250 g) organic wholewheat pastry flour

½ teaspoon salt

4 oz (100 g) vegan margarine (or butter) cut into pieces, at room temperature

about 4 tablespoons water

This pastry is suitable for all pies, quiches and savoury pastry dishes.

1. Mix the flour and salt together on a work surface.

2. Add the margarine and, using your fingertips, rub the fat into the flour. Work quickly and lightly until it is all combined.

3. Now sprinkle the water onto the mixture, a little at first, then more, mixing it in with a palette knife or your fingertips. You will now have a ball of dough. Knead it briefly with the heel of your hand, then wrap in clingfilm and chill for 30 minutes to 1 hour before rolling it out (see page 217).

VARIATIONS

- *Rich organic wholewheat shortcrust pastry* Good for sweet flans and tarts. Substitute 1 chilled large beaten egg for water and add 1 teaspoon fine demerara sugar (or caster sugar) to the egg mix.

- *Rich organic sweet shortcrust pastry* Substitute 2 medium beaten eggs for water and add 3 oz (75 g) of sugar. This pastry is light, crisp and strong – ideal for tartlets and also good for fruit flans.

- *Shortbread* Use 1 egg and increase the sugar to 4 oz. Shortbread cannot be rolled out but should be lightly pushed into the base of the tin, then pricked, chilled and baked.

Note: In all short pastries vegan margarine may be wholly or partially replaced by butter. Butter does of course give pastry a much smoother richer flavour than margarine.

If using a food processor, use the 'Pulse' function as this will help to prevent the overworking of the dough. Mix the flour and salt together in the processor, add the fat and pulse mix it until it resembles breadcrumbs. Pour on the chilled water and continue to pulse mix to a smooth dough. Wrap and chill or chill and use.

Sweet short pastries should be cooked 10–20°C cooler than unsweetened short pastries.

Croissant Dough

Makes 12 croissants, each 3 oz (75 g)

½ pint (275 ml) fresh milk or water

1 oz (30 g) sugar

1 oz (30 g) fresh yeast

1 lb 2 oz (500 g) organic fine white pastry flour

10 oz (275 g) unsalted French butter

½ teaspoon fine sea salt

Croissant dough or 'pastry meets bread' is possibly the most complex recipe in the book, combining as it does the intricacies of puff pastry with the mysteries of yeast cultures. Like all pastry, however, it is only as good as its ingredients and for best flavour only French butter is good enough.

The French allow their butter to mature for 1 month prior to packaging; this allows the development of a distinctive rich creamy flavour that should pervade the perfectly cooked croissant. Flour is the other major ingredient and it is vital that it should be freshly ground, fine and strong. Wholewheat flour will work, but only with French butter and you never get quite the same lift. We now use unbleached untreated flour and the results are excellent. Always use good fresh yeast.

Croissants may be frozen, ready rolled and shaped but must be allowed to defrost at room temperature and then rise in a warm, humid place.

1. Heat the milk until tepid to warm and dissolve the sugar in it.

2. Crumble the yeast into the milk, cover and leave for 10 minutes in a warm place. It should start to foam vigorously.

3. Retain a handful of flour and put the rest in a large bowl with the salt.

4. Pour in the milk and stir, adding more flour if necessary. The resulting dough should come away from the sides of the bowl.

5. Allow the dough to rise in a warm place, covered with a tea towel, for about half an hour. It should double in size.

6. Knock the dough back by kneading it briefly, but do not overwork it. Roll it into a ball.

7. Wrap it firmly in a black plastic sack. Store in the fridge overnight or for at least 6 hours.

8. Lightly flour a surface.

9. Take the dough out of the fridge and cut a cross in the top of the doughball.

10. Roll out the dough ball, making a quarter turn each time to form a rectangle with exaggerated corners.

11. Using your rolling pin, flatten the butter so that it spreads out into a rectangle approximately half the size of the dough rectangle (this is an excellent opportunity to vent frustrations). Place the butter in the centre of the dough and fold in the corners to completely cover the butter.

12. Lightly flour the surface again roll the dough out into a rectangle, fold in three and allow to rise for 20 minutes. Repeat this process three times. Brush any excess flour from the dough and trim the edges of the final rectangle.

Proceed according to the final shape and size of croissant you desire (see pages 4 and 136).

Brioche

Makes 12 Brioche rolls

$\frac{1}{2}$ oz (15 g) fresh yeast
1 teaspoon runny honey
$3\frac{1}{2}$ fl oz (100 ml) warm milk
1 lb (450 g) unbleached plain strong flour, sifted
1 teaspoon salt
14 oz (400 g) unsalted butter, softened
5 eggs, beaten
1 egg, beaten with a little milk

Brioche is the point at which cake meets bread. It has an incredibly rich and buttery taste that is good on its own, with preserves or, more unusually, as a contrast to a savoury sauce like Sun-Dried Tomato Sauce (page 21). Brioche rolls are excellent with savoury fillings like Brie or pâté.

1. Using a whisk, mix the yeast with the honey and the warm milk.

2. Add a quarter of the flour and mix in well. Cover and set aside in a warm place for at least 30 minutes.

3. Put the rest of the flour with the salt in a bowl and make a well in the centre of it.

4. Gradually add the eggs and yeast mixture to the flour until all is absorbed and the dough is uniform in texture. Divide the dough into three.

5. Mix the butter into one third of the dough. When it is completely combined, add a second third. Continue to mix, then add the last third. Knead until the dough is smooth and shiny.

6. Allow to rise in a warm place covered with a damp cloth until at least doubled in volume – about 3 hours.

7. Divide the dough into 3 pieces. Knead each one and allow to rise again. Then place in a cool place for a couple of hours or overnight.

8. Divide the dough into 12 pieces. Remove one third of the dough from each piece. Roll the larger pieces into balls and place into 12 well greased brioche tins. Press a hole into the centre of each roll with a clean finger or wooden spoon handle.

9. Roll the smaller pieces into balls and push them into the holes.

10. Cover with clingfilm or a damp tea towel and leave in a warm, draught-free place for 40 minutes or until approximately double in size.

11. Heat oven to 220°C/425°F/Gas Mark 7.

12. Glaze with the beaten egg and milk, then place in the oven and bake for 20 minutes or until golden brown. Serve hot and fresh, straight from the oven.

VARIATION

Instead of individual brioche rolls make one large loaf. Bake for 40–60 minutes.

Puff Pastry

V *Makes about 1 lb 2 oz (500 g)*

7 oz (200 g) organic wholewheat pastry flour (or unbleached white)

7 oz (200 g) unsalted butter or hard vegan margarine, finely diced into $\frac{1}{4}$ in (5 mm) cubes

1 teaspoon fine sea salt

4 fl oz (120 ml) iced water (must be icy cold – add ice cubes if necessary)

squeeze of lemon juice

Here's a great pastry to top your pies with. Use it for any recipe where puff pastry is required but don't keep it in the fridge for more than 3 days – and don't expect it to rise quite like bought puff pastry.

1. Sift the flour onto a work surface and make a well in the centre.

2. Put the butter cubes into the well and, using your fingertips, gradually work the butter into the flour.

3. When the mixture has become streaky, add the iced water and mix it in. Do not overwork it; as soon as the water is absorbed, stop kneading the dough.

4. Lightly flour the surface, then roll the dough into a convenient sized rectangle. Fold this rectangle into 3 to form 3 layers (like an envelope). Roll it out again. Turn it 90 degrees, then fold it in 3 once more. Repeat the process one more time, then wrap the pastry in greaseproof paper and chill in the fridge for 30 minutes.

221

5. Remove the pastry from the fridge. Roll and fold it twice more before using it.

6. Remember, whatever use you put the pastry to, allow it to rest for 20 minutes in the fridge before baking.

Sweet Pastry

Makes 1 lb (450 g)

8 oz (225 g) organic wholewheat
    pastry flour
4 oz (100 g) butter
2 oz (50 g) demerara sugar
pinch salt
1 free-range egg

Sweet pastry is mainly used for tarts and is often baked blind before being filled with fruit and pastry cream. It is a robust pastry that keeps its shape well, and is easy to roll out. If possible, always make pastry on a marble surface. Sweet pastry will keep well in the fridge for 2–3 days.

1. Sift the flour onto a work surface. Make a well in the centre.

2. Cut the butter into small cubes and place in the well. Work the butter with your fingers to soften it.

3. Add the sugar and salt and mix into the butter, add the egg and gradually work the flour in at the same time.

4. When the dough is smooth, roll into a ball. Wrap in clingfilm and chill for 2 hours before use.

Vegan Sweet Pastry

V   *Makes 8 oz (225 g)*

4 oz (100 g) organic wholewheat
    pastry flour
1 oz (30 g) demerara sugar
pinch salt
pinch cinnamon
2 oz (50 g) vegan margarine
1 tablespoon water

This recipe gives enough pastry to line a 8 or 9 in (20 or 22.5 cm) flan tin.

It is not advisable to make this pastry in larger quantities. It will, however, keep for up to a week in the fridge. Also, this pastry is by nature crumbly to handle, so rather than rolling it out simply push it into a lightly oiled flan tin.

1. Mix all the dry ingredients together in a bowl.

2. Cut the margarine into small cubes and rub into the dry mix until you achieve a fine breadcrumb consistency – do not overwork.

3. Add the water and stir to form a smooth dough. You may need slightly more depending on the type of flour used.

4. Wrap in clingfilm and refrigerate for 2 hours before use.

Fresh Tomato Purée

V G This is best made in late summer when tomatoes are naturally ripe, plentiful and cheap. You will need to adjust the seasoning of the purée according to the natural sweetness of the tomatoes. If they are very sweet add a little salt, if slightly sour add a little honey or sugar.

If the tomatoes really are a bargain and you have the freezer space, make as much as your largest pan can hold.

Purée the tomatoes in a liquidiser, then pass through a fine sieve. Cook the resulting purée gently at first until it is very thick. Adjust the seasoning.

Apricot Purée

8 oz (250 g) dried apricots
1 oz (30 g) demerara sugar to taste
    or 1 tablespoon honey

Here's a handy purée that's good to have in the freezer and which can be served as a savoury or sweet sauce.

1. Soak the apricots in sufficient water to cover, overnight.

2. Next day drain the apricots and add the sugar or honey in whatever quantity you want it. Dried apricots do tend to need some. Cover with water again and bring to the boil.

3. Simmer gently for about 1 hour – adding more water if at any time the mixture looks dry – until the apricots are well cooked.

4. Cool, then purée. Freeze in suitable plastic containers.

VARIATIONS

- Dilute the water or sugar syrup, reboil and pass through a sieve to make a delicious fruit sauce.

- Add Kirsch or apricot brandy.

- Use to flavour cream custards.

Vegan Mayonnaise

V G   *Makes $\frac{3}{4}$ pint (450 ml)*

4 fl oz (100 ml) soya milk
juice of 2 lemons
2 teaspoons English mustard
   powder
2 cloves garlic, crushed
2 teaspoons fresh herbs, chopped
finely ground sea salt
freshly ground black pepper
$\frac{1}{2}$ pint (275 ml) soya oil

Vegan Mayonnaise can be kept in the fridge but may separate, so use it as you make it.

1. Blend all the ingredients except the oil together in a liquidiser.

2. Gradually add the oil, with the machine running, until the mayonnaise is a thick consistency.

Garlic Oil

V G   *Makes 8 fl oz (250 ml)*

8 fl oz (250 ml) olive oil
8 cloves garlic, minced

Every kitchen should have a supply of garlic oil. Apart from obvious applications in cooking and making dressings or brushing vegetables, it also makes a great snack, simply brushed onto toasted bread. Wonderful!

1. Heat the garlic in the oil for 4 minutes.

2. Remove from heat, allow to cool and store in a screwtop jar.

Pesto

V G *Makes about ½ pint (350 ml)*

1 large bunch basil, washed and
    dried
1 bunch parsley, washed and dried
12 oz (325 g) pitted black olives
4 cloves garlic, roughly chopped
1 tablespoon lemon juice
4 tablespoons olive oil (if you want
    to keep the pesto)
4 tablespoons freshly grated
    Parmesan (optional)
fine sea salt
freshly ground black pepper

Pesto is another must in the kitchen. It's probably not a good idea to add Parmesan to it unless you know there are no vegans coming – it will also keep better this way. This version contains black olives instead of the more usual pine nuts.

1. Blend all the ingredients in a food processor.

2. Store in a clean screwtop jar.

Vegetable Stock

V G *Makes 2½ pints (1.5 l)*

1 oz (30 g) butter or 1 tablespoon
    vegetable oil
3 onions, roughly chopped
3 sticks celery, roughly chopped
1 parsnip, roughly chopped
1 turnip, roughly chopped
1 leek, roughly chopped
2 bay leaves
1 bunch parsley stalks
2 teaspoons thyme
6 cloves
10 peppercorns, crushed
2½ pints (1.5 l) boiling water
1 tablespoon tomato purée
    (optional; see page 223)
1 tablespoon soya sauce

This makes a good dark vegetable stock that can then form the base of sauces and soups. For a spicier stock, see the variation below.

1. Melt the butter or heat the oil in a pan.

2. Add the vegetables, herbs, cloves and peppercorns. Sauté in a large pan for 15 minutes with the lid on, stirring occasionally. Do not allow to burn.

3. Pour on the boiling water and stir in the tomato purée and soya sauce. Bring back to the boil and simmer for 40 minutes to one hour.

4. Remove from the heat and allow to cool. When cold, skim the surface, then strain through muslin into your storage receptacle.

5. Freeze or store in the fridge for up to 3 days.

VARIATION

For an Indian feel to your vegetable stock, add 4 cardamom pods and a bunch of chopped fresh coriander.

225

Cranberry and Orange Sauce

V G   *Makes 1 pint (600 ml)*

1 oz (30 g) unsalted butter or vegan
   margarine
1 shallot, finely chopped
8 oz (225 g) cranberries, washed and
   picked over
4 oz (100 g) sugar
3 tablespoons fresh orange juice
1 tablespoon port (optional)

This is a slightly more refined version of a famous sauce that could be served hot or cold to accompany savoury dishes, such as Festive Feasts or Stilton Puffs.

1. Heat the butter. Sweat the shallot in the butter with the lid on the pan.

2. Add the cranberries and the sugar. Cook for 5 minutes until hot.

3. Add the orange juice and simmer until the cranberries are soft.

4. Add the port if required, then pass through a sieve.

5. Store in a jar with a screw top in the fridge.

Mango Chutney

V G   *Makes approx. 3 lb (1.3 kg)*

Point to note: Do NOT use aluminium
   pans when cooking this dish.

5 large unripe mangoes, peeled,
   stoned and cut into thick slices
1½ teaspoons salt
1 tablespoon Sambal Olek (see page
   227) or 4 fresh chillies
3 cloves garlic, crushed
½ oz (15 g) fresh ginger, grated
½ pint (275 ml) white wine vinegar
½ teaspoon garam masala
8 oz (225 g) sugar
4 oz (100 g) seedless raisins or
   sultanas

Mango Chutney is extremely popular and I think it's best to make your own. Proprietary makes are often too sweet or too gingery. It's an ideal accompaniment to any spicy dish or recipe with cheese.

1. Put the slices of mango into a bowl sprinkled with salt.

2. Blend the Sambal Olek or chillies with garlic and ginger. Use a little wine vinegar to moisten the mixture.

3. Add the garam masala and sugar and a little more white wine vinegar and blend again.

4. Put the rest of the vinegar in a stainless steel pot and add the contents of the blender.

5. Bring to the boil and simmer for 15 minutes.

6. Add the mangoes and raisins or sultanas and simmer until thick and syrupy.

7. Allow to cool before packing in airtight sterile bottles.

VARIATION

Substitute apricots for mangoes to make Apricot Chutney.

Roasted Red Pepper and Chilli Sauce

V G *Serves 4–6*

3 large red peppers
2 tablespoons virgin olive oil
2 shallots, finely chopped
2 cloves garlic, chopped
1 fresh chilli, finely chopped (retain seeds for a very hot chilli)
½ teaspoon ground cumin
2 tablespoons fresh tomato purée (see page 223)
4 fl oz (120 ml) water or vegetable stock
fine sea salt and freshly ground black pepper
1 oz (30 g) unsalted butter (optional)

This makes a nice alternative to more conventional chilli sauces and is delicious served with rösti, burgers, pies or used as a sauce for pasta. It's best made when red peppers are plentiful.

1. Bake the peppers on an oiled roasting dish in a moderate oven (200°C/400°F/Gas Mark 6). Turn them occasionally until the skin is starting to blister. This can take up to 25 minutes. It is important that they are coloured evenly.

2. While they are in the oven, heat the oil in a deep pan and gently sauté the shallots, garlic, chilli and cumin.

3. When ready, remove the peppers from the oven and put them into a paper bag for 3–5 minutes. When they are cool enough to handle, core, deseed and skin the peppers using a sharp knife. Cut into strips, then add them to the rest of the vegetables. Add the tomato purée and continue to cook for another 5 minutes.

4. Add the water or stock and bring quickly to the boil. Simmer for 5 minutes, then put the whole mixture into a liquidiser and purée it.

5. Return the purée to the pan and adjust the seasoning. If the mixture is too runny boil it to reduce the amount of water. If too thick, just add a little more water or stock and adjust the seasoning.

6. Whisk in the butter if you want a nice shining sauce.

Sambal Olek

Sambal Olek is a great way to keep fresh chillies preserved, so when chillies are cheap at your market, buy as many as you can afford. Remove their tops, wash and dry. Place in your liquidiser, then add enough white wine vinegar to moisten and get the mixture going. Blend to a smooth paste and store in a sterilised screwtop jar.

Use instead of chilli powder, especially in sauces and dressings.

Sugar Syrup

V G *Makes about 1 pint (600 ml)*

16 fl oz (500 ml) water
8 oz (225 g) demerara sugar
zest of 1 lemon

This basic commodity is good to have at hand when making simple fruit sauces, especially if you use demerara sugar. Of course, when fruits are sweet enough in their own right it is not necessary to use a sugar syrup.

Boil the ingredients together and cook until just starting to thicken. Allow to cool, then strain.

Real Custard

Serves 4

$1\frac{1}{2}$ oz (40 g) cornflour
1 pint (600 ml) milk
4 oz (100 g) demerara sugar
1 vanilla pod, split
4 egg yolks

This smooth creamy custard is the perfect accompaniment to spicy fruit crumbles and sponges.

1. Mix a little of the milk with the cornflour.

2. Bring the rest of the milk to the boil with the sugar and the split vanilla pod.

3. Pour the boiling milk onto the cornflour mixture. Return to the boil, stirring well.

4. Remove from the heat and stir in the egg yolks vigorously.

5. Return to the heat and simmer until the custard has a coating consistency.

INDEX

A

almonds: blackberry and almond tart, 38–9
apples: apple and pear purée, 158
blackberry and apple pavlova, 65–6
Danish applecake, 205
spicy apple cake, 175
apricot purée, 223–4
Arundel tarts, 171
asparagus-filled buckwheat crêpes, 78–80
aubergines: aubergine dip, 154–5
grilled aubergines with fresh tomato salsa, 89
autumn vegetable soup, 25
avocadoes: avocado and fromage frais dip, 154
avocado, red pepper and tomato filled crespolini, 49–50
guacamole, 33
guacamole with corn chips, 178
Hamish's turtle pizzas, 119–20
two pear salad, 98

B

bananas: banana raita, 158
banana smoothies, 17
Banoffee pie, 123–4
BBQ bananas, 189
Banoffee pie, 123–4
barbecue sauce, 178
barbecues, 177–93
barley water, orange, 125
Beaujolais breakfast, 2–9
beetroot: minted beetroot and celeriac salad, 163
peppered mangetout and, 58
biryani, 2–4
blackberries: blackberry and almond tart, 38–9
blackberry and apple pavlova, 65–6
blackcurrants: blackcurrant wine cup, 193
hazelnut and blackcurrant trifle, 52
blackeye bean and mushroom korma, 114
blinis with roasted peppers and sour cream, 61–2
bowls, edible, 166
brandy butter, gingered, 204
bread: black olive bread, 209–10

garlic bread, 188
the perfect toasting loaf, 14–15
sandwiches, 165–6
walnut bread, 6–7, 166
breakfasts, 1–15
brioche, 220–1
broad beans, sweet and sour, 64
broccoli: broccoli and cauliflower coulibiac, 56–7
steamed with lemon butter, 51
brunches, 1, 16–21
Brussels sprouts with chestnuts, 72
buckwheat stuffed mushrooms, 187
buckwheat crêpes, 78–80
buffets, 127–63
bulghar wheat: Indonesian layer bake, 24–5
burgers, friendly, 117
business breakfast, 10–15
butterbean mayonnaise, 151
butters: flavoured, 179
gingered brandy butter, 204

C

cakes: Guinness cake, 44
spicy apple cake, 175
vegan date and walnut bread, 45
carrot, cabbage and onion salad, 110
cauliflower cheese, 105–6
cauliflower cheese sauce, 106
celeriac: glazed courgettes and celeriac with ginger, 58
minted beetroot and celeriac salad, 163
chanterelle salad, hot, 29–30
cheese: cauliflower cheese, 105–6
cheese palmiers, 159
cheesy croquettes, 120–1
cheesy mushroom and spinach toasts, 55
deep fried Brie, 8
Devonshire blue tartlets, 137
fresh spinach and goat's cheese ravioli, 87–8
Stilton and walnut pâté, 197
Stilton puffs, 130
tomato and cheese straws, 160
cheese, soft: potatoes with quark, 65
tiramisu, 37
toasted haloumi with fresh figs and walnut vinaigrette, 93–4

cheesecake, rhubarb and strawberry, 42–3
cherry and red wine sauce, 212
chestnuts: chestnut roast, 210–12
festive feast, 198–9
white chocolate and chestnut pudding, 107
chickpeas: chickpea and coriander pâté, 168
chickpea and olive tapenade, 155
falafels, 144
chicory, orange and pistachio salad, 82
chillies: chilli mayonnaise, 149
Mexican chilli sauce, 32–3
sambal olek, 227
chimichangas, 33–4
Chinese stir-fried vegetables and tofu, 28
chocolate: pain au chocolate, 5
white chocolate and chestnut pudding, 107
white chocolate mousse, 39–40
Christmas, 194–215
Christmas pudding, 202–3
chutneys: mango, 226
tomato, 173
cinnamon shortbread, 174
cocktail sauce, 149–50
coconut custard creams, 35
coffee: tiramisu, 37
corn on the cob with spicy butter, 183
cornmeal: grilled polenta, 186
coulis, 39–40
courgettes: glazed courgettes and celeriac with ginger, 58
hot courgette and tomato salad, 214
couscous, Moroccan, 27–8
cranberry and orange sauce, 226
crisps, home-made, 161
croissants, 4–6, 219–20
tiny leek and Gruyère, 136
croquettes: cheesy, 120–1
parsnip and walnut, 96
sesame and potato, 14
croûtons: cheesy garlic, 102
garlic, 161
cucumber: cucumber fans, 129
mustard and cucumber yoghurt sauce, 110
curried mayonnaise, 149–50

curry tarts, 135
custard: coconut custard cream, 35
    real custard, 228
    real rum custard, 204

D
Danish applecake, 205
date and walnut bread, vegan, 45
Devonshire blue tartlets, 137
dips, 153–8
dressings, 149–53
drinks: barbecues, 192–3
    buffets, 128
    picnics, 176

E
eggs: egg mayonnaise, 149–50
    poached eggs, 7–8
    Spanish fritata, 20
    spinach and Mozarella scramble, 13

F
falafels, 144
fassoulatha, 208–9
festive feast, 198–9
figs: BBQ figs, 190
    fresh figs with blueberries and Greek
        yoghurt, 42
    toasted haloumi with fresh figs and
        walnut vinaigrette, 93–4
flapjacks, Kate's peanut and raisin, 123
fritata, Spanish, 20
fritters, herby sweetcorn, 97
fromage frais and avocado dip, 154
fruit: barbecued fruit, 189–90
    dried fruit compote, 11–12
    exotic fruit salad, 205
    hot fruit salad, 206
    succulent fruit salad, 18
    tropical fruit tango, 38
    two-berry summer pudding, 74
fruit cup, 193

G
garlic: garlic bread, 188
    garlic croûtons, 161
    garlic mayonnaise or aïoli, 149
    garlic oil, 224
garnishes, buffets, 128–30
Geordie mushroom and ale pie, 32–3
ginger: ginger and vanilla ice cream,
    190–1
    gingered brandy butter, 204
globe artichoke mousse, 76–7
gnocchi, semolina, 68–70

gooseberry and lime soufflé, iced, 83
granola, 18–19
grapefruit juice, 11
gravy, vegetarian or vegan, 104
guacamole, 33
guacamole with corn chips, 178
Guinness cake, 44

H
haloumi, toasted with fresh figs and
    walnut vinaigrette, 93–4
Hamish's turtle pizzas, 119–20
hash browns, 201
hazelnuts: hazelnut and blackcurrant
    trifle, 52
    hazelnut pâté, 168
herby mayonnaise, 149–50
Hoffnung's sautéed potatoes, 81
hoisin, soya and plum sauce, 157
honey sultana muffins, 19
horseradish dip, fresh, 153

I
ice cream: ginger and vanilla, 190–1
    pecan and maple tofu, 191
    tofu, 215
iced gooseberry and lime soufflé, 83
Indonesian layer bake, 26
Irish mashed potato, 104–5

K
Karen's unbelievably simple tomato
    soup, 121
Kate's peanut and raisin flapjacks, 123
kebabs: BBQ fruit, 190
    marinated vegetable, 182
Keith's vegetable basket, 148
kidney beans: kidney bean dip, 157
    refried beans, 32–3
kimizu-Japanese salad dressing, 151

L
leeks: leek and vermouth sauce, 50
    sloshed leeks and carrots, 213
    tiny leek and Gruyère croissants,
        136
lemon: lemon and honey vinaigrette,
    152
lemon and lime meringue pie, 124–5
    lemon and tahini dressing, 153
    lemon twists, 130
    Mollie's home-made lemonade,
        125
    very lemon tart, 59
lentil Kiev, 62–3

lima beans: fassoulatha, 208–9
lime and peanut relish, 111
linguini, port and mushroom, 23

M
Madeira mushrooms, 9
mangoes: mango chutney, 226
mango flambé with pistachio cream,
    115
marinades, 180–1
mayonnaise: butterbean, 151
    garlic (aïoli), 149
    vegan, 224
meatless meat sauce, 118
meringues: blackberry and apple
    pavlova, 65–6
    lemon and lime meringue pie, 124–
        5
Mexican chilli sauce, 32–3
mince pies, 216
Mollie's home-made lemonade, 125
Moroccan couscous, 27–8
mousse, globe artichoke, 76–7
muesli, home-made, 12–13
muffins, honey sultana, 19
mushrooms: cheesy mushroom and
    spinach toasts, 55
festive feast, 198–9
    Geordie mushroom and ale pie, 32–
        3
    grilled buckwheat stuffed, 187
    hot chanterelle salad, 29–30
    Madeira mushrooms, 9
    mushrooms on sticks, 138
    port and mushroom linguini, 23
    tofu-stuffed mushrooms, 70
    wild mushroom filo parcels, 94–5
mustard dip, 149–50

N
nearly Caesar salad, 90
new season salad, 163
nori sushi, 141–3
nuts, spicy, 160–1

O
oaties, peach, 175
oils: flavoured, 179
    garlic, 224
olives: black olive bread, 166, 209–10
    black olive pâté, 147
    chickpea and olive tapenade, 155
onions: grilled onion with herb butter,
    185
    onion salsa, 156

onion tartlets, 137
oranges: home-made orange barley water, 125
  orange juice, 4

P

pain au chocolate, 5
pain au raisins, 6
pakora with lime and peanut relish, 111
palmiers, cheese, 159
pancakes: asparagus-filled buckwheat crèpes, 78–80
  avocado, red pepper and tomato filled crespolini, 49–50
parsnips: honey roast sesame parsnips, 202
  parsnip and walnut croquettes, 96
party nibbles, 126
passion fruit coulis, 39–40
pasta dishes, 23, 87–8, 162
pastry: rough puff, 221–2
  sweet, 222
  vegan sweet, 222–3
  wholewheat shortcrust, 217–18
pâtés: black olive, 147
  chickpea and coriander, 168
  hazelnut, 168
  Stilton and walnut, 197
peaches: BBQ peaches, 190
  kirsch-flavoured stuffed, 99
  peach and cinnamon strudel, 36
  peach oaties, 175
peanuts: Kate's peanut and raisin flapjacks, 123
  satay sauce, 146
pears: BBQ pears, 190
  nutty pear and lemon crumble, 39
  two pear salad, 98
peas: fresh pea pilau, 113
pecan and maple tofu ice cream, 191
peppercorn sauce, green, 71
peppers: blinis with roasted peppers and sour cream, 61–2
  peppers on toast, 146
  preserved peppers, 89
  red and green pepper terrine, 167
  red, green and yellow pepper marmalade, 200–1
  roasted red pepper and chilli sauce, 227
  roasted red pepper and pasta salad, 162
  Spanish fritata, 20
pesto, 225

picnics, 165–76
pie, Geordie mushroom and ale, 32–3
pineapple: BBQ pineapple, 189
  pineapple and banana sponge, 40–1
pistachio cream, 115
pitta breads, 166
pizzas, Hamish's turtle, 119–20
polenta, grilled, 186
poppadoms, 109
port and mushroom linguini, 23
potatoes: roast fanned, 72–3
  filled baked potatoes, 184
  garlic potatoes, 215
  Hoffnung's sautéed potatoes, 81
  home-made crisps, 161
  Irish mashed potato, 104–5
  potato and onion roast, 51–2
  potatoes with quark, 65
  rösti, 30
  sauté potatoes, 201
  sesame and potato croquettes, 14
  spicy new potatoes, 141
pumpkin: butternut pumpkin and cider soup, 101–2

Q

quails' eggs, marinated baby vegetables with poached, 85–6

R

radish roses, 129
raisins, pain au, 6
raspberry sorbet, 192
ravioli, fresh spinach and goat's cheese, 87–8
red cabbage, spicy, 106
red Med salad, 31
refried beans, 32–3
relishes: lime and peanut, 115
  rhubarb and date, 78
rellenos, 171
rhubarb: rhubarb and date relish, 78
  rhubarb and strawberry cheesecake, 42–3
rice: biryani, 24
  broccoli and cauliflower coulibiac, 56–7
  fresh pea pilau, 113
  nori sushi, 141–3
  Spanish rice, 122
  Tuscan rice salad, 164
root vegetables, tagliatelle of, 64
rösti, 30
roulade, spinach and carrot, 169
rum custard, 204
rural rolls, 131–2

S

salads: carrot, cabbage and onion, 110
  chicory, orange and pistachio, 82
  hot chanterelle, 29–30
  hot courgette and tomato, 214
  minted beetroot and celeriac, 163
  nearly Caesar, 90
  new season, 163
  red Med, 31
  roasted red pepper and pasta, 162
  Tuscan rice, 164
  two pear, 98
salsa, tomato and basil, 156
sambal olek, 227
samosas, vegetable, 132–3
sandwiches, 165–6
satay sauce, 146
satay sticks, 145
sauces: barbecue, 178
  black cherry and red wine, 212
  cranberry and orange, 226
  fresh tomato and garlic, 80
  green peppercorn, 71
  grilled tomato and coriander, 96
  leek and vermouth, 50
  meatless meat, 118
  Mexican chilli, 32–3
  mustard and cucumber yoghurt, 110
  pesto, 225
  red wine and mustard cream, 57
  roasted red pepper and chilli, 227
  satay, 146
  sun-dried tomato, 21
  tangy tomato and sour cream, 200
semolina gnocchi, 68–70
sesame and potato croquettes, 14
sesame snaps, 147
shallot vinaigrette, 152
shortbread, 218
  cinnamon, 174
sorbet, raspberry, 192
soufflé, iced gooseberry and lime, 83
soups: autumn vegetable, 25
  butternut pumpkin and cider, 101–2
  fassoulatha, 208–9
  Karen's unbelievably simple tomato, 121
Spanish fritata, 20
Spanish rice, 122
spinach: fresh spinach and goat's cheese ravioli, 87–8
  spinach and carrot roulade, 169
  spinach and Mozarella scramble, 13

spinach bhaji, 112
spring onion brushes, 129
spring rolls, 134
steamed winter vegetable pudding, 103
Stilton and walnut pâté, 197
Stilton puffs, 130
Stilton vinaigrette, 152
stock, vegetable, 225
strawberries: wild strawberry tartlets, 91
strudel, peach and cinnamon, 36
sugar syrup, 228
summer pudding, two-berry, 74
sunflower seeds, tamari roast, 160
Sussex pasties, 172
swede and carrot purée, honeyed, 73
sweet potatoes with garlic butter, 184
sweetcorn: baby sweetcorn on sticks, 139
    herby sweetcorn fritters, 97

T
tagliatelle of root vegetables, 64
tahini and lemon dressing, 153
tapenade, 155
tartelettes Niçoise, 131
tarts and tartlets: Arundel tarts, 171
    Banoffee pie, 123–4
    blackberry and almond tart, 38–9
    curry tarts, 135

Devonshire blue tartlets, 137
lemon and lime meringue pie, 124–5
onion tartlets, 137
tartelettes Niçoise, 131
very lemon tart, 59
wild strawberry tartlets, 91
terrine, red and green pepper, 167
tiramisu, 37
toast, 14–15
    herby wholegrain toast, 148
tofu: barbecued marinated tofu, 182–3
    Chinese stir-fried vegetables and tofu, 28
    pecan and maple tofu ice cream, 191
    Tam's tarragon tofu served with satay sauce, 48–9
    tofu ice cream, 215
    tofu-stuffed mushrooms, 70
tomatoes: fresh tomato and garlic sauce, 80
    fresh tomato purée, 223
    grilled tomato and coriander sauce, 96
    grilled tomatoes with herby garlic ciabatta, 185
    Karen's unbelievably simple tomato soup, 121
    roasted cherry tomatoes, 9
    stuffed tomatoes, 143–4
    sun-dried tomato sauce, 21

tangy tomato and sour cream sauce, 200
tomato and basil salsa, 156
tomato and cheese straws, 160
tomato chutney, 173
tortillas: chimichangas, 33–4
trifle, hazelnut and blackcurrant, 52
Tuscan rice salad, 164

V
vegetables: grilled marinated, 181
    Keith's vegetable basket, 148
    marinated baby vegetables with poached quails' eggs, 85–6
    raw and marinated, 170
    vegetable samosas, 132–3
vinaigrette, 152
vine-leaves, stuffed, 139–40

W
walnut bread, 6–7, 166
wine: blackcurrant wine cup, 193
    mulled wine, 206
    red wine and mustard cream sauce, 57

Y
yams, candied, 213
yeasted pastries, 4–6

Z
zhooch, 150